Acknowledgements

Chapter Five, "A Rose by Any Other Name", has been adapted from *Filozofski Vestnic,* Vol. XXVIII, No. 2 (Ljublijana, Slovenia, 2007), pp.151–68. Used by permission.

An earlier, briefer version of Chapter Six, "The Soft Side of Stone", was first presented at the Conference on the Aesthetics of Stone and Rock, 14 June 2007, Koli, Finland and has been published in a Finnish translation. Also reprinted in *Environmental Philosophy*, Vol 4, Nos. 1 & 2 (Spring & Fall, 2007).

An earlier version of Chapter Seven, "Aesthetic Engagement and Urban Ecology", was presented at the international conference on *Environment, Aesthetic Engagement, and the Public Sphere*, Paris, 9 May 2007. Translated into Chinese and reprinted under the title, "Aesthetic Ecology and the Urban Environment" in *Academic Monthly*, Vol. 3, 2008.

Chapter Eight, "Celestial Aesthetics", is adapted from a presentation originally written for "Celestial Aesthetics: The Aesthetics of Sky, Space and Heaven", the 7th International Conference on Environmental Aesthetics and presented in Heinävesi, Finland on 28 March 2009.

An early version of Chapter Nine, "The Negative Aesthetics of Everyday Life", was presented at *Everyday Aesthetics*, VIII International Summer School of the International Institute of Applied Aesthetics, Lahti, Finland on 17 June 2008.

Chapter Ten, "Terrorism and the Negative Sublime", was presented as the keynote address at the international conference on Arts and Terror at Ohio University on 16 May 2009.

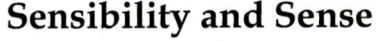

Sensibility and Sense

ST ANDREWS STUDIES
IN PHILOSOPHY AND PUBLIC AFFAIRS

Founding and General Editor:
John Haldane, University of St Andrews

Sensibility and Sense

The Aesthetic Transformation
of the Human World

Arnold Berleant

St Andrews
Studies in
Philosophy and
Public Affairs

imprint-academic.com

Published in the UK by
Imprint Academic, PO Box 200, Exeter EX5 5YX, UK

Published in the USA by
Imprint Academic, Philosophy Documentation Center
PO Box 7147, Charlottesville, VA 22906-7147, USA

ISBN: 978184540 0767 (pbk)
ISBN: 978184540 1733 (cloth)

A CIP catalogue record for this book is available from the
British Library and US Library of Congress.

Contents

Other books by Arnold Berleant

Aesthetics and Environment:
Variations on a Theme (2005)

Re-thinking Aesthetics:
Rogue Essays on Aesthetics and the Arts (2004)

Living in the Landscape:
Toward an Aesthetics of Environment (1997)

The Aesthetics of Environment (1992)

Art and Engagement (1991)

The Aesthetic Field:
A Phenomenology of Aesthetic Experience (1970)
(second [electronic] edition, 2000)

The Aesthetics of Human Environments (2007)
co-editor with Allen Carlson

The Aesthetics of Natural Environments (2003)
co-editor with Allen Carlson

Environment and the Arts (2002)
editor

For R. B.
in appreciation

"Have you been lately in Sussex?" said Elinor.

"I was at Norland about a month ago."

"And how does dear, dear Norland look?" cried Marianne.

"Dear, dear Norland", said Elinor, "probably looks much as it always does at this time of year. The woods and walks thickly covered with dead leaves."

"Oh!" cried Marianne, "with what transporting sensations have I formerly seen them fall! How have I delighted, as I walked, to see them driven in showers about me by the wind! What feeling have they, the season, the air altogether inspired! Now there is no one to regard them. They are seen only as a nuisance, swept hastily off, and driven as much as possible from the sight."

"It is not every one," said Elinor, "who has your passion for dead leaves."

Jane Austen, *Sense and Sensibility*

Preface

The happy suggestion of writing a book that would pursue the aesthetic into the regions of social philosophy was fortuitous, for it became the incentive to follow more deliberately the direction that my work on environmental aesthetics had already begun to take. This was to incorporate more fully the human factor in any aesthetic consideration of environment, and it led me in a series of essays gradually to identify what I called "social aesthetics". It is personally gratifying that circumstance and interest combined to bring together in this book the earliest and most recent of my philosophical interests, for my teaching began nearly half a century ago in the area of social philosophy. Indeed, my very first book-length effort was an anthology of readings I compiled with a colleague to use in such a course. There is thus a particular satisfaction in the intellectual symmetry this book represents.

Placing the aesthetic at the heart of these inquiries was not my original plan. As I pursued the issues, the primacy of aesthetic perception emerged at their center.[1] What such perception consists in and what it implies will become clear in the pages that follow. I hope that they may convey to others the illumination I have gained from the pursuit of a lifetime.

This book owes its existence to the contributions of many. It was John Haldane who first proposed that I undertake

[1] I am reminded of Edmund Burke's perspicacious observation, "…let the virtue of a definition be what it will, in the order of things, it seems rather to follow than to precede our enquiry, of which it ought to be considered as the result." *A Philosophical Enquiry into the Origin of our Ideas of the Sublime and Beautiful*, 2nd edn. (1759) (Oxford University Press, 1990), p. 12.

such a project, and I am grateful to him for the incentive to pursue a course that would turn out to be so personally fulfilling. I have found ironical satisfaction in achieving a sense of completion from work that in method and content must remain incomplete. I am also grateful to John for his careful reading of Chapters One to Four that helped ground my imaginative excesses. Special thanks are due Larry Shiner, whose careful attention to those four chapters also assisted greatly in shaping them.

Yuriko Saito, my co-editor and mainstay at *Contemporary Aesthetics*, has given unfailing support to our joint efforts, making it possible for me to pursue this project. Her intellectual companionship and encouragement have provided great and constant satisfaction. Yrjö Sepänmaa encouraged my deliberations on environmental aesthetics from their beginning, and our friendship over many years has invariably been stimulating. I am grateful, too, for the interest in my work over the past two decades by my many other Finnish colleagues and friends. The more recent enthusiasm of my Chinese colleagues has been both gratifying and stimulating. The warm interest of Cheng Xiangzhan, in particular, continues to infuse spirit into my efforts.

Many other friends and colleagues have offered me wisdom and encouragement, and their friendly comments are reflected in my thinking. I am grateful to Henry Braun, whose opening poem so perfectly encapsulates this book's recurrent theme. With Katya Mandoki I have discovered deep intellectual sympathy and have enjoyed many stimulating exchanges. I have long benefitted from the lucid, subtle wisdom of Ken-ichi Sasaki. I appreciate Anthony Freeman's forbearance with my delays and changes and Lynnie Dall Ramsdell's patient assistance in preparing the manuscript. One debt of gratitude is immeasurable: it is to my wife and intellectual companion, Riva Berleant, whose learning, literacy, and technical skills are reflected throughout this book. My appreciation for her mark and judgment exceeds all words.

Arnold Berleant
Castine, Maine, U.S.A.

Introduction

The function of theory is not only to understand, but also to criticize, i.e. to call into question and overturn a reality, social relationships, the relationships of men with things and other men, which are clearly intolerable. And as far as I am concerned, that is the dimension of politics (Jean-François Lyotard, *Driftworks*).

Assigning central importance to the aesthetic in human experience may seem to be a radical inversion, placing what is usually considered secondary and peripheral at the center of the human world as its nourishing source. Isn't this an ingenuous simplification of the vast range and complexity of experience?

What is at issue here, however, is not the truth of statement but the truth of experience. The question is, how can we best characterize normative experience in our appreciative engagement in the arts and, more widely, in the human world of events and actions? Many forces work to impede our understanding, most prominently in the form of cultural habits and practices and intellectual traditions. We now recognize how difficult, indeed impossible it is to come to inquiry with a clean slate. Conscious understanding is already deeply inscribed with axiomatic premises: that experience is essentially subjective; that it is the composite of different, separate factors; and, perhaps most of all, that it is primarily cognitive.

It may be bold to take issue with these cultural pieties but I propose to try. I do this, not from simple iconoclasm but in the interests of attempting a clearer understanding and so, perhaps, gaining truer experience. There is much to be said for a view that accords with lived experience. Thus, while giving the aesthetic centrality may be unexpected, it is not audacious. Nor is the aesthetic the only force at work. Whatever can be said of the human world, we can be certain that it is neither simple nor uniform. To give the aesthetic a central place is not to ignore other dimensions of experience for, indeed, there are many identifiable ones, such as religious, somatic, mystical, social, practical, and cognitive. One or another may dominate but a multitude of others is certain also to be present, even though less prominent. What may seem at first unexpected, even extraordinary, is the realization that an aesthetic undercurrent is present on occasions when it is not predominant, and this will become part of my principal claim. As in all such matters, recognizing and allowing for proportion, balance, and especially complexity are as important in understanding as in art.

This book, then, is about aesthetics, a concept I take with the utmost seriousness, not for any honorific associations the concept may convey but because it serves as a key to unlock a distinctive and important domain of experience. I find the term 'aesthetics' useful because its etymology, "what is perceived by the senses", holds the perennial center of its meaning, a meaning embodied in the history and appreciation of the arts. Perhaps, indeed, the word has often been evoked by the arts because of their ability to bring perception into definition, as it were, sharper and cleaner.

But the significance of aesthetics goes beyond the arts, for aesthetics points most clearly to primary experience, experience that is the most direct, most immediate, and most pure medium of perceptual apprehension. Each of these characteristics must be specified and can be debated, and it is one of the principal purposes of this book to examine the manifold aspects and implications of the meaning and significance of aesthetic experience. I want to do this gradually so that the richness of that meaning can unfold and be explored freely. As we shall see, this process of exploring aesthetics will lead well beyond the arts to what I call social aesthetics and concerns that implicate ethical, social, and political values.

There is nothing sacred in the word 'aesthetics'. Its denotation has no ontological status for, like all language, its meaning is specified only internally, within a language system. I make no claim, further, for the honorific standing of the term or the objective validity of its meaning. Indeed, there is reason to reject both of these. The concept of aesthetics is useful, however, as a vehicle for drawing our attention to what is true and precious for all humankind — the capacity for intrinsic perceptual experience. Such experience, with its characteristic contents, range, and shadings, is most characteristic of the aesthetic. I speak here of perception rather than sensation because perception includes more than sensory experience. The expression 'sense perception' denotes the sensory part of perception, part of an environment of such influences. But it is sensation mediated, qualified, apprehended, and shaped by the multitude of biological, social, cultural, and material forces that are integral parts of the human world.

Grasping the character of perception leads us to the more general question of experience. Impossible though it be to define, perhaps the poet can help us recognize the ineffable character of experience as well as its passing moods. On rare occasions philosophers can be poets of the human condition, working with evocation as well as statement to locate its various forms. Surprisingly many have their moments of poetic perception, not just the few who, like Plato and Santayana, lift the body of their work on the wings of art.

But it is not with poetry as such that I am concerned here. It is rather with the quality of experience in which poetry attempts to engage us through language. The language of philosophy, despite the carping of some of its internal critics, while not the language of poetry, may attempt nonetheless to lead us by construction and argument toward grasping what in experience is uncomprehended, unshaped, and even ineffable. Philosophers may find their illumination by discerning coherence and fabricating order, or by metaphysical construction. Every philosopher, indeed every person, is thus a poet of order, and what marks each new stage in the history of philosophy is the creativity with which the universe is discerned on the face of the social and intellectual understanding at the time.

In modest emulation of this tradition, I should like to proceed in such a direction. This is not to avoid the rigors of careful analysis, for I hope that a firm armature supports the delicate equipoise of the statements that clothe it, even though it may seem that I am doing just the opposite by dissolving order. On the contrary, I am trying to contribute to a clearer understanding of the human ordering of the world and, in doing this, to offer one of philosophy's distinctive contributions. Lyotard characterized Anton Ehrenzweig by saying that "he believed it more important to assert what is in fact the case than to deny that things work as others claim or have claimed. This is the artistic point of view." I believe that this may be the best way to characterize my own work.

The commitment to undertake this radical re-ordering of the world is not a new turn in my thinking. Prefigured in my previous work, its direction has become increasingly clear as my thinking has evolved. It was social philosophy that first attracted my interest, for where is there a more compelling need for clarity of vision? At the same time the directness of artistic vision has long fascinated me, for this seems to hold a kind of truth that philosophy has not always appreciated. It became increasingly clear to me that the issue lay not in reconciling differences but in discerning connections and relationships. This was the impulse that led me to find in the idea of an *aesthetic field* a context that could provide a common ground for the activities and products of the arts in human experience. I discerned four principal dimensions in the aesthetic field: the artistic, the objective, the appreciative, and the performative. For these aspects of aesthetic experience need to be related on their common ground before they can be better understood and not taken as diverse and separate objects that must be brought together.

Proposed as far back as 1970 in my first book, *The Aesthetic Field, A Phenomenology of Aesthetic Experience*, that idea became the center of an ever-widening theoretical development. From the importance given to performance as one of the constitutive features of the aesthetic field at a time when that subject was largely neglected in the philosophy of art, my understanding coalesced around this as the activating dimension in the arts. It was important not only in the obvious cases of the performing arts but as a critical factor in the active experience of every art. I expanded this contextual aesthetics in the idea of *aesthetic engagement* to characterize the most fulfilled stage of aesthetic experience, and this concept became the guiding theme of the books that followed: *Art and Engagement* and *The Aesthetics of Environment*.

The challenge of understanding environment offered a particularly suitable opportunity for extending and enlarging the significance of aesthetic engagement, as well as for seeing the underlying resemblance of appreciative experience of both art and nature. These ideas — the aesthetic field and aesthetic engagement — became the guiding theme of many essays in aesthetic theory and on different arts and environments, essays collected in three subsequent volumes: *Living in the Landscape*, *Re-thinking Aesthetics*, and *Aesthetics and Environment: Variations on a Theme*. The present book is an extended and integrated statement of the insights gained in these inquiries and, at the same time, of the understanding I could now articulate of my original intuition of the essential relatedness of the aesthetic and the social.

Conceptual thought is the prisoner of language. Setting aside the question of which comes first (for more likely neither does), both conceptual and linguistic practices participate in a developing complex of factors, but the limits of language nonetheless circumscribe and constrict conceptual thought. For words are the product of a cultural historical process that is shaped by circumstances and, while language sacrifices fluidity and freedom for stability and order, at the same time it acquires a powerful instrumental capacity.

Yet despite the philosophic penchant for order, this book is about human continuities. It thus inverts the usual philosophical process of drawing distinctions, identifying differences, establishing divisions, and institutionalizing separations. I therefore eschew fixed categories, even the category of the whole. Yet while this book embraces the processual, it does more than that, for in a world of processes there are stabilities and differences, and identifying and recognizing these is important, as well. The book does not, however, enshrine certain parts, such as mind, consciousness, truth, freedom, even reason, and even being. It holds that there are differences rather than divisions, continuities rather than breaks; and it favors distinctions over separations. A vision is offered that joins ontology with aesthetics and metaphysics with pragmatics, for the aesthetic domain of experience is not ungrounded and free-floating but has its roots deep in the human world. And at the same time the end of most human activity is determinate action, involving decisions, applications, and events. This book, accordingly, rejects conventional certainties and questions many common divisions, such as between universal and particular, theory and application, mind and the world, whole and part. Moreover, it rejects, as unwarranted assumptions, universals such as cognizability and being, as well as alternatives such as permanence or change, all or nothing, and especially human and nature. Given the limitations of philosophical language, it is about more than I can write, about more than I can tell.

How to proceed with such openness and allow for new possibilities is a difficulty of a high order, for it is clear that with the first step we begin to fix the landscape within which we must move. Yet in some sense that step has already been taken by the very condition of inquiry in the world we inhabit and establish. Still we must begin somewhere, and so the sequence of chapters with which this book begins sketches a metaphorical geography of the world, the only world we can speak of, the human world. It is a world replete with interminglings and fusions where nothing stands in pure isolation, nothing is entirely separate. This world is the converse of Leibniz's universe of windowless monads for, in an aesthetic world, monads are a philosophical fiction (as are divisions and separations in general), and windows represent the transparency that reveals the interpenetration that extends everywhere.

Moreover, the commonplace, commonsensical world of independent objects that language offers is not the world we humans inhabit. It is not the world we know directly by acquaintance and struggle to comprehend. For there are no such pristine objects. Not only are things not entirely discrete but the human presence is always a factor and consequently a determining influence. Similarly, we cannot speak of the human factor or agent as self-contained and independent of the world but rather as a constituent in a human-environmental whole. Our understanding of that world is consequently the outcome of a highly complex interplay of factors inseparable from the contributions of human perception, conception, and action. Such understanding, moreover, joins with our collective activities in the ceaseless transformation of the conditions in which we carry on our lives.

Some factors in this differentiated but integral complexity are local, some are regional, some are everywhere present. Among the last of these is the aesthetic, whose aura is the guiding presence in this book. And its demonstrable importance is based not so much on the order of coherence as on the order of experience, much as Dewey's understanding of logic as inquiry confounds the structural logic of rationalists who mistakenly take the former for the latter. For nothing is more primary in human experience than sensory perception, and the satisfactions and dissatisfactions of experience are a principal motivation in our behavior. I take this primacy, then, as the originating idea of the aesthetic, *aisthēsis*, literally, perception by the senses. This merging of the aesthetic with the activities and objects of human life must be acknowledged in aesthetic theory as well as recognized in human practice, not merely as a theoretical claim but also as demonstrable in the elucidation of different situations.

"Man is an animal that lives in a polis." Aristotle's often-quoted observation has never been better understood or exemplified more universally than today. Yet the forms of human sociality far exceed those found in his classification of Greek constitutions. It is almost inevitable that any attempt to discern some kind of order among such social and cultural diversity will overlook the differences and unique adaptations that cumulatively determine the character of a human community. Moreover, the patterns that are distilled from this inventive variety cannot help reflect the dominant interests of the time. Aristotle's classification of constitutions into kingship, aristocracy, and polity mirrors his interest in the distribution of political power, and this continues to be a central concern of the science of politics.

Critical in any discussion of social organization as are the distribution and uses of power, one of the searching questions must be their influence on the character of human experience. The quality of experience, understood most inclusively, is both the first and the final touchstone of the success of any political structure, and there is no necessary correlation of one with the other. Some sort of contentment may occur under autocratic rule and pervasive fear and insecurity may be endemic in a political democracy. Our times have seen both. Still, these characterizations of social atmosphere are crude at best, even though the modern fascination — one might even say obsession — with the psychology of consciousness has led to the refined discernment of many states of being. Because the quality of human experience is the touchstone of such judgment, this gives central relevance to the aesthetic.

Yet an account of human sociality is not exhausted by politics or psychology. Not only are these not separate from each other; they do not include all the experiential dimensions of life. The forms of transactions that occur in social institutions and economic relationships include other strands essential to the complex weave of sociality; and other patterns, shapes, and meanings of personal association, body movement, or diet are inseparable from political order and mental state. We cannot search then, in Aristotelian fashion, for a single essential property that defines society. Rather must we deal in complexes, in complexities that can be arranged and sorted in many different ways, on many different levels, and for many different purposes.

How such complexities can be elaborated from a metaphysical perspective has been demonstrated with striking originality by Justus Buchler. My interest here, however, is rather different: it is partly reportorial, partly classificatory, partly constructive, and partly projective. While some might descry a utopian element, this is not literally so, for cases of what I would call an aesthetic community have occurred in the past and do now exist. What I want to elevate to a dominant place eludes structural analysis, however, for it is the very condition and quality of experience. And this brings us back to aesthetics.

My ideas on what I call social aesthetics have their philosophical roots in phenomenology and the phenomenological method, their empirical roots in the arts and in aesthetic experience of natural and human environments, and their ethical roots in pragmatism as a grounded understanding and application of inquiry joined with the primacy of the social. This book endeavors to bring these together so that they can develop in a coherent yet non-systematic way, more as an artistic creation than a scientific structure. I hope to project here an aesthetic vision of the human world that is both comprehensive and coherent, a vision grounded in the ecological, social conditions of human life. As such it is necessarily aesthetic in the largest sense. I hope this will emerge as we wend our way through the landscape of aesthetic inquiry.

The twelve chapters of this book fall into three parts. The first, "Grounding the World", is unavoidably metaphysical. This is necessary because exposing our preconceptions reveals that many are grounded on self-justifying tradition and are unreflective, arbitrary, or presumptive. There is a wholesome rigor in phenomenological methodology, to which I have recourse, for to suspend assumptions of existence also raises questions about the existence of our assumptions. Chapter One, "Beginning", starts the process by introducing the three main strands of the cord I have already identified that binds this inquiry together: phenomenology as a critical method of experience; pragmatism as the necessity of connecting every idea with its implications, uses, and consequences; and aesthetics as paradigmatic experience and the normative criterion by which it must be judged. Chapter Two, "Understanding the Aesthetic", probes the controversial region of the aesthetic in an effort to locate it, determine the character and value of aesthetic experience, and explore the directions and the domains to which it leads. The third chapter, "The Aesthetic Argument", endeavors to focus directly on aesthetic experience and on what it means for the kind and content of the knowledge that is possible for humans. In doing this, it exposes the extent to which cultures establish a conceptual environment largely populated by things that do not exist and by differences that are taken to be ontological structures rather than conceptual discriminations. It is these considerations that occupy Chapter Four, "The World of Experience".

Part Two, "Aesthetics and the Human World", critically examines varied domains of our world, revealing how thoroughly the world we inhabit is culturally founded. Chapter Five, "A Rose by Any Other Name", shows the prevalence of the aesthetic throughout human culture in constructing the world, whether or not its aesthetic character is acknowledged. "The Soft Side of Stone", Chapter Six, contrasts that most obdurate material with the meanings we assign to it, and shows how thoroughly those meanings are informed by cultural factors and how, in culturally qualified perception, the fusion of meaning and material overrides ordinary claims about the "true nature" of stone or any presumably impersonal object. In Chapter Seven, "An Aesthetics of Urbanism", we see how that most distinctive of human environments, the built, urban environment, thoroughly embodies the human forces that create it. The final study in Part Two, "Celestial Aesthetics", adopts the perspective of outer space and, considering the Earth as a human world, proposes to replace myths about the celestial universe with metaphors that can evoke feelings of awe and mystery. It considers in what sense the idea of a celestial sublime is meaningful and develops the idea of global ecology in the context of the celestial universe.

The final part of this book, "Social Aesthetics", extends and elaborates this grasp of the human world into the full and comprehensive presence of the aesthetic in human society. Chapter Nine, "The Negative Aesthetics of Everyday Life", takes the aesthetic as a standard by which to evaluate aspects of the world we experience, recognizing not only the descriptive character of the aesthetic but also its ability to serve as a basis for critical judgment. For meanings function aesthetically and an aesthetic model becomes an illuminating glass through which to view the human world with a critical eye. Chapter Ten extends the underside of aesthetics by examining its application to terrorism, enabling us to understand more fully something of the use and significance of terrorism. It also enables us to extend the sublime as a negative moral category. A new realm is charted in Chapter Eleven, "Perceptual Politics", where perceptual experience is not only common to all humans but presents the basis for moral and political as well as aesthetic claims. Finally, Chapter Twelve, "The Aesthetics of Politics", charts some recent applications of aesthetic ideas and values in political theory and suggests some implications of proceeding in that direction.

While not systematic in the usual sense of establishing an explicit logical structure, as Spinoza and Kant did so brilliantly, this book has nonetheless an overall consistency. It is the coherence of an embracing vision that finds a place for all, even though the elaborations may be unexpected and the occlusions many. It is, one might say, the coherence of a cantilena and not of a computer. And it is guided by the idea of aesthetics as the theory of sensibility.

Chapter One

Beginning

Nothing really begins
save to emphasize
an already wholly given
elsewhen.

Even amoebas
wriggled in the pre-bloodstream of a middle
eon. Bundles of reeds from the Nile
became columnar
emphases of the Doric.

Begin with noticing the middle,
the Przwalsky horse, say,
a quiet stubby grazer
inheriting, initiating
bloodlines.

Begin with everyday.

The wheels we travel on roll inwardly,
tightening to scrolls
for the Memorial Library
of travel.[1]

First Things

This book approaches two basic regions of human being, the aesthetic and the social, and explores their interdependence. A concern with their relationship is neither new nor recent, for it can be traced at least as far back as Classical Greece. But there are compelling reasons for reconsidering these normative domains now. We are at a point in human history when the momentum of changes that have been building over the last two and a half centuries has increased

---

[1] Henry Braun, "In The Beginning Was the Middle", in *Loyalty* (Weld, Maine: Off the Grid Press, 2006). Used by kind permission of the poet.

to their present culmination in permanent global crisis. It is essential that we refresh our understanding of this condition, and we are in desperate need of new ideas and directions for responding to this demand.

The initial stage of any inquiry is crucial, especially in one that has normative concerns. But in no inquiry are hidden assumptions and presuppositions more prevalent yet difficult to expose and identify than in one that centers on the social, the moral, and the aesthetic. For along with curiosity we come armed with procedures and expectations. All of these qualify the process. While there is no such thing as a free-floating investigator, the less independent the inquiry and the more influential these preconditions, the more compromised the undertaking and the less dependable the conclusions. How, then, to begin?

The search for a beginning has been a human preoccupation ever since the earliest mytho-philosophical speculations. Myths of creation are found in many cultures, providing explanations of the origin of the world they inhabit. These accounts, such as the Greek myth of the origin of the earth (Gaia) and the sky (Uranus) from the two halves of the shell of the golden egg; the Hopis' belief in an ascent through underground chambers; the highly imaginative animal stories from West Africa; the earth-diver myths widespread throughout central Asia and northeastern North America; and the sequence of initiating acts believed by the ancient Hebrews to have dispelled chaos and brought humans into being—these creation myths establish the beginning of time and are situated in a particular place. The locations and explanations differ but they exhibit the common fact that they are cultural constructions.

The earliest philosophers moved from imaginative invention to rational speculation in seeking the one original substance from which everything is made, be that water, air, or atoms. When it took theological form, this quest for a reasonable explanation was embedded in the myth of the world beginning in divine acts of creation, and much ingenuity has been spent in the effort, also much disputed, to provide a rational justification for such originating actions, whether by understanding a deity as a first cause, an onto-logical necessity, or required by a purpose, as in the argument from design. Some few, following Francis Bacon,[2] have concluded that the very presumption of a beginning is itself a myth that derives from an underlying resemblance to basic human experience and need. Many philosophers, and more recently scientists, have nonetheless pursued this quest: the power of myth continues within the house of reason.

Before we can consider the question of cosmic order, or indeed of any order, we have to choose how to proceed and where to begin. In some sense the philosopher's pursuit is like the artist's, having always to start by confronting a blank canvas, a rough block of stone, a sheet of unmarked paper, or a blank computer screen. It is necessary to decide how to proceed and what our instrument of inquiry will be. Moreover, the philosopher's challenge is double, for not only must we determine how to begin an inquiry; we must choose the paint as well as the canvas, the ink and the paper, the chisel along with the stone — the very means with which to begin. And neither the query nor the means by which to conduct it comes first. There is no logical order here, only the pragmatic acknowledgement that matter and means are co-determining. This is the logic of inquiry, not the logic of geometry.[3]

For the means to begin there are at least two contrasting rational ways in which philosophers have proceeded, ways that I shall call critical and substantive.[4] We can say that a critical methodology uses the techniques of doubting, questioning, analyzing, and comparing ideas, claims, proposals, explanations, and language itself. Critical philosophy

[2]   Francis Bacon, *Novum Organum*, xlviii.
[3]   It has been customary for the philosophy of science to order knowledge on a deductive model, i.e., the logic of geometry. It is less common but to my mind truer to the acquisition and grounding of scientific knowledge to follow John Dewey and understand it as inseparable from the process of inquiry. See John Dewey, *Logic, the Theory of Inquiry* (New York: Henry Holt & Co., 1938).
[4]   This distinction differs from C.D. Broad's well-known classification of philosophical methods as critical and speculative. His is a logical distinction whereas mine is a procedural one.

encompasses Socratic scepticism and the Cartesian *dubito*, scientific scepticism, linguistic analysis, and deconstruction. A substantive methodology, on the other hand, endeavors to combine information, ideas, and experiences in a plausible order. Sometimes this entails egregious assumptions and hypostatizations, but it may also forego such imaginative constructions and stay close to the data that we need to explain. Here lie such efforts as Kant's three *Critiques* and Hegel's *Phenomenology of Spirit*. Methodological synthesis includes the great metaphysical systems, whether idealistic or naturalistic, and theory constructions of all sorts, from ethical systems to theories of art. Philosophical synthesis is an effort to discern resemblances and relationships, to give order to phenomena and ideas and, at the same time, to add as little as possible but as much as needed to secure a favored view of the collection of particulars that are being ordered. Both methodological and philosophical synthesis are substantive in intent and achievement, as is this very discussion of philosophic methodology.

Most philosophers combine both procedures, even though they may give priority to one. Thus Plato utilized the dramatic form of the dialogue to promote the critical process, exploring concepts in the effort to synthesize them into forms. Aristotle collected empirical data and invented logical techniques, but these did not deter him from constructing theoretical explanations on a grand scale, both metaphysical and cosmic. Much the same can be said of other influential figures in the history of philosophical inquiry, from Descartes, through Kant, to such recent figures as Dewey and Merleau-Ponty. Of course the balance of both functions may differ, as well as the particulars with which they deal. Spinoza exemplified this to an extraordinary degree, joining them in equal proportion and with forceful effect in his *Ethics*. Because matters of procedure and data are so basic and critical in any attempt at beginning, let me try to articulate how I shall construe them in the pages that follow.

It is almost universally true that efforts at substantive aesthetics and at synthesis are compromised by the incursion of presumptions of one sort or another: logical, methodological, ontological, and cultural.[5] Assumptions take many forms, some of which may seem to be unexceptional and unavoidable, such as a two-value logic of truth and falsity, a dual order of matter and spirit, and beliefs about human nature. Some of these assumptions will be examined critically in the discussions that follow. What is different in this inquiry will become clearer as it is exemplified in the process.

I dwell on the matter of presuppositions, whether consciously endorsed in an inquiry or hidden in the intent or the implications, because assumptions profoundly influence the issues that follow. To a greater or lesser degree they qualify the inquiry, rendering it partial or circular or even vitiating it entirely. Yet the candor that must guide philosophical inquiry leads me to pursue a course as free as possible from unarticulated assumptions, the usual pitfalls that entrap philosophic inquiry. To avoid all assumptions is impossible, for the very conduct of inquiry entails many, such as the presumption of personal existence, of language, and of thought, itself. That these are really the conditions rather than the assumptions of inquiry will soon become apparent. It is well, in any case, to acknowledge the unavoidable.

My starting point in this inquiry is to move along three tracks at the same time, although not always simultaneously, following one or another more prominently as the demands of the discussion require. I shall adopt the philosophic rigor of radical scepticism, combining the methodological approach of phenomenology and the centering of pragmatism on practice and consequences with the perceptual focus of aesthetics — all with the view of re-shaping the landscape of social philosophy. Phenomenology enters as a methodology, aesthetics as the source of data, and pragma-

---

[5]   Despite claims to be free of metaphysics, critical approaches to aesthetics are equally laden with ontological assumptions associated with atomism, divisibility, and the like.

tism as the criterion of judgment, the validating test. As movements and disciplines these are widely known and it is unnecessary here to attempt to establish the case for any of them. While I use them freely, my understanding is, I think, not idiosyncratic. However, taken in combination they will lead us in directions that are transformative. Let me describe how I shall understand and use them here.

Phenomenology as Method

The phenomenological reduction, the idea that fundamental philosophical inquiry should proceed by suspending all assumptions, including that of existence, stands as one of the great marks of twentieth century philosophy. In the rationalistic form Descartes gave such scepticism in the seventeenth century, the idea of suspending all preconceptions inaugurated the modern era in philosophy. And in our own time, the same impulse led Husserl to introduce the phenomenological *epoché* as the first stage in the originary process of philosophical investigation. The resemblance of these two philosophers, separated by three centuries, is no coincidence; Husserl, in one of his late works, the *Cartesian Meditations*, made it explicit by deliberately emulating the procedure of his predecessor. What both philosophers shared was the primary philosophical impulse to cut through the accumulated layers of habit and cultural history and return to beginnings. That one based his procedure on reason and the other on perception is an obvious difference that overlays a greater consanguinity.

The critical cast of philosophical inquiry is, as I have noted, one of its perennial features. It endeavors to liberate us from the multitude of cognitive habits and prejudices we unknowingly adopt, to set aside so-called common sense,[6] and to open all our presuppositions to examination. In principle this would seem to be a useful cognitive procedure. In practice it is both difficult and dangerous, as the intellectual

---

[6]   Consider Thoreau's unforgettable characterization of common sense as "the sense of men asleep, which they express by snoring." Henry David Thoreau, *Walden* (New York: W.W. Norton, 1966), p. 215.

history of the West testifies. Philosophical analysis (not of language but of thought) has been, from Socrates on, one of the great intellectual skills and a valuable instrument for intellectual purgation. The difficulties with the radical form it took for Descartes are now well known, but I should like to reconsider its efficacy in phenomenological analysis. For while the procedure of "bracketing" our assumptions of existence, as Husserl termed it, is a useful way of calling attention to the often insidious intrusion of these presuppositions, it is inadequate as a technique for re-grounding philosophy. It cannot be adequately practiced, I believe, for it is itself assumptive and misleading. It assumes that one can return to beginnings, to a pure starting point, and indeed that there is a very beginning to which we can return if only we can successfully identify and set aside all assumptions.

This is the fundamental Cartesian error, for it assumes that there is a logical sequence, indeed a *deductive* order to knowledge, together with the underlying premise of such an order that there is a *first* step. There is, moreover, the additional assumption of a neutral investigator, even though one cannot avoid influencing that process. And, most interesting of all, it unwittingly postulates pure consciousness as the originating point of inquiry and indeed, for Husserl, its terminus. That its metaphysical conclusions are ideal essences is the result of the method, not of the inquiry. No concept is more rich and complex in modern philosophy than consciousness, and none more problematic. These difficulties are not overcome when we make consciousness incarnate, as Merleau-Ponty did in regarding the flesh as foundational. This risks succumbing to the other side of the same dualism, although for Merleau-Ponty it was only a stage in the transition to an experiential unity of humans and the world.[7]

---

[7] See Maurice Merleau-Ponty, *The Visible and the Invisible* (Evanston, Northwestern University Press: 1968). Merleau-Ponty, moreover, recognized the insoluble difficulties inherent in psycho-physical dualism. In this, his last, unfinished work, he was groping toward transcending that endemic assumption of Western philosophy, and he was one of the first philosophers to attempt to emancipate himself

The phenomenological method has double utility here, not only for its rigorous exposure and suspension of assumptions, but also for its focus on perceptual experience as the originating point of inquiry. It is here that phenomenology shares common ground with aesthetics, which, as we shall soon observe, is grounded in sense experience. The phenomenological method provides a purgative procedure and a direct one by which aesthetic inquiry can proceed.

Pragmatism and Practice

Starting inquiry without a firm place from which to begin and with no absolute, whether in the form of a being, a beginning, or an axiomatic "truth", leaves us with the problem of how to judge an idea, a proposal, or a claim. We seem to be free-floating in ontological space with neither a fixed point nor any point at all from which to begin. How, then, can we proceed? To what can we appeal?

These are critical questions and they bring us to the second dimension of our methodology. This consists in making use of the central thesis of pragmatism, namely that the meaning of an idea is found in the actions it implies and its truth and value are determined by the consequences that follow from its use. Here no idea or practice is self-con-

---

from its dominance in his incompletely developed notion of the chiasm. Merleau-Ponty represents here two stages in this process, first in his emphasis on the flesh of the world, including humans, and then by passing beyond that two-sided metaphysical coin and trying to articulate an experiential unity of humans and the natural world.

We find a remarkable parallel to that effort in Eastern thought. "In the unenlightened state, however, what we take for our world of reality is only the world of discrimination (*vikalpa*), which is manifested on the *tathata* basis. In this world of discrimination, subject and object, representation and name, are revealed. But by penetrating these ideas through skillful means, we come back to the world of *tathata* and true wisdom. That does not imply the disappearance of the world of phenomena. What disappears is discrimination-imagination. The world of phenomena is revealed in true wisdom without being veiled by *vikalpa*. *The world of phenomena is but one with the world of tathata in the same way that waves cannot be separated from the water.*" Thich Nhat Hanh, "Footprints of Emptiness", Ch. V in *Zen Keys* (New York: Doubleday, 1974, 1995), pp. 138–9. *Vikalpa* is a Sanscrit term meaning "the true being of phenomena that lies beyond conceptual thought." *Tathata* means 'thusness' or 'suchness'.

tained. It is essential to look at what follows from its acceptance and application in order to determine its meaning and its value.

The inquiry that occupies us here involves a critical re-casting of ideas, of ideas about everything. And it is critical because of the rigorous excision of hidden but tendentious presuppositions. The pragmatic method offers a criterion for this re-casting. Living in a condition of uncertainty, of scepticism, of the fallibilism of all beliefs, we would be helpless without some way of choosing and judging among particular beliefs and practices. The pragmatic standard of judgment, moreover, is not chosen arbitrarily; it is imposed by the conditions of inquiry and by the circumstances under which life is carried on. By considering where beliefs lead and what follows from putting them in force, we are left with a criterion that is on the same level as the beliefs and practices, themselves. This is not a handicap but rather a condition of inquiry, for there is nothing to which we can appeal that is outside or beyond the domain in which we think, live, and act. This domain is inevitably the ground condition of all inquiry.

One can, of course, ask what the standard imposed by practice itself presupposes. This may appear to be a legitimate question, and it is hard to resist the temptation to play a game of recursion. But just as we find ourselves as part of a world already established in some fashion or other, so we cannot inquire with a blank slate. Since nothing lies beyond the human context against which we can measure ideas and practices, we must then recognize that it is we who construct the criteria for judgment, and these must derive ultimately from the conditions that constitute our world. All we can assert must be judged by a standard that rests on the physical, social, and historical conditions of a human environment.

I believe, moreover, that this standard is not arbitrary or even optional. Just as we do not choose our organic condition, we do not select the basic interchanges that proceed from the drive to carry on our biological functions, themselves not chosen of endeavoring to protect and preserve, and to promote our well-being. It is for this reason that ultimate scepticism is self-invalidating, since to place everything in doubt assumes that the doubter is excluded.[8] The firm conditions of living are a sobering corrective to high-flown conceptual puzzles. So while we never start from nowhere and with nothing, to start with everything in the form of complete and finished "truths" is self-deceptive. We cannot, then, avoid starting with something, but we must nonetheless place the particularities of our condition on the stand.

This basic condition has brought pragmatists of many stripes to embrace a naturalistic world view. It is a view that affirms the idea that the sciences, with their theories and practices constantly subject to confirmation and modification, provide not an arbitrary path to knowledge of our physical world but a dependable, trustworthy, and credible method. Philosophy, then, cannot stand prior to or apart from science but must endorse scientific method and the knowledge it produces, where it has been established, and must work in harmony with it.

At the same time it is essential to recognize that this naturalistic metaphysics, like all claims to knowledge, must itself be tempered by recognizing the assumptions that scientific knowledge makes. These include its self-justifying presupposition that scientific method is the only legitimate method of inquiry, vitiating every other path to human understanding, and that it is, therefore, by its very nature, universal. From a meta-critical point of view, this claim is neither necessary nor desirable. It does not diminish either the validity or the value of scientific knowledge by recognizing that it succeeds in certain broad domains of the human world but not universally.

This recognition does not require us to endorse logical or metaphysical limits to the domain of scientific inquiry, as Descartes, Kant, and many others did. But at the same time we need to acknowledge that, while the boundaries of scientific investigation and knowledge are not fixed, there are

[8] See A. Berleant, "On the Circularity of the Cogito", *Philosophy and Phenomenological Research*, XXVI, 3 (March, 1966), 431–3.

regions of experience and understanding about which science has had little or nothing to say. This inapplicability of science does not require us to dismiss these realms of meaningful understanding as pure fantasy, as mere speculation, or as unknowable, but rather to recognize and accord them the significance and value they occupy in the wide range of human experience. We would do far better to try to comprehend, evaluate, and utilize what such experience has to teach us. There are domains such as religious experience, aesthetic appreciation, poetic meaning, moral sentiment and compulsion, and contemplative or meditative illumination that make their own contribution to human understanding. Aspects of these domains are certainly open to scientific inquiry but such inquiry does not necessarily exhaust their scope. Therefore, we must not take science and the naturalistic world view as necessary presuppositions but open these, along with everything else, to critical philosophical inquiry. It is inconsistent with the pluralism and provisionalism of pragmatism to replace a religious or metaphysical absolute with a scientific one. Philosophical pragmatism is, then, not prior to scientific method and knowledge but accommodates them.[9]

The Aesthetic

The third strand in the fabric of this inquiry, its warp, so to say, is the aesthetic. It is central to my case here, even though the nature and scope of aesthetic inquiry are being debated widely and vigorously. Indeed, the concerns of aesthetics may be more controversial at present than at any time since the eighteenth century when Kant gave modern aesthetics its classic formulation.

Aesthetics provides no comparable logical structure that can compete with science in its study of the natural world. And it can muster no physical object or institutional agent to place against the powerful forces of society and culture.

---

[9] John Dewey, for example, held that philosophy is not prior to science but reflects and generalizes from it, a position that Quine later reaffirmed.

Only in rare instances does the museum take a stand. And artists raise brave cries for change but they are often heard only to be co-opted and put into service by the very social forces of which they may be the only uncompromised critics. Nor do the arts provide any palliative in the form of comforting visions. Yet at the same time, the arts, and the aesthetic, more generally, offer the clearest ground from which to recognize and confront the experiential conditions of contemporary life. Empowered by forceful experiences of both transcendence and repugnance, the aesthetic offers a powerful criterion of value.

What is the field of study called aesthetics? What is the aesthetic? These are critical questions here, for the aesthetic provides the guiding vision that directs my inquiry, and in a sense this entire book endeavors to respond to these questions. As we shall see, the aesthetic offers methodological, normative, judgmental, and experiential dimensions that are central to our purposes. At the present stage of this study, the aesthetic, together with its phenomenological and pragmatic companions, enters as part of the triangular armature on which this inquiry is being constructed. And so I shall confine my discussion here to the critical contribution the aesthetic makes to the beginning of this inquiry and gradually sketch a fuller picture as we proceed farther.

The etymology of the word 'aesthetics' is of cardinal importance for it provides the core meaning that runs through its various uses. Introduced by Baumgarten in the middle of the eighteenth century, 'aesthetics' is the name he gave to the science of sensory knowledge that is directed toward beauty and that attains perfect sensory awareness in art.[10] In effect, Baumgarten gave an identity to a field of active philosophical discussion that reached back to Classical times, and the name has remained. He drew the term from the Greek, literally, "perception by the senses", and the field of aesthetics continues to retain a close association with sensory experience. In naming this descriptive science "aesthetics", Baumgarten kept close to the original Greek

---

[10]   Alexander Gottlieb Baumgarten, *Aesthetica* (Frankfurt a. O., 1750), Vol. I.

meaning of *aisthēsis* (αἴσθησις), when he defined the domain of this new science. I take its core meaning seriously.[11]

Aesthetics, however, has long exceeded its traditional meaning as the study of beauty in art and nature and has been extended from the ugly and grotesque to the ordinary and the repulsive. Experiences of art need not be elevating; they can also be repugnant. Yet how broadly the range of the aesthetic may be extended is debated, and even though its boundaries may be contested, its wider application must nonetheless be taken into account. Being guided, however, by the etymology of 'aesthetics' prevents us from losing touch with its core significance. Acknowledging that the aesthetic begins and ends in sense experience, we can at least on principle consider aesthetically any object and any experience that can be sensed.

At the same time it is essential to recognize that there is no such thing as pure perception. All sensory perception passes inevitably through the multiple filters of culture and meaning: the concepts and structures supplied by language and the meanings instilled by culture.[12] To these influences

---

[11] Katya Mandoki pursues a parallel analysis in her recent *Everyday Aesthetics: Prosaics, the Play of Culture and Social Identities* (Aldershott: Ashgate, 2007). See especially Part 2, "On Aesthesis".

[12] Peter L. Berger and Thomas Luckmann, *The Social Construction of Reality* (Garden City, NY: Doubleday, (1966) 1967). See also Alfred Schutz and Thomas Luckmann, *The Structures of the Life-World*, trans. Richard M. Zaner and H. Tristram Englehardt, Jr. (Evanston: Northwestern University Press, 1973). The same conclusion can be drawn from the analysis of language as Davidson suggests. We cannot obtain direct knowledge of the world nor is it necessary that we do so "because the causal relations between our beliefs and speech, and the world also supply the interpretation of our language and of our beliefs." He concludes that we cannot base interpretation on the foundations of knowledge for "there is no clear meaning to the idea of comparing our beliefs with reality or confronting our hypotheses with observations." Thus "we are left ... in a situation where our only evidence for a belief is other beliefs .... And since no belief is self-certifying, no set of beliefs can supply a certain basis for the rest." We have, then, a linguistic system that underlies meaning, and language is necessarily intersubjective. What remains seems to be a self-enclosed system not unlike Saussure's, a linguistic system that expresses beliefs and that is variable because of the cultural factors that affect it. See Donald Davidson, *Subjective, Intersubjective, Objective* (Oxford: Clarendon Press, 2001), pp. 164, 173–5, 203–4.

we must add personal experience in the form of the many activities that constitute daily life, education, and the influences that inform acculturated experience.

The breadth and variety of occasions and experiences that have at various times and places been described as aesthetic are striking. These have led to the word 'aesthetic' achieving such wide currency that it is glibly applied to a large collection—a garbage heap, some might say—of objects and occasions. And aesthetics has acquired a range of associations that spreads across the spectrum of values. Thus the epithet 'aesthetic' is often applied to maquillage, employing cosmetic processes to enhance personal appearance, and it is applied to surgery that has the same purpose—cosmetic surgery. The aesthetic is considered to be a feature of labor and a form of success. It appears on plans for land use in environmental impact statements that are obligated to consider "the effects on the aesthetics" of the area. It is attached to design, to fashion, to style, and even to the artistic life. There is also aesthetic consumption and the aesthetic consumer, as when the term is applied to wine. 'Aesthetic' is often used as a synonym for beauty, and even sociability is considered an aesthetic quality. And on the other side of the normative coin, one suffers "aesthetic outrage" when an object or practice deeply offends our sensibility. Is there anything that these various usages have in common? Is there a family resemblance that binds them together?

If the multiple uses of 'aesthetic' have any feature in common, it lies in their explicit or their implied reference to sensation, to the realm of perceptual experience. In this respect, aesthetics retains a connection with its origin, with *aisthēsis*. Of course the bond of sensation is never unqualified, but it does identify the principal component of the kind of experience we call aesthetic. It is freely applied to the pleasurable experiences evoked by the arts and by natural scenery and landscape, so that we identify that kind of appreciative experience by calling it "aesthetic". Clearly more is involved in the appreciation of the arts and of nature than simply sensory satisfaction: personal and cultural associations enter immediately and color that experience. So, too, do the knowledge and meanings we bring to all experience. Still, the sensory base in aesthetic appreciation is never wholly obscured without turning the experience into something different, such as religious, mystical, or cognitive experience.

At the same time it is necessary to be sensitive to the difference between meaning in the cognitive sense and the *experience* of meaning, i.e. between cognitive meaning and experiential meaning. So in speaking about the invasion of perception by meaning, we must go beyond sense perception to include the *awareness* of meaning. Experienced meaning is both complex and indistinct. It harbors feeling tones, bodily stance, mnemonic resonances, associations, and intimations that cannot be articulated except, in their own ways, by the arts, particularly, perhaps, literature and music. In speaking of aesthetics, we must therefore go beyond beauty, we must go beyond *objects* that are pleasing, and focus on our *experience* of such objects, since only through experience can we grasp them.

Aesthetic experience, then, has two principal aspects: a *sensory* one that is primary, and the *experience* of meanings. It can be studied in its relation to art when art is understood as a dramatic shaping of intrinsic experience through objects and situations, actual or imaginary, in ways that intensify their distinctive character. Aesthetic experience can also be studied in the perception of the qualitative processes of the natural and the social world. And aesthetics can inquire into the ways that join the natural and the social in the qualitative experience of the many modalities of environment: in environmental art, in the consummatory perception of landscape, and in the many forms of the built environment.

Moreover, there is, in my view, a further, important aspect to such appreciation. Aesthetic experience seems to transcend the barriers that ordinarily separate ourselves from the things we encounter in the world. In aesthetic appreciation we often have emotions that are diffused rather than localized, and we may feel exposed and vulnerable to forces we cannot easily enclose in ready-made ideas. This has led some commentators to see a liberating quality in such appreciation, while others find it a danger to established conventions. Both may be right.

The intimate quality of this appreciative experience may overcome the sense of separateness that divides us from things so that we become an integral part of the aesthetic field. The intimate involvement that often characterizes aesthetic appreciation and makes it so difficult to encapsulate and categorize is an essential quality of that perceptual experience. And it is so distinctive a feature of aesthetic appreciation that we can describe such experience as a kind of engagement, as "aesthetic engagement". Thus we cannot only use aesthetic perception as direct experience; we can recognize such perceptual experience as the clearest measure by which to assess the values that emerge. Aesthetic perception may indeed stand as the touchstone of human values.

Let me pursue the use of aesthetic experience by returning, with a clearer understanding of the aesthetic, to the question with which we started, the question of beginning. And let me weave together the three strands I have been elaborating: phenomenology as a window to perception free of presuppositions, including the assumption of existence; aesthetics as the model for the directness and immediacy of perceptual experience; and pragmatism as the requirement to consider the meanings and consequences implicit in the practice of ideas and beliefs. Together these will contribute to a better grasp of how we can know and understand the human world. Ultimately, too, this inquiry must be judged by that same standard. But let me now turn from aesthetics as a methodological tool to aesthetics as an investigative one.

Chapter Two

Understanding the Aesthetic

As a domain of normative experience, the aesthetic has a powerful and pervasive presence in the human world. This book's central purpose is to reveal that presence and to explore how the aesthetic is incorporated in the texture of the world. Further, by recognizing the profound implications and the transformative possibilities of the aesthetic, we can help shape that world to make our place in it more generous and fulfilling. This may sound both presumptuous as well as opaque but, as we proceed, I hope that the deep and penetrating significance of the aesthetic will become both lucid and inevitable.

Let me begin this chapter by considering the aesthetic, not so much as the central influence in the methodological procedures that will guide this inquiry, but rather by developing its place in our concerns in the human world. To do this I need to develop still further some of the distinctive features of the aesthetic. But at the same time it is important to expose some of the misconceptions that discolor the term. Most significant of all is to recognize that the aesthetic stands as a source of value and a factor in judgment, and that these underlie its power as a social instrument. How such value occurs and can be applied, the final topic of this chapter, will bring us still closer to the central concerns of the book.

Traditional Preconceptions and the
Axioms of Aesthetics

I want to start by brushing aside some of what Francis Bacon called "reasoners", who resemble spiders and "make cobwebs out of their own substance."[1] These have gravely misunderstood the aesthetic as well as much else in human experience. Aided by tendentious misreadings, the force of the aesthetic has been dammed up and its influence channelled so as to flow only within carefully constructed banks. To begin, let me indicate where these channels lie and then proceed to re-direct their course and flatten their banks.

Two common constrictions impede the Western understanding of the aesthetic (apart from its appropriation by the body-care industry). The first is the misguided idea that aesthetics concerns only the fine arts and the beauty of nature. The second impediment is the presumption that to call something aesthetic is to honor it. Both of these conventional misunderstandings unnecessarily restrict the applicability the aesthetic, diminish its vitality, and largely divest it of its profound normative power. These are strong claims and it will take the considerations that follow to give them body and life.

We have seen how, in the eighteenth century, aesthetics as a field of scholarly inquiry attracted attention and acquired a distinct identity. During the same period, the idea of art, in a complementary development, became increasingly focused on five mostly visual arts: painting, sculpture, architecture, music, and poetry. These were considered the major arts, the "fine" arts, and they represented the noblest human achievements. Other arts were also recognized, such as dance, theater, prose literature, and garden and landscape design, but these five were taken to embody beauty in its purest form as the distinctive achievement of civilization.[2] It is still common to honor these arts as

---

[1]   Francis Bacon, *Novum Organum* (1620), xcv.
[2]   The classic account of this historical development is P.O. Kristeller's "The Modern System of the Arts" originally published in the *Journal of the History of Ideas*, Vol. XII (1951), No. 4, 496–527, and Vol. XIII (1952) No. 1, 17–46, and often reprinted.

"high", while the term 'fine art' commonly denotes the visual arts alone. Placing these five arts at the pinnacle shaped the landscape of aesthetics and carried with it consequences that were liberating at first but soon proved problematic. It will be useful to consider some of these consequences, but first, however, its strengths.

One effect of this way of ordering the arts was to institute a protective barrier between these arts and certain others considered primarily practical, such as garden design, weaving, basketry, and pottery. Like the fine arts, these require considerable skill combined with creative invention, and this leads to the enjoyment of them for their own sakes. What sullies their purity, however, is their inseparable bond with practical concerns. For in this tradition beauty was commonly idealized and considered incompatible with use, and it is the fact of their utility that separates these practical arts from the realm of pure art. The sense of art as skill, a meaning found in the etymology of the term,[3] relates these useful arts to the fine arts, but many today still hold that their utility is a distraction from the pure contemplation of beauty.

This deep-seated prejudice against the aesthetic worth of the "practical" arts has Classical Greek roots in the essentially class-based distinction between theoretical knowledge (*theōria*) and practical knowledge (*phronēsis*). The first is enjoyed in pure, detached contemplation while *phronēsis* is exhibited in action. This is one of the most deep-seated distinctions in philosophy and carries profound social and cultural implications as well as aesthetic ones. For here lies the origin of the difference held to exist not only between the fine and the practical arts, between beauty and use, but between intellectual and manual labor, theory and practice, white collar and blue collar jobs, and the like. The fine arts require detached contemplation and are bound up with the senses that seem to thrive on such receptivity. Thus, of a piece with that distinction, it has been held traditionally that the proper aesthetic senses are the distal senses of sight

---

[3]   See Chapter 1.

and hearing, whereas the proximal senses of touch, smell, and taste — the bodily senses that are central to the practical arts — have been excluded because they presumably impede the contemplative detachment required for aesthetic enjoyment.[4]

It is essential to note, however, that the difference does not lie so much in the experience as in the implicit value judgment that raises contemplative over practical knowledge and is applied here to categorize sensory experience. Thus the fine arts and natural beauty are elevated over practical, utilitarian, and functional considerations so that only those arts and nature may enter the domain of the aesthetic. This restriction, one might remark facetiously, turns the aesthetic appreciation of art and nature into a spectator sport. It is the first of several constraints imposed on the aesthetic by conventional wisdom. And the judgment then applied to the senses that raises sight and hearing over the contact senses leads us to a second limitation.

Another restriction that emerged in traditional aesthetics is expressed in the common tendency to think that calling something aesthetic is to praise it. 'Aesthetic', then, is taken as virtually synonymous with beauty. To show why this unduly narrows the meaning of aesthetics and is misleading, let me return to the meaning of the concept.

As we have seen, the concept 'aesthetics' derives from the Greek *aisthēsis* (αἴσθησις), literally, perception by the senses, and was introduced by Baumgarten to name the science of sensory knowledge that is directed toward beauty. On this reading, art epitomizes sense perception as the perfection of sensory awareness. I find the perennial center of the meaning of 'aesthetics' in its etymology, and it can serve as a key to unlock a central domain of experience. Perhaps,

---

[4]   Plato's *Hippias Major* is often cited as one of the most prominent classical expressions of this distinction among the senses, where the pleasure found in sight and hearing is associated with the beautiful, while the pleasures found in smell and love-making are not. *Hippias Major*, 299a. My essay, "The Sensuous and the Sensual in Aesthetics" (1964), was early among recent efforts to expand the esthetic relevance of all the senses. Reprinted in *Re-thinking Aesthetics, Rogue Essays on Aesthetics and the Arts* (Aldershot: Ashgate, 2004), Ch. 5.

indeed, the word 'aesthetics' is easily associated with the arts because of its ability to bring the arts into focus, as it were, sharper and clearer. Its etymology, "what is perceived by the senses", is embodied in the history of the arts and points clearly to what we may call primary experience, experience that is a direct, immediate, and pure form of perceptual apprehension.[5]

Each of these characteristics of aesthetic apprehension must be specified, and one of the purposes of this chapter is to examine such aspects of its meaning. But I shall do this gradually so that its richness can unfold freely. At this point it is clear that to identify an experience as sensory should say nothing in its favor or disfavor: it is entirely neutral. Sensory experience may be hurtful or harmful, as well as enriching or exhilarating. And it may merely offer perceptual information. It is simply experience in which sensory input is central, even though, as we have noted, sensation is always affected by variable factors — biological, social, cultural, and historical. Therefore, by keeping close to this source of its meaning, we can speak of the sense experience to which the aesthetic refers without ascribing any value, whether positive or negative, to whatever is termed "aesthetic".

Finally, there is nothing sacred in the terms 'aesthetic' or 'aesthetics'. As concepts they have no ontological or normative status. Like all the words in a language, their meaning is specified only internally, within a language system, as Ferdinand de Saussure made clear. I make no claim, therefore, for any universal and unchanging truth located in the aesthetic, but I find the term useful as a vehicle for drawing our attention to what holds for all humankind — the capacity for perceptual experience, experience whose full range and shadings are realized only rarely. I speak of perception rather than sensation because, as we must constantly remind ourselves, perception incorporates more than sen-

[5] "All experience is aesthetic by definition because to experience is equivalent to aesthesis." Katya Mandoki, *Everyday Aesthetics: Prosaics, the Play of Culture and Social Identities* (Aldershott: Ashgate, 2007), p. 35.

sory experience. It is sensation mediated, quantified, apprehended, and shaped by psychological and cultural
characteristics and patterns of apprehension, and by the
multitude of forces that are part of everyone's world. The
expression 'sense perception', then, denotes the sensory
aspect of perception, the central character of a collection of
such influences. But let us now return to the aesthetic in its
etymological and historical signification.

Aesthetic Experience

Experience is central to the meaning of the aesthetic, not
only from the origin of the word but because of its content
and significance. At its simplest and most direct, we may
have aesthetic experience in the pure sensuous delight in
gazing at a lone trillium blooming amid the leafy debris of a
woodland in spring. Aesthetic experience can refer to the
feelings of uplift and wonder when we marvel at the ever
unique cloud streaks and shapes in the sky, regardless of
whether they seem to resemble a basket of washing or can
be accounted for by a meteorological explanation.[6] Here,
too, one might place the mysterious contact with Rem-
brandt in one of his late self-portraits or the shiver of delight
from the dramatic sequence of broken octaves in the solo
violin in the first movement of the Brahms Concerto. Aesthetic experience encompasses our unending wonder at the
beauty of nature and our awe of the power of the arts to penetrate deep into our emotional lives, encounters that lie at
the high point of aesthetic value. At the same time experiencing the aesthetic can make us aware of the delights of
ordinary life that may hold our pure attention for a moment
– the glint of sunlight on spring leaves, the full moon rising
above the horizon at dusk, a child's ingenuous smile. In all
such things the force of the aesthetic lies in its capacity for
distinctive perceptual experience.

---

[6]   R. W. Hepburn, "Wonder", in *'Wonder' and Other Essays. Eight Studies
in Aesthetics and Neighbouring Fields* (Edinburgh, Edinburgh University Press: 1984).

In one way or another, every attempt to explain the aesthetic, every theory of the arts or of values in nature, must take stock of experience, experience that encompasses imaginative as well as actual perception. And it is not uncommon for aesthetic theory to acknowledge this, from Kant's transcendental aesthetic, in which knowledge rests on the capacity for experience[7] and flowers in his critique of aesthetic judgment, to Dewey's development of an aesthetic theory from an inquiry into experience that, at the same time, focuses his entire philosophical vision. As experience is necessary for many forms of knowledge, so it is necessary for the aesthetic. And as the aesthetic exceeds the limits of cognitive knowing and grasps the very heart of experience, it may be considered all the more essential. How, then, to characterize aesthetic experience? This is the point from which all theoretical paths diverge.

To give a full account of the many directions in which they lead and to explore the attempts to describe and justify their legitimacy would require an exhaustive study of its own, and that is not my purpose here. Indeed, a clear insight lies behind the vision of the aesthetic that guides this book. Its central, distinguishing features can be described in brief and can be contrasted with some other influential views. This is what I want to do at the present stage of my inquiry. An inclusive understanding of aesthetic experience, one that takes account of its fullness, its ramifications, and its implications, is best built up out of the specific issues, particular cases, and examples that will appear as this we proceed. That is where we can hope to locate its critical features. It is not question of definition as much as a quest for elaboration.

Underlying most accounts of aesthetic experience lies an idea endemic in Western civilization, the view that sets consciousness apart from nature. Appearing in Plato, incorporated into scholastic theology, assuming many guises and penetrating deeply into Western cultural belief systems, this idea reached its clearest, its classical formulation, in

---

[7] Immanuel Kant, *Critique of Pure Reason* , trans. N.K. Smith (London: Macmillan, 1929), p. 65, §1.

Descartes' dualism of mind and body, and it continues to pervade contemporary thought. Often challenged, this fundamental understanding is difficult to circumvent for, as a central ideological premise of Western philosophy, it undergoes many mutations and continues to reveal its presence in diverse disciplines and in theoretical accounts of all sorts. Few thinkers have been able to free themselves from its grasp.

In aesthetics, Cartesian dualism occurs in the common way of speaking of appreciation as the subjective experience of a work of art, in thinking of the work of art as a separate object to which we must direct our appreciative contemplation. It is manifested in the appreciation of natural beauty as an inner joy or an overwhelming feeling when one's "heart leaps up" on beholding a towering mountain, a tree that bears the scars of wind and weather, a spring flower, or "a rainbow in the sky". It underlay Kant's recognition of the subjectivity of the judgment of taste,

> the feeling of pleasure and pain, by which nothing in the object is signified, but through which there is a feeling in the subject as it is affected by the representation.

And it lay behind Kant's unsuccessful attempt to surpass such subjectivity by insisting on the necessity of attaining universality.[8]

Traditional aesthetic theory is nonetheless bound by the same difficulty in relating subjective experience to an external object that Descartes encountered in attempting to regain the "external" world. We have had theories that endeavor to correlate emotion, when it becomes aesthetic, with formal qualities. We have seen the widespread, manifestly subjective accounts of appreciation based on what is termed the aesthetic attitude, a distinctive attitude of contemplative detachment, of aesthetic disinterestedness still considered essential by many for the kind of appreciation appropriate to the arts. All such attitude theories resolve into psychological ones where it is considered necessary to

---

[8]   Immanuel Kant, *Critique of Judgment*, trans. J.H. Bernard (New York: Hafner, 1951), pp. 38, 76-77 (§1 and §22).

adopt a mental set, a state of mind, so to say, in relation to what is variously called the work of art, the artwork, or the aesthetic object, in order that appreciation that is distinctively aesthetic take place. We find it in recent variations of social-psychologistic thinking as institutional theory in which the art status of a presumably aesthetic object is decided by the art public's acceptance. This resembles the view that what determines when something is a work of art and not a "mere real thing" is someone's declaring that it is and acting as if it were. This last case, Danto's well-known philosophical conundrum, rests on the double, perhaps even treble, division into reality, imitative works of art, and non-imitative, indiscernible actual objects whose meanings are presumably decidable by intuition, by a theory of art, by some other belief system held by a separate knower or appreciator, or by the conventions of the art public. In ways from naïve to sophisticated, this dualism endemic to Western culture persists, and it is difficult, for some perhaps impossible, to seriously question its ontological frame.

Of course there have been daring thinkers who challenged this metaphysic, most notably Spinoza, whose understanding of ontological unity remains a lonely but steadfast beacon to those who share his clarity and independence. But few others after this flash of brilliance in the seventeenth century have been illuminated by it. Among the most original and influential in recent times have been John Dewey and Maurice Merleau-Ponty. Dewey's naturalistic metaphysics of experience locates the human as part of an all-inclusive natural world, engaged in a continuous activity of "doing and undergoing" in constant transaction with the conditions of the natural and social environment. Merleau-Ponty, coming from the very different French cultural-philosophical tradition whose pervasive Cartesianism seems to make any alternative inconceivable, persevered in an independent course by giving phenomenology an existential cast. This led him to discern a perceptual continuity in "the flesh of the world" joining both "seer" and "seen", touching and the touched, a continuity that exemplifies a "reversibility" in perception.

Merleau-Ponty was working his way toward a vision of existential continuity, "the antecedent unity of the me-world" that he gropingly characterized as the "chiasm".[9]

This ontological issue underlying experience bears some relation to another division of aesthetic experience in which what is a complex contextual condition is broken up into parts more easily identified and named in terms of common understanding. Thus debates have persisted over generations about emotion in appreciative experience, about expression and symbol, about the resemblance between an artistic rendering of an object and the actual object—all dimensions of a single continuous process of appreciation. Obviously one cannot dismiss issues debated with complex prolixity by a verbal gesture. But it is worth considering whether such accounts mistake undeniable and significant aspects of the experience of art or nature, such as feeling, communication, language, meaning, and resemblance with the world beyond, for the whole of the experience.

This can be seen as a kind of philosophical metonomy, leading to what I have elsewhere called "surrogate theories of art", theories that are misleading not so much by being mistaken as by being incomplete.[10] It is common, for example, to identify an emotional component or quality in appreciative experience. Yet to attempt to associate a specific emotion with the aesthetic experience of particular objects or occasions vastly simplifies a quality that pervades appreciation but cannot be separated from that full, complex experience. Similar claims of incompleteness can be made of other common theories. Each fastens on a dimension of aesthetic experience and, like the blind Indians trying to tell what an elephant really is, senses a partial truth that it takes

---

[9]   Maurice Merleau-Ponty, *The Visible and the Invisible* (Evanston, Northwestern University Press: 1968), pp. 249, 261, 249m, 256ff.

[10] Arnold Berleant, *The Aesthetic Field, A Phenomenology of Aesthetic Experience* (Springfield, IL: CC Thomas, 1970), ch. 1.

for the whole. As Wordsworth put it, "We murder to dissect."[11]

Domains of Aesthetic Value

Earlier in this chapter I observed that value is commonly associated with the aesthetic, and that value can actually originate in the aesthetic. At the same time it is important to remember that aesthetic perception is, at center, a somatic event or activity, however complex and culturally appropriated it may be, and that sensory experience, taken in itself, is an event that is value neutral. Sensation just *is*, but experience is screened through normative filters that usually assign moral standing. Experience in general derives value from its context and its associations; and aesthetic experience is associated with the fine arts, whose value casts its glow over it. But taken alone, sensory perception is simply a complex neural and more generally somatic event in a person's history. Sensory stimuli are just that, and under ordinary conditions they are occluded by external strictures, often moral ones, that are embedded in those experiences and appear to be inherent in them. Cultural features do indeed meld with sensory events, but it is important not to ascribe those features to the physical sensation.

It is common in the West to regard visual and auditory perception as inherently superior to other sensory modalities, hence the elevated status assigned to the visual arts.

---

[11] William Wordsworth, "The Tables Turned". The full stanza reads, "Sweet is the lore which Nature brings;/Our meddling intellect/Mis-shapes the beauteous forms of things:/We murder to dissect."

John Haldane has called my attention to the 19th century Scottish philosopher (and phenomenology pre-figurer) James Ferrier, who gave wonderfully graphic illustrations of the same point: "The human mind, not to speak it profanely, is like the goose that laid golden eggs. The metaphysician resembles the analytic poulterer who slew it to get at them in a lump, and found nothing for his pains.... Cut into the mind metaphysically, with a view to grasping the embryo truth, and of ascertaining the process by which all these bright results are elaborated in the womb, and every trace of 'what has been' vanishes beneath the knife; the breathing realities are dead, and lifeless abstractions are in their place". *An Introduction to the Philosophy of Consciousness* (1838).

But when experiences involve bodily functions and activities, or when perception is overtly physical, as in touch, smell, and taste, they are automatically accorded a lower status and are immediately suspect. Indeed, designating perception "lower" or "higher" imposes a moral, or should we say a moralistic standard on experience, and it is a criterion that is irrelevant to aesthetic value as such. This is an insidious instance of the long tradition of the moral oppression of art. A classical expression of this judgment is the comment attributed to Plato that, although the beautiful is invoked by the pleasure of sight and hearing, viewing the act of love is far from agreeable to the sense of sight or beautiful.[12] This is no rare example, for sense perception is never pure sensation but is always affected by a multitude of factors. Common influences frame aesthetic experience in various ways and it is important in characterizing such experience to try to identify them. Notwithstanding the qualifications just mentioned, experience is central in any discussion of aesthetics and is the source of the value we ascribe to the aesthetic.

As I have noted, sensation denotes neural activity and is simply a bodily event. It is rarely, if ever, "pure". If we could extrapolate sensation from every cultural influence and consider it just as organic activity, in such a limited context its value as a healthy sensory process would be relatively modest. Yet much sensory experience itself, especially when involving bodily functions, is colored by moral judgments. This is important to recognize, for normative claims are often made about the arts that ascribe moral value to the experience of those arts. Regardless of whether such judgments are supportable or not, they must be kept distinct from aesthetic (i.e. sensory) perception. Here is where the

---

[12]   *Hippias Major*. While some doubt has been cast on the authenticity of Plato's authorship, this bears little on the point being made here. We might remark that the subtlety of the exchanges and their dramatic embodiment in this presumably early dialogue are comparable to those of the dialogues whose authorship is not in question. The skill with which the dialogue is composed does credit to whomever its author may have been and, most important here, the prevalence of that view of aesthetic senses does not rely on its author. See also Note 4.

phenomenological method is invaluable, for it can help us remain clear about what we are actually perceiving and how we are judging it.

Distinguishing between aesthetic experience and aesthetic value can be useful in understanding art that challenges or ridicules or even supports widely held beliefs, such as those concerning sexual morality and religious orthodoxy, social values about gender and racial equality, and political ones about human rights. Convention typically reacts violently to such artistic criticism, often in blasphemous contradiction to the very values it espouses. Thus religion is turned into a shield to justify and protect the intolerance or animosity of its believers who nominally follow its teachings of brotherly love, compassion, and generosity. Love of one's country may become the incentive for suppression and persecution in the name of democracy, belying the freedom and tolerance that it parades beyond its borders.[13] The sanctity of human life is used to justify legal and illegal violence directed toward those endorse and engage in practices that promote human life values, violence that belies those very values. Thus the unending controversy over abortion, for to proscribe its choice would inevitably produce pain, self-violence, and damage to life already existing. It would not be difficult to extend this list to an appalling length in this age of deeply conflicting values.

Perceptual experience itself is direct and immediate. It is inherently valuable and may be universally sought. As we noted earlier, such value is traditionally taken to be self-sufficient and separate from any utilitarian interest in the object with which it is concerned, using the common distinction between intrinsic and instrumental value. It is usually assumed that these are exclusive and exhaustive.

It takes little effort to recognize, however, that normative experience rarely observes this distinction, and this is true in the arts as everywhere else. All intrinsic experiences have

---

[13] An egregious example is the persecution of political dissenters as unpatriotic or un-American, while that very persecution blatantly contradicts the very values it purports to uphold.

effects and these effects must necessarily be associated with those experiences, even if unrecognized or unknown. We may prize the aesthetic pleasure and illuminated understanding we gain in visiting a museum of fine art, but consequences are inseparable from such valuing. The visit may lead us to become more aware of our immediate surroundings, we may become more discerning in our apprehension of minute differences of color, of qualities of light and of shapes and their interrelations, or we may view people or places with finer attention to detail and nuance. These are some of the personal effects a museum visit may produce, but there are many consequences less directly but no less significantly involved: environmental effects from travelling to the exhibition, social effects in changing one's understanding of, say, illness, poverty, dissipation, or careless consumption; political effects in the attempts of governmental bodies to censor or suppress an exhibition; economic effects in the costs of maintaining the museum, in the employment of staff, in the cost of admission; cultural effects in the results of the scholarship required to research the background of the exhibition, in the pedagogical utility of visits by schoolchildren or student assignments. This list of effects could easily be doubled or trebled.

Aesthetic experience, like mystical and religious experience, is characteristically immediate and is experienced directly and without intermediary. This gives it a certain, unequivocal authenticity. Unlike the mystical, the aesthetic never loses touch with its origins in body activity and receptivity; we remain aware of and actively engaged in somatic perception. And unlike the religious, it requires no myth or doctrine to explain and justify itself, nor does it lead us beyond to a different realm. The aesthetic is content to remain exactly what and where it is, and to elaborate skeins of memory, understanding, and especially of active and intense perceptual awareness on its own. In this sense, the aesthetic is self-sufficient and self-gratifying, and therefore, I believe, most authentic.

Even though immediate, aesthetic experience, as I have noted, is never pure, never simple sensation. Like all perceptual experience, the aesthetic is not only mediated by culture; it is itself inherently cultural. Cultural influences pervade our sensory perceptions. At the same time, these influences also profoundly affect our values, for inasmuch as values are not an extraterrestrial incursion into human affairs but assimilated in living situations, the aesthetic has a certain originality.[14] Indeed, it may be the point from which all other values spring and the base on which all values ultimately rest.

Just as aesthetic values are rarely if ever exclusively intrinsic, taken wholly in themselves, so they are not necessarily positive. Resting on perception, the aesthetic may be experienced at any place in the range of values from highly positive to unqualifiedly negative. With greater perceptual sensitivity one's capacities for experience will enlarge. This enlargement may not only lead to wider and more subtle pleasures; the experience of art is as likely to produce greater awareness and sensitivity to pain, from Daumier's social and political caricatures to Anselm Kiefer's dark visions of the present world humans have made. And there are questions puzzling for aesthetic theory that arise in the painful pleasures of watching a performance of *King Lear* or reading *The Old Curiosity Shop*. Leaving the worlds of art and turning to the aesthetics of the urban environment, we are quickly overwhelmed by the superabundance of occasions for negative aesthetic experience.

---

[14] The positive value associated with the aesthetic has been appropriated by many cultural interests, some tangentially related even to an enlarged sense of the aesthetic, others shamelessly exploiting its favorable connotation. Examples of the first are its use in plans for land use in environmental impact statements that consider the "effects on aesthetics", and in the explicit appeal to the aesthetic in promoting fashion, style, and in advertising design. Instances of the second occur when reference is made to success as aesthetic, and to aesthetic labor. Cosmetic surgery and dentistry (to achieve "facial aesthetic harmony") are a major industry, as are aesthetic cosmetics. It is no surprise to find reference to aesthetic consumption and the aesthetic consumer, including the aesthetic view of wine, and its social use occurs in judgments of social quality and social facilitation ("sociability is an aesthetic that needs to be considered when designing social software"). These just begin the list.

Taking aesthetics broadly again to refer to the immediacy of sense experience, it is difficult to find places of aesthetic equilibrium in the ordinary course of things, let alone occasions of elevation. There is not a sense modality that remains unscathed in the urban environment, from the cacophony of the roar of traffic and the blaring of loudspeakers in public places to the soporific blanket of canned music and intrusive private conversations over cell phones. In the gaudy, intense colors of advertising circulars and the bath of all the commercial impingements on our sensibility, hardly a sense survives unoffended. Is this the aesthetic equivalent of Descartes' evil genius, rendering every perceptual occasion not a deception but an affront? This partial catalog of sensory offences anticipates an aesthetic critique of the social environment, a matter that will assume major importance later when we explore the implications of the aesthetic for social judgment.

The Scope of the Aesthetic

Let me turn finally to those normative occasions, themselves. Examples such as I have just been citing may seem to stretch the range of the aesthetic beyond recognition. Yet if we apply the extended sense of the aesthetic with sensation as its center and focus on intrinsic perceptual experience, nothing in the human world is excluded. By excluding nothing on principle, by adopting no pre-determined limits, any thing or any situation may become an occasion for aesthetic experience.

Universality, however, does not imply uniformity. To say that any situation can be the occasion for aesthetic appreciation does not put everything on the same footing nor does it give everything equal value. A complex field lies before us in which differences occur and discriminations apply. The visual arts, for example, vary in materials, styles, subject matter, and uses and are therefore incomparable; precise determinations of value become impossible. The same can be said of every other art, including music, architecture, literature, and dance, and this raises problems of comparative value that may be unsolvable. Should punk rock be judged against the nineteenth century symphony? Hummel figurines against Paleolithic ones? Magazine illustrations against the masterworks of studio art? Differences in media, style, intent, and appreciation do not necessarily translate into quantitative differences in value. A democracy of the arts would allow each art a legitimate place without imposing an external normative standard on it. Is an insolvable problem a legitimate one?

Let us consider what we can say and what is worth considering. An important factor is not only the difficulty but the undesirability of constructing a comparative order of aesthetic value in any art or between arts. It would be better to let sleeping differences lie and turn rather to discriminating our experiences of appreciation. As with the arts, however, experiences allow no normative scale of appreciation. Some listeners are caught up in the feelings stimulated by rock music, others are transported by the Mozart *Requiem*. It is easy to discriminate differences between those experiences of appreciation, but the choice should be left to the listener. Perhaps the most that can be said about comparative judgments is the insight found throughout the history of philosophic thought, from Augustine to Mill, that it takes genuine experience of both to be able to determine value. Here it is the auditor who has had such a breadth of experience who is the best judge, and for him or herself only, with relevance perhaps for those of similar background and sensibility. This is the origin of public evaluation, where similarity of experience leads to generally accepted normative judgments.

Part of what makes differences of judgment so difficult to resolve comes from the fact that values, in this case aesthetic values, are not scalar. Such values do not differ quantitatively but only qualitatively, and qualitative differences cannot be measured. While values may vary in extent, in intensity, and normatively (that is, in being experienced and considered as positive, neutral, or negative), they admit of no precise degrees, only differences. Differences must be acknowledged but judgment reserved. Differences in appreciative experience are unavoidable, but at the same time the fact that similar valuations cluster around the same art objects suggests the possibility, indeed the likelihood, that judgments will concur. Rather than looking for differences in value, let us look for differences in experience and knowledge, recognizing that the ultimate criterion is personal. Normativity is inherent in the experience of values. They may be contrasted modally as positive, negative, different, indifferent, etc. but their variability is qualitative rather than quantitative. And we must recognize all the while that value, itself, is an indeterminate category and perception always unique. Particular experiences of aesthetic value have properties or characteristics that can be identified and distinguished. At the same time appreciative experiences also have holistic properties recognized in the 'tone' of an experiential whole, its pervasive character.

Finally, this discussion of normative judgment would benefit from some basic distinctions. We can think of these as discriminative orders of normative experience. First (logically as well as empirically) is recognizing the experience finally and ultimately *as* normative experience, as the social, moral, or aesthetic experience that it is. A second order of value experience, here aesthetic value, is not only as simply experience but experience cognized, that is, as value identified, recognized, discriminated, and associated with aspects of an art object or an aesthetic situation. A third order of normative judgment is the assessment of aesthetic value. The difference between aesthetic experience and aesthetic judgment is critical. And to return to the point that opened this discussion, admitting the universal applicability of normative judgment puts neither their types nor occasions in the same pot. Here it is possible to discriminate numerous domains of value, aesthetic or other, distinctions that depend on the need and the occasion.

One of the broadest and most widely recognized domains of normative experience is that of the arts, and it is here that the possibilities of aesthetic experience may be realized most fully. In the arts the aesthetic is at its most direct and intense, and is most fully developed. This capacity to evoke appreciative experience creates an incentive to develop an aesthetics of the arts that describes and clarifies what aesthetic appreciation consists in. Such an aesthetic understanding would identify the loci of appreciation and justify the grounds for judgments of beauty and skill—all founded on such experience. In its narrowest, most traditional meaning, aesthetic experience focuses on an art object. Along with broadly expanded art activity and production and their diffusion throughout the larger culture, the range of aesthetic appreciation has been extended to environment, and environmental aesthetics has grown from an interest in natural beauty to the aesthetics of the human environment, including the built environment and the environment of everyday life. In all of these regions the scale and scope of aesthetic experience have grown, as well, and with this greater inclusiveness new domains of appreciation have emerged. In addition, the aesthetic significance of the sublime has re-entered aesthetic discourse and so, more recently, have judgments of transcendence.[15]

Finally, the aesthetic has expanded to include what I call social aesthetics, social values manifested in the relations among people, individually and in groups, and in discussions that recognize aesthetics and ethics as inextricably intertwined. From Plato's acknowledgement of moral beauty and his suspicions of art's social effects up to the present day, philosophers have occasionally touched on such values. Dewey, like Schiller, saw art as a means of enhancing social cohesion, and Jürgen Habermas has turned

---

[15] The most influential modern discussions of the sublime were initiated by Edmund Burke and Immanuel Kant in the seventeenth century. Contemporary aesthetics has reaffirmed its importance, as in Jean-François Lyotard's *The Postmodern Condition: A Report on Knowledge* (Minneapolis: University of Minnesota Press, 1984). Ronald Hepburn has explored the transcendent quality of aesthetic experience. See R.W. Hepburn, *'Wonder' and Other Essays. Eight Studies in Aesthetics and Neighbouring Fields* (Edinburgh, Edinburgh University Press: 1984), "Landscape and the Metaphysical Imagination", in *Environmental Values*, Vol. 5, 1996, 191–204, and *The Reach of the Aesthetic* (Aldershot: Ashgate, 2001). Chapter Ten, below, extends the range of the sublime to encompass the negative as a distinguishing feature of the contemporary world.

to the aesthetic as a means of overcoming the splintering of society. The critical question here lies in the connections between the aesthetic and the social and in the relevance of the one to the other. This book endeavors to use the aesthetic as a way to renew and rehabilitate social experience and value and not consign it to a derivative role in culture.

Chapter Three

The Aesthetic Argument

Beginning to Know

I have been pressing the question of how and where to begin. The first phase of this inquiry examined how, and I proposed three courses that are least assumptive: using phenomenology as a methodology for approaching and grasping perception, aesthetics as a model for developed and focused perceptual experience, and pragmatism as the imperative to consider, as part of its meaning, the implications and consequences of every proposal to which inquiry may lead.

Turning to the meaning and scope of the aesthetic, we determined that its core rests on sensory perception together with the personal and cultural factors that affect perception. And we found that inasmuch as the aesthetic can encompass the negative as well as the affirmative, there is no necessity on principle and no need in practice to confine it within eulogistic parameters. Nor must the aesthetic be restricted to the arts. All perception and every condition can have an aesthetic dimension, at times invisible or unnoticed, at other times minor, but sometimes dominant. I intimated, too, that a revived perceptual aesthetic carries important implications for criticism and provides powerful grounds for social judgment.[1]

---

[1] All these claims for the aesthetic will be developed at length in the chapters that follow.

With a reinvigorated understanding of the aesthetic and how it functions pragmatically as well as phenomenologically, we are better prepared to make full use of it as a perceptual model. Even so, it may seem unexpected, in exploring the origins, complex meaning, and implications of the aesthetic, to turn to questions of knowing. Yet the processes of cognition, inseparable from their conditions and limitations, provide one avenue among others along which human experience proceeds, and the cognitive processes undoubtedly influence the way we begin, however we wish to proceed. There is knowing in not knowing, as Socrates realized long ago, and not knowing takes multiple guises.

Even so, it may still seem presumptuous to enter into a consideration of knowing under the guidance of the aesthetic. In fact, some inquiries into the aesthetic regard the two processes as widely different and even incompatible. It is often said that aesthetic experience is pre-cognitive or non-cognitive. If the first, the aesthetic precedes reflective consciousness, retaining its own identity and place. It may, however, influence reflection, dominate it, or be entirely displaced by it. If the second, the aesthetic and the cognitive are held to be separate, incomparable realms such that the directness and immediacy of aesthetic perception make it qualitatively unlike deliberate, mediated cognitive reflection.

It is important to consider the nature of these two modes of awareness, aesthetic and cognitive, especially since the history of Western aesthetics has been shaped and dominated by an epistemological model. On this basis aesthetics gradually became codified in the eighteenth century, achieving its classical formulation in Kant's theory of aesthetic judgment. This understanding, still prevalent, is dominated by a contemplative ideal clearly separated from any purposive, utilitarian practice and bound to the epistemological desideratum of universality. Universality, however, can be claimed, on the Kantian model, only on the assumption that human nature possesses a common subjectivity. With its roots in the Aristotelian ideal of theoretical knowledge as the highest form of knowledge, that such knowledge is contemplative and separate from practice, together with the requirement that it have universal validity, it is little wonder that Kant grounded pleasure on reflection and excluded desire from the aesthetic.

There is, moreover, a different large and complex set of relationships between the aesthetic and the cognitive that concern the relevance of knowledge for proper appreciation. It appears in questions concerning the significance of representation and verisimilitude in aesthetic appreciation in controversies generated by formalist aesthetics, and in the doctrine of aesthetic autonomy, where the debate concerns the aesthetic relevance of the resemblance and comparison of pictorial and literary representations to the world outside. A similar issue arises when it is questioned whether moral concerns should be taken into account in making aesthetic judgments: Is it possible to completely set aside moral beliefs and judgment in considering the arts, inasmuch as they function as a social institution and a social force? The question of the relevance of the cognitive process for aesthetic appreciation is at the center of the current debate in environmental aesthetics over whether scientific knowledge is requisite for the aesthetic appreciation of nature.[2]

Let me turn from these observations on the historical origins of aesthetics and their continuing influence in the current debate over the aesthetic relevance of the cognitive to consider the question itself. Qualitatively different though they be, may there indeed be a relation between the aesthetic and the cognitive? If we take the perceptual immediacy that is most fully exercised in aesthetic perception as the originating stage of the cognitive process, then instead of the aesthetic being governed by an epistemological ideal, the knowledge process may itself be grounded on aesthetic perception. Is it the case that experience comparable to the experience we have in the arts lies at the origin of knowing in every cognitive domain, and that aesthetic experience

---

[2]   See Allen Carlson, "Nature and Positive Aesthetics" in *Aesthetics and the Environment* (New York: Routledge), 2000, pp. 72–101; Emily Brady, *Aesthetics of the Natural Environment* (Edinburgh: Edinburgh University Press, 2003), pp. 86–119.

underlies knowing in general as it gives shape to organic consciousness in the sensory realm? To regard aesthetic perception as the source of the knowledge process and as the test of knowing constitutes what we might call the aesthetic argument in epistemology. What is central here is the originary status of aesthetic perception.

The issue, moreover, is not entirely theoretical. It is concerned with the grounding experiences of life, and the way in which the aesthetic process is understood has foundational social and political significance. We touch again here on the underlying theme of this book. Critical though this understanding be, it has gone largely unnoticed even though not entirely unremarked. These words of Harold Laski harbor a deep and powerful insight:

> Our business if we desire to live a life not utterly devoid of meaning and significance, is to accept nothing which contradicts our basic experience merely because it comes to us from tradition or convention or authority. It may well be that we shall be wrong; but our self-expression is thwarted at the root unless the certainties we are asked to accept coincide with the certainties we experience. That is why the condition of freedom in any state is always a widespread and consistent skepticism of the canons upon which power insists. [3]

For Western societies where science and technology are twin deities, the appeal to experience may seem almost oxymoronic. In the sciences, what we understand by experiment is actually controlled experience. Such experience is considered the origin of knowledge and the test of its truth. Until recently this understanding was both simple and incontrovertible. Nothing seemed as concrete and undebatable as experience, whether in scientific research or in appraising technological innovations. Sometimes in all innocence (and often not), experience became a screen for hidden allegiances and purposes, and was fashioned to promote presumptive motives and to confirm certain expectations. Further, with the spread of subjectivism in the twentieth century, encouraged by Freudianism, Eastern

[3]   Harold J. Laski, "The Dangers of Obedience", *Harper's Monthly Magazine*, Vol.159 (1919), pp. 1–10.

religions and disciplinary practices, and new forms of philosophical idealism, inner experience became prominent and even dominant.

What, then, does experience, in its multiple and often incompatible forms, provide? Is there anything that the various forms and modes of experience have in common? Whether it be considered subjective or objective or neither, experience is the test of ideas, the grounds for establishing and verifying beliefs, the court of appeal for settling disputes, and the ground of authenticity. This is a heavy burden for experience to carry, especially with its multiple meanings and inherent ambiguities. These dimensions and uses of the aesthetic anticipate a discussion we shall pursue later, but for now it will serve us best to probe further into the issues around beginning.

The self-conscious search for a philosophical beginning, the deliberate consideration of how and where to begin, may be considered the hallmark of modern philosophy. It arose at the moment science emerged as the corrective to the dogma of received authority, which was the foundation of scholastic knowledge. The deliberate choice of a starting point for investigation and the clearing away of all that would compromise it was Bacon's purgative for freeing scientific inquiry by dispelling the false beliefs—idols, he called them, significantly enough—that obstruct and distort our understanding.

But at the early stages in establishing scientific knowledge it was Descartes who went about this more systematically and rigorously, even though he utilized what may seem today to be a thoroughly unscientific procedure in his turn to subjectivity. Descartes found in consciousness, exemplified in the act of doubting, the deciding point in deliberate, rigorous inquiry and, by using the processes of internal reflection, established in subjectivity the foundation of knowledge, which for him took the form of mathematical science. Edmund Husserl, in the twentieth century, emulated Descartes' example still more deliberately and intensively in his attempt to install philosophy as a rigorous science that would be foundational. He did this by devising the philosophical *epoché* as a technique for removing the influence of mundane beliefs, a procedure he called the phenomenological reduction or bracketing. By this Husserl meant setting aside "the natural attitude" so that no prior claim would be made for the existence of anything. Through this technique of radical skepticism he gained a new kind of experience, a direct intuition he claimed was transcendental.

By starting with consciousness, first Descartes and then Husserl introduced a critical and determinative basis for knowledge, establishing a course that has dominated much philosophy since then. Yet subjectivity, radical or otherwise, is no pure beginning. It reflects a prior determination about what evidence is most to be trusted (i.e. that of consciousness); and even more, it consists in structuring the human world in such a way as to incorporate dualistic and anthropocentric preconceptions, thus compromising and, indeed, vitiating its methodological claims of achieving a pure beginning.[4]

The Aesthetic Argument

The problems arising out of the turn to subjectivity have preoccupied much of modern philosophy. To review them would require a history of the discipline since the seventeenth century, and that is not my purpose here. What it is necessary to say about subjectivism in the context of this discussion can best be approached in considering issues that place its premises in question.

Let me begin with a word of caution against assuming that taking the aesthetic as the start of inquiry is itself an endorsement of subjectivism. In fact, it is a widespread misunderstanding to regard perceptual experience as subjective and be compelled as a consequence to endorse some form of subjective idealism. There are disciplinary move-

---

[4]   Edmund Husserl, *The Paris Lectures* (The Hague: Nijhoff: 1967), pp. 12–13; "Philosophy as Rigorous Science", in *Phenomenology and the Crisis of Philosophy* (New York: Harper, 1965), p. 147. *Cf.* A. Berleant, "On the Circularity of the Cogito", *Philosophy and Phenomenological Research*, XXVI, 3 (March, 1966), pp. 431–3.

ments that deliberately deny this, such as the use of physiological psychology to explain consciousness as neural events in the brain, and biological reductionism to claim that mental processes like thinking and knowing, and psychological conditions like depression, as well as human behavior, can be fully accounted for by organic conditions such as neurobiological brain processes, genes, hormones, and other such biochemical conditions. But one does not have to replace subjectivism by materialism to achieve a plausible explanation, for both alternatives rest on the mind-body dualism that Descartes so kindly bequeathed to us. Later we shall consider contemporary efforts, such as those of Dewey, Merleau-Ponty, and Lyotard, to release philosophical inquiry from the grip of metaphysical dualism.

On what experience, then, *can* we ground knowledge? To come to basic experience Husserl turned to the intentional consciousness of the transcendental ego, Dewey looked to the doings and undergoings of humans as biological creatures in social and technological exchanges and, as we saw in the passage from a political and social critic quoted above, Laski advised skepticism toward anything that contradicts our basic experience so that our freedom not be compromised and we be able to achieve a life that has meaning and significance.

To specify such experience more clearly is the challenge of this inquiry. I believe that the aesthetic provides the firmest ground on which to acquire an understanding that makes a meaningful and significant life possible, and this conviction is the beacon that guides this book. The success of this endeavor rests on whether aesthetic experience — perceptual experience at its most direct and least assumptive — offers the soundest basis on which to build the structures knowledge can justifiably take and directs us in being true to the truth of that experience in the social, the human, world.

In turning to the aesthetic here, I am using it as a critical process, not as a method but as the standard of judgment. Like Descartes' doubt, aesthetic experience is purgative, exposing that which is ungrounded in perceptual experience. And like Descartes' doubt it is skeptical, inclined to question rather than accept. As with Plato's dialectic, the aesthetic harbors an ontology in determining what can be accepted as real, and why and how, and what should be discarded as ungrounded. Inverting Plato, however, the aesthetic method directs us not to dismiss sense experience because it is variable and inconstant but to withhold credence from whatever cannot be experienced perceptually. Unlike both Plato and Descartes, an aesthetic standard is not bound by the meaning and acceptance of epistemological or logical criteria of universality, stability, permanence, and coherence. These are demands imposed on experience so that knowledge can be structured and made consistent. By using the authenticity of perception rather than the formalism of reason, we cannot read more into experience than is actually there, and so experiences sometimes taken as self-verifying and compelling are accounted for in the least presumptive way. Thus visions turn into dreams, revelations into powerful intuitions, eternal verities into cultural dogmas, and objectivity into agreement that is socially grounded and widely accepted.

It is well understood that our human experience is so heavily layered with patterns of thought, structures of understanding, mandatory convictions, and prescribed behavior that direct experience is virtually impossible. Perhaps it cannot be achieved at all. Perhaps, in fact, there is no such thing. We have already noted that perceptual experience is never pure but is always filtered through cultural lenses and ordered in traditional structures. To speak of immediate experience, then, experience that is direct and unburdened, is to propose a standard against which actual experience can be measured rather than to impose a prescribed and necessary precondition. Like all standards, that of direct experience functions heuristically as a goal that may not be fully achievable but toward which we must strive. The knowledge process must endeavor to remove filter after filter and dig beneath the layers in an effort to identify and dispel the factors and forces that influence perception. At the same time we must realize that, even though we must constantly return to perception, absolute immediacy and purity are unattainable and will forever elude us. Perception can, however, function as an ideal, and we can recognize the liberation that comes as we approach it.[5]

There are, then, two meta-cognitive requirements. One is to identify, describe, and account for the kinds and varieties of cognitive constructions that have emerged over time and place. The other is to use perceptual experience, especially aesthetic experience, to consider them critically. The first of these is greatly aided by ethnologists, linguists, sociologists, cultural geographers, and the various cultural critics who describe and explain such beliefs from political, historical, social, philosophical, and literary perspectives. Recognizing the perceptual grounds of criticism is the second requirement and it provides the basis for the aesthetic argument. But how can we base critical judgments on aesthetic experience?

The answers to this question are themselves various. Often critical standards are taken from the constructions of other political or moral worlds, as in socialist realism or ecclesiastical doctrine. They may be imposed from within the same belief system in the name of consistency or given higher priority: moral, religious, social, or political. Yet these standards allow only partial and limited judgments, since they come from the very fabrications that are in question. Indeed, what makes criticism so difficult to justify is that judgments are always made within a context. This context may sanction the kinds of structures that are themselves being considered or it may nurture imaginative structures that owe themselves to that context. For the human situation is inescapable: we cannot help but think within the worlds in which we are implanted. Language, history, belief systems, social institutions all direct and

---

[5]   Such influences lead to the investigations that are the subject of the sociology of knowledge, a subject we shall examine more fully in the next chapter. An excellent general introduction to the issues can be found in Peter L. Berger and Thomas Luckmann, *The Social Construction of Reality* (Garden City, NY: Doubleday, (1966).

delimit any critical gaze. And language is the primary mechanism by and through which we attempt to articulate a cognitive understanding of our world.

The desire to establish a stable groundwork for a system of belief has stimulated great ingenuity. Apart from the various realisms that posit an external, independent world of things to which appeal can be made, the history of philosophical thought reveals many ways in which ontological stability has been attempted. Plato provides the most common illustration of such a construction, and his proposal is well known: a realm of ideal forms behind the multiplicity of phenomena, using Socrates as a masterful dialectician in leading inquiry from individual instances to a common underlying form or universal. Kant inaugurated the modern era of philosophical speculation by proceeding in a similar way, finding it necessary to posit a noumenal realm, unchanging and unknowable, that underlies all phenomena and on which he based the metaphysical and moral requirements that cannot be satisfied by experience alone. And when, in the case of judgments of taste, the structure of the understanding could not provide the basis for the universality that he believed knowledge requires, Kant projected a "subjective universal" to resolve the problem of terminal subjectivism by the speculative assumption of a *sensus communis*.[6] A century earlier, Descartes had cleared the way for the objectivity of scientific inquiry and knowledge by constructing two distantly related but independent realms of body and mind, the one providing a basis for the investigation of the physical world and the other permitting a safe haven for religion and morality. Neither solution is free from the charge of proof by postulation and indeed of circularity.[7]

These are some of the most influential proposals thought to make it possible both to acquire independent, objective knowledge and to still recognize the claims of human experience. However, there is, I think, a corrective that is inevitably influenced by the world from which we view things, but

[6]   Immanuel Kant, *Critique of Judgment*, §9.
[7]   A. Berleant, "On the Circularity of the Cogito", *op. cit.*

a corrective nonetheless. It lies in the qualified directness and immediacy of perceptual experience as I have already described it: experience best characterized as aesthetic in the large, inclusive scope of the word and on which the creative force of the different arts is founded. The traditional seat of the aesthetic in the appreciative experience of the arts is important to recognize and highly instructive. Much lies in how we construe such experience and on recognizing that, though largely direct and immediate, it is inevitably qualified by cultural and cognitive filters. The argument of this book rests on such an account of aesthetic experience, and on appreciation as engaged, not disinterested. I have developed and applied the idea of aesthetic engagement extensively elsewhere, and it underlies the understanding and application to which the aesthetic is put here.[8]

Because social and historical settings are always changing, the clarity of aesthetic perception may intensify the disaffection that arises from the outrages of injustice or the pangs of hunger. The aesthetic can provide an eloquent outlet for the estrangement of one generation toward its immediate predecessor, and it can also ennoble or equally well condemn visions of the human world that emerge in the robes of religion, systems of philosophy, or the sword of politics. Such visions develop constructions of their own, but they are likely to be bound by the same non-aesthetic constraints as in the past. Moreover, it is often the case that these revolutionary moves are quickly co-opted and emasculated by the prevailing orders of power. Sometimes an improvement in human conditions may occur, but there is no inevitable course from barbarism to a just and humane social order — the true meaning of civilization. In fact, some

---

[8] Understanding aesthetic experience as engaged is a major theme in my work and I have developed and applied it to the arts and to human culture more generally, especially in *The Aesthetics of Environment* (Philadelphia: Temple University Press, 1992), *Aesthetics and Environment, Variations on a Theme* (Aldershot: Ashgate, 2005), and, most extensively, *Rethinking Aesthetics, Rogue Essays on Aesthetics and the Arts* (Aldershot: Ashgate, 2004). Chapter 5 will offer an extended discussion of the meaning and applicability of aesthetic engagement, and the concept will be further enlarged in subsequent chapters.

of the very developments that may be considered advances
in wellbeing—population growth or greater technological
and productive capacity—themselves often become the
very means and agents of the barbarism they have supposedly replaced. Hence wars that destroy civilians as readily
as combatants, technologies that produce weapons of massive, even universal destruction, irrepressible production
whose most profitable by-product and hapless victim is the
insatiable consumer. How can the capacity for aesthetic
experience counteract and unbalance this quantitative
expansion and qualitative decline?

Aesthetic experience offers no competitive logical structure and no institutional agent with which to face these conditions other than the direct encounter with them through
engagement in the arts and its diffusion into the other
regions of human experience. The aesthetic may provide
the palliative of comforting visions or it may utter calls to
action to achieve a revolutionary alternative, but none of
these is inherent in aesthetic experience. What the aesthetic
offers is the direct force of specific experiences in encountering and recognizing what harms or otherwise diminishes
human values, together with the intrinsic rewards of gratifying and fulfilling experiences. In such ways the aesthetic
becomes a modest but irrepressible instrument of human
betterment.

The aesthetic argument cannot be made dialectically alone
and its proof cannot be established by general principles. But
by a cumulative process of both aesthetic experience and aesthetic critique we can begin to emancipate ourselves from
being in thrall to a world of things that do not exist and the
inhospitable world that humans have made of things that do,
and learn to be content in a world of fluidity, variability, and
uncertainty. We can gain the deep and infinite satisfactions
of positive experience without the intrusion of social and cultural filters that distort, misrepresent, or discredit it. And we
can live more freely without being burdened by the *impedi-
menta* of external meanings, beliefs, and judgments. This is a
high vision. Can it become more than that? Let us begin the
uneven process of finding out.

Chapter Four

The World as Experienced

I'm thinking about the aurora borealis. You can't tell if it really does exist or if it just looks like existing. All things are so very uncertain, and that's exactly what makes me feel reassured.[1]

A World of Things That Do Not Exist

We can recognize the force of the aesthetic argument both in the experience on which it is based and in the standard of an aesthetic critique by exploring its transformative effects. Indeed, my primary mission in this book is to show how and where it can lead. At this point let me illustrate the force of the aesthetic by pursuing what may be called a phenomenology without ontology at the stage when the knowledge process attempts to cognize the human world through language.

It is well and truly known that, of all the formative influences on grasping experience, language and the powerful force that language exercises on thought stand first. For language in some form provides the means for both the structure and the content of all cognition. Language reflects the social world of which it is a part and the environing conditions under which humans live. Since these conditions change with changes in climate (e.g. global warming), technology (e.g. digitizing information and communication), and the social and political organizations and practices that

[1] Tove Jansson, *Moominland Midwinter*, trans. Thomas Warburton (London: Ernest Benn Ltd., 1958), p. 28.

adapt to them, the human world varies widely both historically and geographically. The sociology of knowledge studies the constructions and changes in vocabulary and
grammar that reflect the many factors and influences that
comprise the human world insofar as cognitive constructions, a body of knowledge, and collective practices constitute that world. Thus it is claimed that reality is entirely a
social construction.[2]

To explore this observation would be a valuable undertaking but it is not the one I am following here. At this stage
of my inquiry I want to consider a small segment of this
sociological study and show how, in the human world, perceptual experience is at the same time both mediated and
obscured by language, and more generally by culture,
which is its home. Let me illustrate this in a preliminary way
by turning again to Francis Bacon.

> The human understanding is of its own nature prone to
> abstractions and gives a substance and reality to things
> which are fleeting... The Idols imposed by words on the
> understanding are of two kinds. They are either names of
> things which do not exist ... or they are names of things
> which exist , but yet confused and ill-defined, and hastily
> and irregularly derived from realities.[3]

We humans are extraordinary creatures. We feel our
needs and desires so intensely and have imaginative capabilities so convincing that, unawares, we fabricate worlds to
explain and justify them. Language becomes the sometimes
inadvertent ally of such efforts. These linguistic constructions may be as satisfying as they are ingenious, and they
appear to gratify our equally strong cognitive need to identify and account for the fabrications. But they are, nonethe-

---

[2]   I deliberately exclude from this characterization of knowledge those
      claims based on intuition, feeling, revelation, or any other non-ratio-
      nal process. However, these, too, respond in their own ways to the
      same factors I have been describing. An informative account of the
      development and influence of these conditions on knowledge is Pe-
      ter L. Berger and Thomas Luckmann, *The Social Construction of Reality*
      (Garden City, NY: Doubleday, (1966). See also Marcia Muelder
      Eaton, "The Social Construction of Aesthetic Response", *British Jour-
      nal of Aesthetics*, 35/2 (April 1995), 95–107.
[3]   Francis Bacon, *Novum Organum* (1620), li, lx.

less, constructions. We employ the imaginative capabilities of language to achieve magical effects, constructing our conceptual home by linguistic contrivance alone. Put simply, we build a world that contributes to our social ends, satisfies our psychological needs, and achieves our dreams all through the magic of words. This is done by using words as vehicles to establish the existence of things that have no basis in actual sensory experience but rest solely on need, custom, rote learning, education and the other institutions of acculturation, and the habits of thought we have assimilated but of which we are likely unaware.

Religious beliefs and doctrines are replete with reference and appeal to things that do not exist. It is all too easy to expose the visionary grounds of words that populate the dominions of theology. *Soul* is one such word and the origin of many others, and it has had a long historical development.[4] As its meaning first began to be codified in the ancient world, 'psyche' (ψυχὴ) or 'soul' meant simply 'breath', the life force in a living being, especially as a sign of being alive. By the fourth century BCE in ancient Greece, soul began to be thought of as something inherent in living beings that is the seat of both thought, feeling, and desire, and it was early associated with life after death. Plato codified this idea in *The Republic* in the form of a tri-partite soul composed of distinct though interrelated parts: the rational, concerned with knowledge and truth and guided by wisdom; the spirited part, the motivating force from which come drives that, when frustrated, produce emotional responses; and the part that is the seat of the appetites manifested in the desire for physical pleasures, especially of food, drink, and sex.

Plato's theory of the psyche, formed during the flowering of Classical Greek civilization, has been a powerful influence on the major intellectual watersheds of Western civili-

---

[4]   "Soul" is one of the many myths Mary Midgley exposes so effectively in *The Myths We Live By* (London & New York: Routledge, 2003). See esp. pp. 50, 54–5. Indeed, in chs. 1–11 Midgley develops critiques of many of the intrusive assumptions that are exposed and challenged not only in the present chapter but throughout this book.

zation, continuing to the present. Striking parallels (though obviously with differences) appear in Aristotle's hierarchy of souls: the rational soul that is the distinguishing mark of humans; the sensitive soul that is the seat of sensation, of sensory awareness, that all animals possess; and the nutritive soul that energizes organic functioning in plants as well as animals. Plato's echo resounds in Kant's division of reason in his three *Critiques* of knowledge, morality, and judgment, with pure reason grounding science and knowledge in general, practical reason providing the theoretical justification for morality and channeling desire, and judgment, establishing the basis for aesthetic value. And we may even detect the Platonic soul in Freud's division of the human psyche into id, ego, and superego.

Like other such key words, the meaning of 'soul' changed over the course of centuries. By the time of Aquinas in the thirteenth century, soul was thought of as immaterial and distinct from the body. And this ever-deepening division, also prefigured by Plato, received its most emphatic expression by Descartes in the seventeenth century, who considered soul and body so distinctly different and separate that in humans they were tangentially connected only in the pineal gland. What seems to have been common throughout its history is the idea of soul as the vital force in living things and the intelligible part in humans, in contrast to the material body.

It is clear from this brief account of its historical course that soul is a concept that was constructed to underlie and account for thinking, acting, and feeling in humans, and it was further enhanced, especially since it could not be apprehended directly, by being associated with a life force that was considered distinct from the body. Yet if we consider this idea without prejudice and on the basis of what can be directly perceived, it becomes clear that soul merely postulates an entity purported to be the source or seat of these different forms of conscious functioning, forms that themselves are abstractions from experience. It is a fabrication that takes the functions of thought and action and simply stipulates invented entities as their source, such as reason, will, desire, and feeling. Like many other such ideas, 'soul' is an hypostatization projected to provide an explanation of various experiences, and eventually to offer a comforting justification of immortality.[5]

Yet our conscious activities of living, thinking, feeling, and desiring are just that—activities in which we humans engage. No entity such as a mind or a self is needed to underpin these experiences. They are experiences, solely and fully, of the human organism, and to posit a soul to account for them is entirely gratuitous. Nothing in these activities requires us to go beyond the awareness of them to postulate, discover, or create an entity as their origin. We might paraphrase William of Occam, the fourteenth century Franciscan monk, who recognized the tendency to devise explanations by stipulating entities to explain them. To correct this he devised the rule that came to be known as Occam's Razor affirming that, in reasoning, one should not construct or multiply entities beyond necessity.[6] It is entirely possible to be comfortable and content with these

---

[5]   One reader commented, "But there are ranges of cases in which concepts are introduced to identify unobservable dischargers of causal and other roles postulated in theories of observable phenomena. In fact it is pretty standard to say that the semantic value of theoretical terms is given by the generalisations in which they feature and that the relationship between explanatory claims in which they feature and observation reports is indirect. In this respect 'soul' is no worse off than 'field' 'quark' 'multiverse' or indeed 'thought'. From the fact that something is postulated to explain observables but is itself unobservable it doesn't follow that it is 'a pure fabrication'." (John Haldane, personal communication, 8 March 2008.) I have no quarrel with this re-statement of my point, for science has its own mythology, as do most human institutions. The principal factor here is the difference in the "explanatory value" of their concepts and in the other consequences of their acceptance and use.

[6]   "*Pluralitas non est ponenda sine necessitate*", "Plurality should not be posited without necessity", William of Occam's (ca. 1285–1349) famous principle of parsimony. John Haldane points out that "it is one of the ironies of the history of philosophy that Ockham's principle 'entia non sunt multiplicanda praeter necessitatem' is not to be found in the writings of Ockham. The term 'Ockham's razor' first appears in the C.19th in Sir William Hamilton. What Ockham says is 'Frustra per plura quod potest fieri per pauciora' it's vain [pointless] to do with many what can be done with fewer." Personal communication, 10 March 2008.

experiences alone without resorting to fabrications to explain them. In any case, merely inventing such "explanations" is poor comfort.[7]

Many other imaginative constructions developed out of this early one: *spirit, mind, consciousness, self* — to name some of the most familiar. It is common to think of these as entities of some sort that are the source of our different mental activities. This is exactly what, in a distant echo of Bacon, Dewey warned against: false knowledge that comes from turning an activity into a force that becomes the cause of that same activity, as in the explanation that a match sets fire to a piece of paper by its calorific power, that the force of magnetism enables a magnet to attract iron or the force of gravity causes an object to fall.[8] Cautions such as Occam's and Dewey's are still largely ignored.

Consider these related concepts: Like 'soul', 'spirit' is true to its origin in the Latin *spiritus*, breath. For whatever additional meaning it has acquired, spirit, like breath, is immaterial and is often contrasted with matter or with the flesh. It again gives substance and stability to the insubstantial by turning an idea into an entity. 'Consciousness' and 'mind' are other such concepts, and all have been powerful forces in learned as well as popular discussion from Classical times to the present.

Consciousness is associated with mind and thought and their purported contents, entities all. How is consciousness experienced? As the passage of fleeting awareness, James's metaphor of a stream is helpful except that it suggests a continuous, flowing sequence in awareness. Here, too, the inveterate tendency to hypostatize gives more coherence and continuity to awareness than we actually experience. Ever inconstant, our awareness appears and recedes, meanders, splits into different, concurrent streams, blanks out, flows back on itself. Continuity, coherence, and order are difficult achievements, the outcome of a rigorous process

---

[7]   "Spiritual experience is simply an aspect of normal experience [and] belongs to the subject-matter of psychology." Midgley, *op. cit.*, p. 42.
[8]   John Dewey, *Human Nature and Conduct* (New York: Henry Holt, 1938), p. 450.

that selects, excludes, and arranges what we may conveniently call "psychic" phenomena, and applies logical criteria to them. Consciousness, thus, is transformed into an entity, making it an agency of the activities of awareness in order to produce these very experiences. That is to say, the entity "consciousness" is taken as the cause of conscious experience. 'Mind' is another such word that gains stature by contrasting it with matter or the concreteness of reality. The reasoning is irrefragably circular.

The concept underlying all these fictitious entities is undoubtedly that of the 'subject.' Indeed, subjectivism may be regarded as the principal theme of modern philosophy, surviving and appearing in one form or another from Descartes' epistemological subject to Kant's transcendental one, from the metaphysical subjectivism of nineteenth century idealism to the constitutive subject of phenomenology[9] and the inescapable subject of existentialism. From psychoanalysis to drug-induced hallucinations, its manifestations are virtually inexhaustible. Yet I venture to suggest that 'subject', too, is a word for something that does not exist. It is the transubstantiation or, better, the refinement and hypostatization of conscious experience into an entity that supports it. Here, again, we venture onto sacred ground but, if we are going to probe as clearly and as cleanly as possible into an examination of perceptual experience, we must take that step.

Others have already transgressed. One was Merleau-Ponty, especially in his late writings and notes, where there are many fragmentary intimations of non-subjective experience and of the primary unity of self and world. He finds this in the world of silence that he claims was always there as a non-thematized *Lebenswelt*, a transcendental field comprising the relation between the agent (i.e. the actor) and the sensorial field (the body), and in the principle of reversibility that joins inside and outside, making apparent "the antecedent unity me-world". Merleau-Ponty's notion of the chiasm, expanding on this

---

[9]   Cf. Levinas' critique of egology in *Totality and Infinity*.

reversibility, is the most direct formulation of this idea of unity:

> Chiasm I—the world
> I— the other
> chiasm my body—the things, realized by the doubling up of my body into inside and outside—and the doubling up of the things (their inside and their outside).

Thus Nature is "in one way or another the primordial being which is not yet the subject-being nor the object-being".[10]

Lyotard also considered the subject suspect. He removed it from its pre-eminent place as a philosophical category and considered the subject not as transcendent but as one of many elements and the product of social and political forces, open to the libidinal "irrational" forces of feeling and desire. Nor is the self the master of incommensurable language games but rather their point of intersection, existing in a network of relations that constitute one of many possible language games and capable of mobility within it.[11] And Lyotard's extraordinary analysis of the sublime in the presentation of the unpresentable, so indicative of postmodernism, exposes how avant-garde twentieth century art calls the subject into question.[12]

---

[10] Maurice Merleau-Ponty, *The Visible and the Invisible* (Evanston, Northwestern University Press: 1968), pp. 260–4, 273. There are many passages that reflect the continuity of thought, body and world: "The bond between the soul and the body ... is to be understood as the bond between the convex and the concave, between the solid vault and the hollow it forms..." (p. 232) "The flesh of the world ... is indivision of this sensible Being that I am and all the rest which feels itself in me, pleasure-reality indivision..." (p. 255) "The *antecedent* unity of me-world, world and its parts, parts of my body, a unity before segregation, before the multiple dimensions... All this is *exhibited* in: the sensible, the visible." (p. 261)

[11] François Lyotard, *The Postmodern Condition. The Postmodern Condition: A Report on Knowledge* (Minneapolis: University of Minnesota Press, 1984), p.15. Cf. Ashley Woodward, entry on Lyotard in *The Internet Encyclopedia of Philosophy*, http://www. iep.utm.edu/l/Lyotard.htm#H9, esp. Section 6; *The Postmodern Condition*, p. 79 ff.

[12] *The Postmodern Condition*, pp. 77–82. Stefan Morawski criticizes postmodernism strongly for what he claims is its loss of the dignity and independence of the subject. See "On the Subject of and in Post-Modernism", *The British Journal of Aesthetics*, 31–1 (January

The list of such words as I have been discussing can easily be extended. These concepts raise issues that are extensive and inclusive, and a whole field of philosophical inquiry has developed to inquire into these and related concepts, the philosophy of mind, which itself must be qualified by the same considerations raised here. The scope of the present discussion, however, is deliberately limited to its relevance for my larger purpose, and I engage in it largely as an example of the transformative consequences of insisting that thinking remain true to *aisthēsis* , to aesthetic perception.

Nonetheless, these concepts, widely accepted and used, weave an ephemeral web of thought into a world of things that do not exist. These may take the form of invisible entities, a pantheon of gods, spirits, and devils — all mythical or supernatural beings whose existence is exclusively hypostatic but, because they are venerable, they are considered real: fabrications that acquire their plausibility as part of a hallowed or official belief system. Invisible insubstantial entities may also originate in visible things and still not exist: abstract ideas derived from particulars that become forces in their own right, such as justice and injustice, freedom, and even truth. Or they may be constructions that are inferred from specific instances and then applied back to supervene on them. Some examples of this are society and the state, whose distributive origin in certain relations of mutuality is replaced by an abstract collectivity. These various forms of hypostatization do not function in identical ways but they share their non-existence in common, if one may so put it! We shall later consider the functions and uses of some of them.

This is not to deny the experiences that such words intend to signify and to which they respond — experiences of consciousness, of powers, of emotion, of deeply felt needs, of personhood, of feelings of helplessness or of being overwhelmed, and the like. But if we wish to understand the human world as it is directly and truly experienced, we

1992), 50–8. See *The Troubles with Postmodernism* (London: Routledge, 1996) for Morawski's general critique of postmodernism.

must remain faithful to our perceptions not only at the beginning but also at the end of knowledge.

It is important to add that this understanding of the fictitious nature of such constructed entities is not a reversion to Berkeleyan nominalistic idealism. Just as materialism depends on a metaphysics of division, subjective idealism is possible only in a dualistic universe in which the independent existence of a natural world is denied. In contrast, an understanding that rests on the phenomenology of experience takes that and only that experience as what is real. We might call the view that results naturalism in a broad sense, not restricted to scientific knowledge alone but based on the natural world *en tout*, which includes the course and content of human living. Dewey's observation is both profound and true:

> things ... are what they are experienced as. Hence, if one wishes to describe anything truly, his task is to tell what it is experienced as being... [W]e have a contrast, not between a Reality, and various approximations to, or phenomenal representations of Reality, but between different reals of experience.[13]

The belief in such entities presumably denoted by the words of which I have been speaking represents a curious kind of thinking. We can think of it as emulating, in a naïve form, the famous ontological argument for the existence of God. According to that argument, God's essence as a perfect being, "that greater than which nothing can be conceived" in St. Anselm's classic formulation, infers the necessity of God's existence from the essence of His nature as a perfect being. For if we could conceive of a perfect being but one that does not exist, it would be possible to conceive of a still more perfect being, one that does exist. And so, the concept of the nature of God as a perfect being *requires* that He exist.[14] That the ideas I have been discussing denote realities seems to be assumed implicitly in quite the same way. Simi-

[13] John Dewey, "The Postulate of Immediate Empiricism", in *The Influence of Darwin on Philosophy* (New York: Peter Smith, 1951), pp. 227–41.

[14] Anselm reasoned, "[I]f that, than which nothing greater can be conceived, exists in the understanding alone, the very being, than which

larly, such powerful and ennobling ideas as gods, spirits, angels, devils, and the like must surely designate the entities which they denote. Thus, thinking goes from the idea to existence.

In the case of abstract faculties like mind, consciousness, and reason, the thinking is similar. Their presumed "reality" results from passing, with blithe disregard of the ontological consequences, from the processes, experiences, and activities of awareness and of the many forms of thinking in which we engage to an entity that is taken as their source. Clearly, such activities may be designated by substantives, but simply as processes extended in time they do not become substances. We discover, again, that the simpler explanation is the preferable.

The inference of realities underlying abstract ideas such as truth, justice, and morality follows a similar, misleading pattern. It is not surprising that such intriguing ideas have generated centuries of debate and, while the basic issues may be clear enough, they are easily obfuscated. [15] The ontological argument, presumably put to rest by Kant, continues nonetheless to be disputed and still often accepted. We continue to live in a world that we explain by ideas of things that do not exist. A phenomenology without ontology can liberate us from such illusions. A reality that is more modest and on a human scale is not only less fraught with ghostly fears and tormenting uncertainties; it is truer to experience. Like the emperor's new clothes in Hans Christian Andersen's tale, there's nothing there but what you see.

---

nothing greater can be conceived, is one than which a greater can be conceived. But obviously this is impossible. Hence, there is no doubt that there exits a being, than which nothing greater can be conceived, and it exists both in the understanding and in reality." *Proslogium*, trans. S.N. Deane (Open Court, 1903).

[15] Derrida skirts close to such issues in his fascination with words and with questions implicated in the Heideggerian search for Being through a unique word. Cf. Jacques Derrida, *Différance,* in *Margins of Philosophy*, trans. Alan Bass (Chicago & London: Chicago University Press, 1982), pp. 3–27.

Words, Edges, Boundaries

The magic of words shows itself in still other ways than the construction of an invented reality of fictitious entities.[16] It also provides a structure for that world. Let me not attempt here either to duplicate or summarize the conclusions of structural linguistics or the critical insights of the sociology of knowledge. What I want to do is to reconsider, starting from direct, aesthetic perception, how we are able justifiably to identify differences and discriminate objects. What kind of world is it that we can directly know? What is our knowledge of the world by acquaintance?

The question at issue is the kind of world we humans inhabit. For our world consists not just in inferred or constructed entities but in structures, divisions, and relationships that distinguish, separate, and connect them, all influenced by the historical, cultural, environmental, and technological conditions under which we construct human reality. Where do things, things from unicellular protozoa to galaxies, begin and end? Common sense seems to guide us in ordinary circumstances, for the microscopic world is not our habitual dwelling place, except perhaps in a metaphorical sense, nor is interstellar space, although this limitation may not last much longer.

Not just at the borders of perception but even in daily life the boundaries of things may be ambiguous. Where, for example, is the exact point of division between the lanes of a two-lane unmarked road or the precise point on the baseline of a tennis court that determines whether the ball is in the court or out? How are masculinity and femininity distinguishable in humans: when, exactly, do biological differences become gender differences? Where in the distribution of wealth is the poverty level and where does the middle class begin? When ocean-front property extends to the high tide mark, where does that lie, since it is always slightly different because of the phase of the moon, the season, and

---

[16] Katya Mandoki provides a trenchant analysis of the fetishes of aesthetics in *Everyday Aesthetics: Prosaics, the Play of Culture and Social Identities* (Aldershott: Ashgate, 2007), Ch. 2.

storm turbulence?[17] And then there's the infamous conundrum posed to logic students: At what point in the gradual loss of hair does a person become bald? Indeed, there is no impersonally determinable mark by which social distinctions, physical differences, or personality types can be identified. Studies of such human differences must always stipulate for heuristic or practical reasons where these lie. Examples of the indeterminacy of boundaries proliferate: where are the edges of a rippling brook? the precise width of the Gulf Stream at any given location? the temperature at which a room becomes cold? Must the pitch of A above middle-C be 440 cycles per second, as present convention in the West specifies, or can it be at 480 as it was on the organs Bach played or at 409 as a pitchfork associated with his contemporary, Handel, declares? Even today when international convention stipulates that A=440, some orchestras in America and the European continent may tune to 442, others may tune to A=445, while many Baroque ensembles choose A=415, nearly a semi-tone lower.

Some instances of such ambiguity are trivial and many are simply stipulated for practical purposes and vary with time and place. Certainly, for purposes of social function or practical demand, distinctions are made and judged on pragmatic grounds by the uses for which they are drawn. The case of musical pitch is particularly interesting because what determines the choice of pitch to which an instrument or an orchestra tunes remains entirely a perceptual choice by the conductor or by custom. The situation isn't much different with other phenomena. We can make a visual determination in deciding whether a cloud is a cumulus or cumulo-nimbus type with no precise measure such as pitch has in cycles per second. As an airplane rises through the cloud layer, it moves through a gradually dissipating mist, while once through and looking down, the cloud blanket appears to be dense and with a clean surface. Land boundaries are unavoidably approximate. Even if they are designated by latitude and longitude, the surveyor's line is never

[17] The reference to mean high or low tide line is a calculation, not a location.

razor thin and ruler straight on the ground. Neither, *a forti-ori*, are the borders of nations.

It appears then that many words appeal to sharp bound-aries that have no physical counterpart, for what they demarcate may be inherently ambiguous or arbitrary. This is not to mention the fuzzy edges of common physical objects at the molecular level, which we cannot ordinarily perceive. Not only may it be difficult to discriminate things, since there are no precisely determinable objects: the very identity of an object is an abstraction from experience. And when words are used to identify and relate ideas, the abstraction is even more distant, as in Kant's distinction between the imagination and the understanding. When we move from objects to concepts, and from concepts to their order and relationships, the only ways they can be distin-guished are by convention or simple stipulation. Isn't this what occurs in legal decisions, when the determination of a judge or the vote of a jury marks the legal difference between guilt and innocence, all examples of Austin's performative utterances?[18] Distinctions and connections do not come from words that denote an ontological difference but from their source in perceptual experience and their application in practice. We regularly disregard Aristotle's caution not to confuse a distinction with a separation.

The question of difference has fascinated some contem-porary philosophers, and the ontological implications of various considerations of difference resemble those that emerge from placing meanings against their perceptual ori-gins and recognizing distinctions not as ontological but as perceptual and pragmatic. Lyotard, for example, argued that difference, *le différend*, occurs in situations, such as those involving the double bind, where a conflict cannot be resolved because no rule of judgment can be found that applies to both sides of a dispute. He notes similarly that the meaning of a phrase can be fixed only within a "phrase uni-verse" and not by reference to reality since reality is not fixed but chosen from competing senses that derive from

[18]　J.L. Austin, *Philosophical Papers*, 2nd edn. (Oxford University Press, 1970), pp. 233–52.

different universes. We have, then, no single Reality against which meanings and knowledge can be judged but only competing realities whose authenticity comes from the ends or goals that are at stake.[19] Dewey comes to mind again:

> [W]e have a contrast, not between a Reality, and various approximations to, or phenomenal representations of Reality, but between different reals of experience.[20]

Derrida's concept of *différance* reflects a similar indeterminacy. Here meaning is never complete, for there is no objective referent, but it is always deferred. *Différance*, he states, is neither a word nor a concept and there is no ontology to which it can be reduced. Hence meaning is never final and can never be fixed; its indeterminacy always lies within itself or between texts. Difference is ineradicable.[21]

Another recourse to an ontology of indeterminacy to account for the shifting character of the human world appears in the work of Gilles Deleuze. In his early writing and subsequently elaborated, Deleuze challenged the philosophic tradition that utilizes reason to discover overriding abstract principles of a transcendent reality. This led him to reject the Good, the True, the Just, and other such constructions, considering them superstitions and delusions. Instead we must get at things from within, we must "trace a field of immanence",

> construct a space of thought in which there are no longer transcendent elements, that is to say, superior categories that dominate and organize things, as the One, the True, the Good, God, Reason, the Subject.

In their place Deleuze discovered only multiplicities: feelings, forces, signs, tendencies that surround the process of events. This is a level of experience that is pure and with no

[19] Jean-François Lyotard, *The Differend: Phrases in Dispute*, trans. Georges Van Den Abbeele (Manchester: Manchester University Press, 1988). Cf. Woodward, Section 4c.

[20] John Dewey, "The Postulate of Immediate Empiricism", in *The Influence of Darwin on Philosophy* (New York: Peter Smith, 1951), pp. 227–41.

[21] Jacques Derrida, *Différance*, (http://www.hydra.umn.edu/derrida /diff.html).

subject or consciousness to originate or underwrite it. It is a world of change and difference with new shapes, multiplicity, and heterogeneity in which we must re-order the very process of thinking.[22]

In collaboration with Félix Guattari, Deleuze later introduced new terminology to reflect the radical re-shaping of reality that deconstruction enjoins. Speaking metaphorically, Deleuze and Guattari adopted the term 'deterritorialization' to refer, among other things, to the shifting of order and control where an "arborescent", hierarchical model is replaced by the "rhizomatic" formation of interconnected, dynamic entities whose boundaries are not fixed and whose identity, meanings, and interconnections are constantly changing. We have thus a continuum and not a structure of divisions. Deleuze and Guattari refer to the earth as

> a body without organs. This body without organs is permeated by unformed, unstable matters, by flows in all directions, by free intensities or nomadic singularities, by mad or transitory particles

formed by forces and powers that are not apparent but that produce the world we see and touch. The things we find in the world, such as mountains (slow-moving), living things (flows of genetic material), and language (flows of words and of information), are not relatively stable but are made up of different sets of flows that move at different speeds. The earth, then, can be understood as a body, a body without organs, with a fluid substratum of forces and powers in constant flow.[23]

Perhaps we can best think of language as a functional symbol system that is applied to the world of experience to assist us in gaining our goals but that has no outside correlative. Isn't this what de Saussure taught us about language,

---

[22] Arnaud Bouaniche, *Gilles Deleuze, une Introduction* (Pocket, 2007), pp. 50–2, my translation. Deleuze first developed these ideas in his early books on Hume, Nietzsche, Bergson, and Proust, and elaborated them later in *Différence et répétition* (Paris: PUF, 1968), *Logique du sens* (Paris: Minuit, 1969), and subsequent books.

[23] Gilles Deleuze and Félix Guattari, *A Thousand Plateaus* (Minneapolis: University of Minnesota Press, 1987), p. 40.

that it is a closed system of meanings in which words are defined by their relation to other words and that they do not descend from or denote anything outside a linguistic system? The mistake in assuming that they do is committed constantly. But the unavoidable fact is that all we have is perceptual experience ordered by language on historical, conventional, and pragmatic grounds, and this ephemeral bond of praxis is the only connection there is between language and experience. For words are always false to experience except in their poetic use, and the truth of poetry lies in making experience virtually tangible. *Vide* Kant: "To call the ocean sublime we must regard it as poets do, merely by what strikes the eye...."[24] To be led by words is to be seduced by their conceptual power, their ability to form a world out of the chaos of perceptual experience, and it is on their deceptiveness that their preemptive power rests. "The feeling that one feels, the seeing one sees, is not a thought of seeing or of feeling, but vision, feeling, mute experience of a mute meaning... ."[25]

It may seem that, by taking perceptual experience as primary, by affirming the primacy of the aesthetic, we relinquish the very authority of reason. This, however, is not a case of "relinquishing" something but of recognizing that language has no ontological basis and that its authority comes from other, equally non-absolute sources. Here again we arrive at a fork in the road to knowledge where a major cognitive decision must be made. It might be thought that this decision is a choice between rationality and anti-rationality, so that if we choose to forsake the former we return to the chaos of a world before Creation. But here, too, the choice is wrongly placed. For the issue is not about rationality itself but rather about the nature of the rationality we can rightly claim. That rationality is not ontologically

---

[24]   Immanuel Kant, *Critique of Judgment*, trans. J. H. Bernard (New York: Hafner, 1951), pp. 110–11 (§29).
[25]   Maurice Merleau-Ponty, *The Visible and the Invisible*, p. 249. See also Maurice Merleau-Ponty, "The Primacy of Perception", in *The Primacy of Perception and Other Essays on Phenomenological Psychology, the Philosophy of Art, History and Politics*, ed. James M. Edie (Northwestern University Press, 1964).

grounded is not to say that it has no validity whatsoever but rather that the cognitive claims of what we take to be real vary with who is making them and with the context in which they are made. Such claims are not arbitrary but depend on our grasp of the natural world, the social world, and the various divisions in either that we may choose to make. The sciences remain intact and unchanged; it is only our understanding of their grounding and their authority (and hence their presumed immutability) that must change. Everything that can be asserted thus rests on the theoretical and pragmatic procedures that are utilized. Whether we start from pragmatic or deconstructive grounds, our knowledge is neither universal nor immutable but loses none of its validity.

The nature of rationality and the dichotomy of "rationalism and anti-rationalism" at the horizon of knowledge has long evoked deep concern and in diverse traditions. A.C. Graham encountered this in his picture of ancient Chinese philosophy, and he was careful to distinguish between anti-rationalism and irrationalism: anti-rationalism, when he took Chuang-tzu as exemplary, who contrasted spontaneity with reason; and irrationalism, exemplified by the Marquis de Sade, Nietzsche and Hitler.[26]

I realize that this chapter considers issues close to the heart of the philosophic tradition and that so brief a treatment of these ontological concerns cannot fully counter the historical force of the deeply-rooted traditions that identify standard problems and the nuanced discussions of alternative resolutions. At the same time, the general approach I have followed has the purgative effect of locating and clearing out ways of thinking that evade solution because of their basic assumptions or their ways of structuring the problems. By demonstrating the application and force of the aes-

[26] See "Rationalism and Anti-Rationalism in Pre-Buddhist China", in A. C. Graham, *Unreason Within Reason. Essays on the Outskirts of Rationality*, La Salle, Ill.: Open Court, 1992, pp. 97-119; A. C. Graham, *Reason and Spontaneity*, London & Dublin: Curzon Press, 1985, pp. 156-227. See also Kwok-ying LAU, "To What Extent Can Phenomenology Do Justice To Chinese Philosophy?" Unpublished paper.

thetic argument, this discussion has its place here. It will be put to use in the chapters that follow, which will apply the aesthetic method to some of the philosophical issues and values central to social philosophy. But tradition is difficult to overcome and the return to experience not easy to achieve. Consider Creon's advice to Antigone:

> Life flows like water, and you young people let it run away through your fingers. Shut your hands; hold on to it, Antigone. Life is not what you think it is. Life is a child playing round your feet, a tool you hold firmly in your grip, a bench you sit down upon in the evening, in your garden. People will tell you that that's not life, that life is something else. They will tell you that because they need your strength and your fire, and they will want to make use of you. Don't listen to them. Believe me, the only poor consolation that we have in our old age is to discover that what I have just said to you is true.[27]

Using the investigative and critical capabilities of the aesthetic with the help of the methodology of phenomenology and a pragmatic process of determining and evaluating meanings and consequences has a dramatic effect on our basic understanding of the human world. That its results are transformative is not the consequence of applying the aesthetic irresponsibly but of recognizing the unfounded intellectual constructions that we have become accustomed to think of as "natural" or as simple "common sense" from the force of tradition, custom, and habit. With this powerful aesthetic instrument in hand, we can now pursue its critical and constructive use in rediscovering and reconstructing our human world.

---

[27] Jean Anouilh, *Antigone*, trans. Lewis Galantière (London: Methuen, 2000), p. 56.

Chapter Five

A Rose by Any Other Name

What's in a name? That which we call a rose
By any other name would smell as sweet.[1]

Having laid out an aesthetic grounding of the human
world, I want to move in the next four chapters in a
wide-swinging arc to offer an aesthetic consideration of
diverse regions of experience, showing how their content
has been formed as the work of the thought and actions of
human culture. This chapter begins the trajectory by bringing together claims I have been making for the scope and
importance of aesthetics, presenting it as an important, substantive, and inclusive approach grounded on perceptual
experience. Aesthetics will emerge as a field that ranges not
only over the arts and nature but that illuminates the full
range of human culture and delineates a far-reaching, het-
erogeneous domain of knowledge and value.

It has sometimes been said that aesthetics is a secondary
discipline, peripheral to philosophy or, like the arts, themselves, peripheral to the study of human society. I do not
think that this is the case; moreover, I believe that such an
appraisal distorts both sides of the comparison. The history
of philosophical aesthetics shows a gradual and growing
development from particular questions to concerns that
have greater scope and that confer increasing identity on
aesthetics as a distinctive field of inquiry. This development
has gained increasing momentum, apart from some brief

---

[1]   William Shakespeare, *Romeo and Juliet*, Act II, Scene II.

intervals when, with supreme arrogance, the intellectual respectability of aesthetics was questioned. We are now, in fact, witnessing a vast expansion of the scope of aesthetic inquiry. It is possible to consider aesthetic value, not only in nature and the arts but in technology, popular culture, environment, social relationships, and political theory. And we recognize that aesthetic values and ideas have implications for a whole range human concerns, including those that lie at the center of human community.

Identifying these wide-ranging aesthetic interests can also promote their further expansion and application. Yet the field of aesthetics has long labored under handicaps, cognitive as well as professional, that have kept its focus limited and narrow. I believe that broadening the scope and application of aesthetics as both a recognized dimension of experience and as a field of study offers the possibility of transforming the human world, not by physical or material change but by altering the kind and quality of our experience and so the ways we live in our world. I want to show how examining the facets and dimensions of experiences we call aesthetic can be expansive and revelatory. This can also help us see how aesthetics relates to other areas of knowledge, such as social and cultural studies, and conversely, how different disciplines bear on our aesthetic understanding.

Let me consider, first, how aesthetic inquiry can take a clearer and more productive direction, beginning with the name of the discipline. I commented earlier on the historical origin of aesthetics and used this as a springboard to argue for its greater breadth. Yet aesthetics has often been used to restrict appreciative experience and, in fact, the term itself may be a liability. But what we label aesthetic is not significant: appreciative experience is. Aesthetic theory is easily caught up in secondary, unproductive, and even possibly false issues, such as the definition of art, the boundaries of art, and the proper designation of beauty. It is in avoiding this danger that this chapter receives its title. What is important, I want to argue, is not what we call beautiful or designate as art but where we find the kind of value experiences traditionally associated with appreciating beauty, natural and artistic, and how we can enhance and develop such experiences. However, this also requires recognizing the converse of these values in the loss, the negation, the desecration of this mode of experience.[2]

The Scope of Aesthetic Experience

Aesthetics is unlike any other field in the central place it gives perceptual experience, experience that is never surpassed or transcended. Since this is where any inquiry must start, I consider aesthetics a foundational discipline, perhaps *the* foundational discipline, not logically or ontologically but temporally and heuristically. This is a powerful claim, but I assert it to recognize how important are those normative experiences we call aesthetic.

It is useful to recall that aesthetic experience has been a subject of discussion since Shaftesbury and Hutcheson inquired into the experience of beauty early in the eighteenth century and regarded aesthetic appreciation as largely disinterested. This view was institutionalized by Kant at the beginning of the nineteenth century and since then has become axiomatic. I have challenged its hegemony, arguing that, among other liabilities, disinterestedness confines appreciation to a state of mind, that is, to a psychological attitude, and unduly excludes the somatic and social dimensions of experience, thus directing aesthetic appreciation improperly.[3]

Aesthetic experience became increasingly important during the nineteenth century and even more in the mid-twentieth, the principal figure in this re-focusing of aesthetic

---

[2]   The negative and critical capabilities of experiencing aesthetic value are the subject of Ch. 9.

[3]   Cf. Jerome Stolnitz, "On the Origins of 'Aesthetic Disinterestedness'", *Journal of Aesthetics and Art Criticism* 20 (1961), pp. 131–44; Ronald Hepburn and Arnold Berleant, "An Exchange on Disinterestedness", *Contemporary Aesthetics*, 1 (2003) (www.contempaesthetics.org); Arnold Berleant, *Re-thinking Aesthetics, Rogue Essays on Aesthetics and the Arts* (Aldershot: Ashgate Publishing Ltd, 2004), Chs. 2 and 3.

inquiry being John Dewey.[4] Somewhat in eclipse during the latter part of the last century, interest in aesthetic experience has returned in recent years, both in artistic practice and aesthetic theory, with renewed vitality and a broader scope. Following the groundwork laid by Dewey in centering discussion on the active human organism, recent interpretations of aesthetic experience stress its sensory character and interpret sensory perception far more widely than before. In contrast to a tradition originating in Classical Greece that confines the perception of beauty to sight and hearing, it is now often acknowledged that all the senses, including proprioceptive and kinesthetic sensation, are involved to varying degrees, and that the senses do not demarcate discrete and separate perceptual channels but rather are experienced synaesthetically.

Yet another expansion of aesthetic experience in the late twentieth century has been to reject disinterestedness entirely, not only because of its psychological cast but because it is unduly restrictive in excluding objects and activities that may be functional or have a practical purpose but that one can still appreciate aesthetically in ways similar to the traditional fine arts. Intrinsic perception must therefore be understood more broadly. It may occur alongside practical interests, as in architecture, automobile design, or an English cottage garden, or it may be inseparable from functional uses, as in the appreciation of a smoothly running machine or a well-designed article of furniture. Social, cultural, and technological influences are also important factors in aesthetic experience. Because the range of aesthetic value has become vastly greater, so also has its significance as a cultural phenomenon.[5]

Thus with the expansion of perceptual experience to include all the senses and to extend beyond a merely psy-

---

[4] John Dewey, *Art as Experience* (New York: Minton, Balch, & Co., 1934).

[5] There is a large and growing literature here, some of it coming from sources in the phenomenological movement and some from the pragmatic. Among the more notable contributors to the enlargement of our understanding of aesthetic experience are Maurice Merleau-Ponty, Mikel Dufrenne, and Wolfgang Welsch.

chological attitude or mental state to the aware, sensing body, the meaning and characterization of aesthetic experience have undergone major changes. What remains of critical importance, however, is the strong emphasis on sensory perception and on the intrinsic character of such perception. The active participation of the appreciator, indeed the appreciator's contribution to the art work as well as to the experience, has become widely recognized in the contemporary arts. Artistic practices, such as including the reader's response and the multiple forms of interactive art, call on the overt and active contribution of the appreciator for their completion. Indeed, we recognize that absorption in aesthetic appreciation may at times be so complete that the viewer, reader, or listener abandons entirely the consciousness of a separate self and enters totally into the aesthetic world. This is familiar to many people in the experience of being caught up in a novel or in the virtual world of cinema. When we are not misdirected by contrary expectations, we can cultivate the ability to become appreciatively engaged on many different artistic occasions. I call such appreciation "aesthetic engagement", and when it is achieved most intensely and completely, it fulfills the possibilities of aesthetic experience.

An Enlarged Domain of Aesthetic Value

At the same time as such experience achieves intensity and completeness, its scope becomes correspondingly greater. Appreciation then is not confined to the art museum or concert hall but extends in all directions. Not only can any object be appreciated aesthetically but so can every situation. Consequently, aesthetics has generated a proliferation of sub-disciplines such as environmental aesthetics, the aesthetics of everyday life, the aesthetics of popular culture, the aesthetics of sport, and the politics of aesthetics. The theoretical scope of aesthetics has also grown, developing new relations with other disciplines and new regions to explore. Comparative aesthetics is one such development, and it extends our understanding of the aesthetic by introducing other cultural and historical traditions to the classic Western one. Social aesthetics is another, looking into ways in which aesthetic experience and value enter human relationships and institutions.

There is yet another direction in which aesthetic experience has enlarged its scope. In giving primacy to intrinsic sensory perception and to meanings and ideas grasped through such experience, we must acknowledge that this condition is not always positive simply but may be normatively complex. The very inclusiveness of aesthetic experience demands that we take account of experiences that are similar in kind but different in value. Intrinsic sensory awareness perceived through cultural meanings and influences may intensify those objects and situations that range from the unfulfilled to the demeaning and destructive.

In short, we may speak of a negative range of aesthetic experience, of negative aesthetics. This can not only reflect lost or frustrated possibilities for enrichment, as in the design of a banal building or martial music that evokes loyalty to false or destructive myths of national or cultural superiority. Aesthetic experience can also produce outright pain, as we may experience on entering a favela or urban slum, of dismay in witnessing the clear-cutting of an old growth forest, or of revulsion when encountering kitsch in literature or art. These experiences can produce not only aesthetic pain but moral suffering, both of which are, at times, inseparable. Its capability of identifying negative aesthetic values gives the aesthetic the possibility of becoming an incisive force in social criticism, a largely untried region of aesthetic activity but a potentially powerful one. Thus aesthetic theory and experience are intimately bound up with the moral, negatively as well as positively.[6] Recognizing the dark side of aesthetic experience is another reason for exceeding traditional constraints.

The aesthetic has not only a history but also a future. It is unwise to attempt to predict the aesthetic capacities of experiences as yet unknown. We can nonetheless see, at our

---

[6]   The meaning and forms of negative aesthetic value are considered in
       Chapter 8.

present stage, some of the revealing possibilities offered by new directions of inquiry. Negative aesthetics is a hidden region of perceptual experience that is closely bound up with ethical issues. We might indeed argue that ethical criticism often harbors an aesthetic dimension. Every decrease in human good may entail a beauty unrealized, and moral transgressions always bring with them a diminution of aesthetic capabilities. It is even possible to say that an aesthetic affront is embedded in every immoral act. This is clearly a complex interrelationship; it identifies a direction in which aesthetic inquiry can move into new ground and enlarge our moral as well as our aesthetic understanding. We shall develop this at some length in Chapters Nine and Ten.

Then there are perennial issues that can acquire new meaning. One of these concerns the interrelationships among the various arts, always an intriguing question and even more so now with new arts and new artistic technologies. Some relationships that were challenging not so long ago have become more or less settled as the presumed conflict has dissipated or at least become less interesting. Obvious examples are the relation of photography to painting, of film to the novel and to video art, and of assemblages and environments to sculpture. It is a task for aesthetic theory to help us understand how these historically related art forms can engage us in different ways and what is distinctive about our experiences with them.

We have already noted new perspectives in experience that can be identified in different historical periods, and how or whether such historically qualified experiences can be grasped clearly enough to establish an identity. Is there, for example, a Victorian sensibility that moves across pre-Raphaelite painting, didactic poetry, gothic novels, and the dark romanticism of nineteenth century symphonic music? What of the baroque in music and architecture or, more recently, dada and surrealist art, and pop art and mass culture? Thus our appreciation also requires examination, and a rich and complex range of aesthetic experiences lies open to inquiry. Does appreciating seventeenth century Dutch landscape painting entail experientially entering the world of van Ruysdael and Hobbema, and, if it does, how authentic is that world to us and to the world of those painters?

A somewhat parallel issue concerns the comparative understanding of the characteristic aesthetic sensibilities found in different cultural traditions. Can we discern, for example, a tangential connection between the experience of the x-ray paintings in aboriginal art with, say, cubist art of the early twentieth century, or between medieval Indian erotic temple sculpture and the sensual sculptures of Rodin or Maillol?

Other related and underlying issues need to be exposed and clarified. Where is aesthetic value located and how is it identified in different cultures? Some obvious complications reside in the frequent fusion of aesthetic with religious and other cultural forms of experience and meaning. Can they be distinguished and, if they can, how much do they resemble one another? To consider a familiar, puzzling case, how can we best understand the interrelations of Christian history and beliefs with the aesthetic experience of the masses of Bach, Mozart, or Schubert? I suspect that a somewhat different understanding will emerge in each instance and, perhaps, in each individual work. What is the aesthetic dimension in the statuary of Hindu deities, of Western medieval and Renaissance religious art, of the carved wood crucifixions and altarpieces of Riemenschneider from the late Middle Ages, for example? Perhaps this cognitive complexity can be seen most directly and generally in the names different cultures use to identify what we may call beauty: the Hebrew *yapha*, the Greek *to kalon*, the Japanese *wabi-sabi*, the Indian *rasa*.[7] While a beginning has been made in comparative aesthetics, fascinating issues remain. Comparative aesthetics, historical aesthetics, the multi-dimensional richness of aesthetic experience in different arts — these are some of the productive directions in which aesthetic inquiry can move.

Such promising possibilities may augur an optimistic future for aesthetic theory. Unfortunately, however, aes-

[7]   *Cf.* Crispin Sartwell, *Six Names of Beauty* (New York and London: Routledge, 2004).

thetics is burdened with many so-called "problems" that are either contrived or misdirected. Here grows the rose referred to in my title. Indeed, such problems often rest on theoretical assumptions originating in cultural belief systems, or on premises that derive from quite different philosophical sources. We may therefore want to regard some of these problems as false issues in aesthetics, all the more unfortunate in their tendency to deflect us from larger concerns and more productive directions. This is not a vague and general criticism; it rests on specific assumptions and practices.

One of these is the widespread practice of centering discussion on the object, the art object, alone. The question is often asked, "But is it art?", rather than inquiring into the experiential situation in which alone that question is meaningful. This object orientation leads to many minor issues that have produced major efforts at conceptual identification, such as locating aesthetic qualities, determining the meaning and boundaries of beauty or the definition of 'art.' It is the distortion that results from taking aesthetic inquiry to be about art objects that produced the controversy between formalism and representation in the visual arts, the conundrum over the difference between art and real things, and the persistent puzzle over the aesthetic significance of artistic representation, as well as uncharitable responses to new materials, styles, and subject-matter. What we should ask instead is "Are we experiencing this situation aesthetically or how can we develop the capacity to so appreciate it?" One consequence of making aesthetic experience central is that it demands the recognition that art is not an object at all but a situation, an aesthetic field, and that every art object functions and can be understood only as part of a experiential situation involving appreciative, creative, and performative dimensions, as well as one that focuses on an object.[8] It does not matter whether we call

---

[8]   I term this "the aesthetic field" and it has been the guiding idea throughout my work in aesthetics. It was first developed in my book, *The Aesthetic Field, A Phenomenology of Aesthetic Experience* (Spring-

something art or not; what is important is how the object works in appreciative experience. It is such experience that lies at the heart of the aesthetic.

In considering obstacles to the expansion of aesthetics, it is useful to recall the distinction between the different modes of inquiry I called critical and substantive aesthetics.[9] Clarifying key concepts, considering the boundaries of art, puzzling over whether and how we can designate and characterize the aesthetic properties of objects that function in appreciative experience, specifying the precise nature of the relation these objects have to aspects of the world independent of art — all these are directions that critical aesthetics may take. So, too, is the concern with the logic of those concepts and the structure of aesthetic theory. Substantive aesthetics, on the other hand, is not directed so much toward objects and their corresponding ideas as toward understanding the content and conditions of appreciative experience. Like the integrative endeavors of philosophical and methodological synthesis discussed in Chapter One, substantive aesthetics attends to the conditions, content, and effects of such experience as much as with the second-order activity of defining and characterizing that experience.

In their extremes, these represent two different and incompatible intellectual cultures, but happily they are not often carried to exaggerated lengths. Most aestheticians employ procedures and goals that are both critical and substantive. The differences among them result from the degree of importance or emphasis given one or the other. Still, even when not extreme, these differences may be significant, indeed fundamental.[10]

Another obstruction to progress in aesthetic thought results from hierarchical thinking, which leads to invidious

---

field: C.C. Thomas, 1970) and has been extended and refined in subsequent publications.

[9]   See the contrast between critical and substantive aesthetics developed in Chapter One.

[10] A fuller discussion of this distinction occurs in A. Berleant, *The Aesthetics of Environment* (Philadelphia: Temple University Press, 1992), pp. 25–6.

distinctions as, for example, between the "higher" arts and the popular arts.[11] Instead of making normative distinctions, we can gain greater understanding from investigating differences in appreciative experience that occur in the artistic modes, materials, and styles associated with such classifications. Here we should also include the folk arts, arts that have histories, styles, and experiences of significant value in their own right. Weaving, basket making, quilting, sculpture using recycled materials, and folk sculptures and environments constructed out of discarded objects can offer deep satisfactions to a perceiver and introduce rich insights into the worlds of people who may be too modest or naïve to claim the title of artist.

Moreover, it would be misleading to consider the popular arts as a homogeneous group. Significant differences exist among them, and subtle yet important discriminations can be made of appreciative experience between arts in the same modality. Popular music encompasses an enormous range of sub-genres that differ significantly from one another. What makes swing, ballad, blues, jazz, rock, hip hop, and rap distinctive and different from one another? This, moreover, is not to deny the qualitative difference between Bartók and be-bop. It is rather to recognize that each kind (not level) of music is the occasion for distinctive appreciative experiences. Differences in quality, in refinement, complexity, and subtlety do not tendentiously demarcate degrees of aesthetic value but rather differences in normative experience. Investigation into those differences is an important but largely unexamined field for aesthetic research.

Related to this traditional hierarchical assumption is the distinction between the fine arts and the practical arts or crafts. This, of course, has cultural and historical roots in the superiority that the Classical Greeks attributed to theoreti-

---

[11] Cultivating the "higher arts" is seen as an important source of creative inquiry in European culture. See the program of The European League of Institutes of the Arts (ELIA) and the Association Européenne des Conservatoires, Académies de Musique et Musikhochschulen (AEC)

cal over practical knowledge. Its modern form appears in the assumption that objects of fine art must be regarded for their own qualities and not for any practical interest. I have noted how the doctrine of the disinterestedness of aesthetic appreciation has been an axiom of modern aesthetics. While it served to identify the distinctiveness of the aesthetic, at the same time it excluded from aesthetic significance and even legitimacy those arts that are inseparable from practical interests, such as the design arts, and it led to such anomalies as considering architecture a fine art and furniture design a practical one.[12] Resting aesthetic value on appreciative experience undermines these false oppositions and makes possible the illuminating study of finely discriminated qualities of appreciation.

The Future of Aesthetics

Finally, a word about the implications of the aesthetic vision I have outlined here. Some of these are fairly obvious from what has already been said. Others may not be immediately apparent. Let me indicate several possible directions.

Once we extend the range of the place and the experience of art and the aesthetic, we can recognize their critical position in human society. Every design decision affects people's experience, and the aesthetic is a critical part of that experience. Instead of being thought of as a "frill", we begin to grasp the pervasiveness and importance of aesthetic factors. These, then, must be assigned greater importance, and decisions about the design of human environments and institutions and of the activities that are part of their functional processes come to take on a broader significance. Social decisions, such as those implemented through architecture and city planning in residential development and urban design all have aesthetic consequences. Once their importance is acknowledged, all social decisions would have to consider aesthetic effects in addition to economic

---

[12] I have developed an extensive critique of aesthetic disinterestedness in several places. See *Art and Engagement* (Philadelphia: Temple University Press, 1991) and especially *Re-thinking Aesthetics*, cited above.

constraints and technological requirements. Before any major construction project is begun, communities should require an "aesthetic impact study" as many now require an environmental impact study. Money can no longer rule as an autocratic god, for economic values are never the only values at stake. Such forethought is necessary not only for design decisions in the physical environment but for designing institutions, political processes, and other forms of social organization.

The aesthetic also has an important place in human relationships, both personal and social, and it affects people's daily activities. I call the aesthetic here "social aesthetics", an area that will be explored at greater length in Part Three. A social aesthetic is present not only in friendship, family, and love, but even in education and employment. Aesthetic decisions and experiences are also embedded in the design and use of factors and features in the everyday environment that have social ramifications. These extend from the choice of clothing, the use of appliances, the packaging of articles, the care and management of one's home, and the other objects and aspects that constitute daily life, to personnel policies and the structuring of employer-employee relations, i.e., the social organization of production and commerce. This is not to overlook the major importance of the ethical factor in these last cases for, indeed, ethical values lie at the heart of social aesthetics. We should also not overlook the influence of aesthetic decisions on political life and on social institutions. Aesthetic distinctions are easily transmuted into class distinctions, and class distinctions are quickly institutionalized in political distinctions and discriminatory social practices. Influences *on* the quality of aesthetic experience and influences *of* such experience pervade the human environment.[13]

The assumption that there are universal aesthetic standards and the quest for them have colored the history of aes-

---

[13] The key study here is Terry Eagleton, *The Ideology of the Aesthetic* (Oxford: Blackwell, 1990). See also Arnold Berleant and Allen Carlson, eds., *The Aesthetics of Human Environments* (Peterborough, ON: Broadview, 2007).

thetic thought, but such standards have never been established successfully.[14] The individual human factor in aesthetic judgment is ineradicable, and with it come the other contextual factors that influence appreciative experience. Yet while specific aesthetic judgments may not be universal, the aesthetic in experience is valued everywhere, and more research needed in exploring this. Not only do all peoples seem to consider aesthetic satisfactions important; there is a similar breadth in the occurrence of the aesthetic in every corner of experience in different cultures. The boundaries that have circumscribed art and the aesthetic have been forever breached.[15]

One of the consequences of such a renewal of aesthetics as I have projected here cannot be categorized easily. This is a vastly enlarged vision of human understanding. Here artists can be our guides and philosophers our cartographers. Experiential understanding is a legitimate mode of knowing the human world. Our awareness deepens from the revelations novelists give us into human conditions, both historically and culturally different.[16] Poets reveal the nuances of particular occurrences and sensibilities and playwrights the peculiarities of an endless range of social situations. As fine artists bring to light new sights and new ways of seeing, composers lead us into the experience of an inarticulable realm of being.[17] So with every art and every

[14]   The question of whether it is possible to establish such standards has been a preoccupation of philosophers from Hume and Kant to the present day.

[15]   For a revealing account of this, see David Novitz, *The Boundaries of Art* (Philadelphia: Temple University Press, 1992).

[16]   In her analysis of literary works, Nussbaum probes into the kind of understanding that literature offers. See Martha Nussbaum, *Love's Knowledge* (New York & Oxford: Oxford University Press, 1990).

[17]   Vladimir Jankélévitch draws a penetrating distinction between the ineffable and the untellable, and assigns the former to music. The ineffable cannot be explained but "acts like a form of enchantment", dealing with mystery and provoking bewilderment. *Music and the Ineffable* (Princeton & Oxford: Princeton University Press, (1961) 2003), p. 72. Also see Ben-Ami Scharfstein, *Ineffability: The Failure of Words in Philosophy and Religion* (Albany: State University of New York Press, 1993).

original artist.[18] Not only are the range and subtlety of human experience vastly enlarged through our aesthetic understanding. Artists are also able to penetrate beneath the protective layers with which we shield ourselves. For aesthetic appreciation is not sensory delectation but an entrance into domains of understanding that lie outside the boundaries of empirically verifiable scientific knowledge, of linear rationality, as it were.

It is possible, however, to discover intimations of such "poetic understanding." Heidegger, for example, found the meaning of an artwork's "coming-to-presence" in poetry, for poetry uses language to reach toward what words cannot say directly and literally. Thinking, he wrote, "must think against itself", and poetry discloses being by offering a presence that touches us. Poetry thus becomes the language of being.[19]

Merleau-Ponty approached aesthetic understanding by another route, through vision rather than language, painting rather than poetry. His problem was somewhat different: how to grasp "our mute contact with the things, when they are not yet things said." How can we make the "transition from the mute world to the speaking world." To do this we must confront "brute vision" and recognize the ineradicable influences both of our corporeal body and of the world of human encounters, culture, and history. What we are seeking, he stated, is being, neither in itself or for itself but at the intersection of both, before the chasm between them that reflection interposes.[20] In pursuing this, Merleau-Ponty invoked original and powerful ideas. One of them is the concept of reversibility, the kind of interdependency that holds between touching and the touched, between the visible and the invisible. This led him to speak of more than interdependency but of a joining together into

[18] Cf. Derek Whitehead, "Artist's Labor", Contemporary Aesthetics (www.contempaesthetics.org), Vol. 5 (2007).

[19] Martin Heidegger, Poetry, Language, Thought, trans. Albert Hofstadter (New York: Harper Colophon Books, 1975), pp. 8, 93. Cf. also pp. 137, 216.

[20] Maurice Merleau-Ponty, The Visible and the Invisible (Evanston: Northwestern University Press, 1968), pp. 36, 38, 63–4, 95, 154.

what he called "the flesh of the world", the "indivision of this sensible Being that I am and all the rest which feels itself in me, pleasure-reality indivision...." [21] His fascinating investigation of this led him to the idea of a 'chiasm' or intertwining. This rich concept, whose full elaboration he left unfinished, points to yet another direction by which we attempt to grasp the non-reflective human world where words cannot take us. [22]

These brief accounts cite only a few of the important efforts to achieve a kind of understanding that is, by its very nature, non-conceptual. Indeed, this sense of understanding is especially apposite to the experience of the arts, which is the paradigmatically non-conceptual. [23] Yet the inarticulability of the end point is hardly a new discovery. One cannot help but be reminded of Plato's recognition of it in the incommunicability of the vision of the forms. [24] A comparable case is Kant's projection of a noumenal realm of things-in-themselves that lies beyond the capabilities of human knowledge but at the same time functions as the ground of its possibility.

In these times when it is widely claimed that scientific knowledge is exclusive and exhaustive while, on the other side, gross irrationality runs madly amok on an international scale, it remains a challenge for philosophers to recognize this realm of the inarticulable and determine its significance. This is something to pursue, not in the manner of an investigation into an objective, universal structure and not by following the artist's intuitive path, but as a cognitive exploration of the pre-cognitive and the non-cognitive, an

---

[21] *Ibid.*, pp. 254–7.
[22] See Ben-Ami Scharfstein, *Ineffability, The Failure of Words in Philosophy and Religion.*
[23] This is a debatable claim, of course, but the theory of aesthetic experience that underlies this book makes the case that such experience, as direct and unmediated, precedes cognition. This bears a close relation to what Jacques Rancière called "the aesthetic regime of the arts" that he characterized as "the regime of the sensible", finding it anticipated by Vico, Kant, Schiller, Schelling, Proust, and Surrealism. See Jacques Rancière, *The Politics of Aesthetics* (2000) (London & New York: Continuum), pp. 22 ff.
[24] *Republic*, VII, 540A.

elusive region of experience, a domain that may be grasped even though not known.

Here aesthetics has much to offer, for the ultimate inarticulability of the aesthetic provides a model as well as an occasion for acknowledging and clarifying the character and range of a region of human awareness insufficiently acknowledged. To recognize it as terrain that is contiguous and perhaps co-extensive with aesthetic experience is to concede that aesthetic inquiry possesses wide philosophical importance. But while the ultimate inarticulability of experience is a challenge, its place in inquiry, like the arts themselves, is substantive rather than critical. It is substantive in offering a beginning, if not a grounding, as we grope toward an understanding that is authentic in its directness and not constrained by external specifications. Aesthetics, both as experience and as theory, has a central place In this process, but to succeed in making its distinctive contribution to the process, aesthetics must enlarge its scope and become ready to move in new directions.

In sum, it is clear that a revival of aesthetics has begun. The place of the arts and aesthetic experience in human society has expanded and become increasingly prominent. Aesthetic values are discovered, from their presence in the objects and situations of daily life to the various forms of social relationships. This enlargement offers a basis for social and environmental criticism, thus giving aesthetic judgment an important social role. Aesthetic experience also has had to grapple with the challenges presented by new arts and artistic technologies. All these have enlarged the range of experience, which then must be understood in ways that can account for these changes. Part of this expanded experience is a growing appreciation of the value of differences among cultures, something an aesthetic sensibility is particularly capable of recognizing and valuing. We can think of this variety in aesthetic perception as part of the culture pool of humankind, as a resource comparable to the human gene pool, a rich fund from which ever-new possibilities of perceptual experience can be brought to experience. And as the value we find in cultural perception

increases, our appreciation of the importance of these differences grows accordingly. And finally, the greater
breadth of human cognitive and perceptual awareness in
knowing leads to a recognition of its limits and a more balanced vision of its range.

There is clearly much room for expanding aesthetic
inquiry and it faces many possibilities. New and different
theoretical questions emerge, from re-examining aesthetic
appreciation to disclosing the shape of aesthetic understanding. Moreover, aesthetic theory has a whole other side,
and applied aesthetics is becoming increasingly important
both theoretically and practically. Indeed, both of these
must come together, for they are different faces of the same
coin. In the process of its expansion, some traditional issues
may be abandoned and, with them, the comfort of familiar
ground. But this is all to the good, for it reaffirms the freshness of this inquiry and the continuing importance of aesthetic value in the global cultures of a post- industrial
world. While we may have to relinquish the rose, we can
detect whiffs of its fragrance everywhere. Let us then
proceed.

Chapter Six

The Soft Side of Stone

Introduction

This chapter is a study of cultural meaning. It examines how stone, a material that is matter-of-fact, firm, dense, and obdurate, is layered with meanings in striking contrast to this conventional understanding. As a philosopher I might be expected to write about meaning and leave the hard side of stone to the geologists and other practitioners of earth science. And as a phenomenologist I might be expected to think about the perceptual experience of stone, a material that, shrouded with significance and associations, is infinitely malleable. To fulfill both expectations, I shall glance quickly over the perception and appropriations of stone but give most of my attention to exploring some of the significance embedded in that experience and to pursuing its implications. For a multiplicity of diverse meanings lies hidden in the space between the hardness of stone and its cultural applications. Yet meaning, one expects, must be grounded in the stabilizing presence of a common world, and what could be more stable and insistently present than stone?

Let me approach the sphere of meaning gradually, briefly considering the role of stone in the geological history of the earth, and then describing some of the sensory qualities, direct and indirect, commonly associated with stone. Then I shall review the variety of uses for which stone is appropriated and consider its transformative possibilities. All this is introduced for the sake of comprehensiveness, but it will lead to the crux of the issue here: the kinds of meaning we can find in stone, its soft side, so to speak.

To begin with the obvious, stone embodies the history of the region in which it is found, a history that can be unearthed, so to say, largely by observing the principle of uniformitarianism. This fundamental doctrine of geological science holds that the processes we observe modifying the earth's crust today have been at work in the same fashion throughout geological time. Similarly, present day earthquakes, volcanic action, and tsunamis caused by the shifting of geological plates cast light on how the earth continues to be reconfigured from the effects of its cooling. Geological strata, of course, literally embody the history of its surface. Careful study of such phenomena and the evidence they have left both on and beneath the earth's surface has led geologists, using radiometric dating methods, to estimate its age to be about four and a half billion years. Finally, the erosive forces of wind and water are constantly working to alter the earth's surface. We can observe these processes, such as the effects of erosion and the action of glaciers in collecting and depositing moraine and in forming lakes. They illustrate how the same processes worked in the past, and such observations assist us in reconstructing the geological history of the earth. In a similar way, the effects of global warming cast light on major climatological shifts in planetary history.[1]

Description and Appropriation

Of course, the operation of these forces is rarely visible to the naked eye. What we see, what we directly encounter with our bodies as we move on the earth's surface, are the directly perceived sensory qualities of stone, its derivatives, and their uses. These include stone's hardness, firm and unyielding; its weight and density; its coldness in shadow and beneath the soil and its warmth under the sun; the insistence of the dampness of stone over its dryness; the roughness of its surfaces over its smoothness and configurations; stone's varying color, usually transformed when wet as well as under different kinds and directions of light. Per-

---

[1]   The complementary theory of catastrophism has been revived also.

haps most insistent is our physical apprehension of the size, massiveness, weight, and distribution of stone in particular locations. To these we must add its indirect sensory features, such as the color or grain that emerge when stone is polished. Stone has an interior, too, that is revealed when it is split. While all this is well known, the large number and broad range of these sensory qualities may still be surprising.

Further complexity comes from the fact that stone rarely stands in noble isolation. It is usually found under conditions that complement or contrast with it. Stone is often encountered, sometimes by deliberate design, in combination with water, one of the most tractable of substances, in thought as in nature.[2] Yet at the same time the strength of water can exceed that of stone, as pebbles worn smooth by a mountain brook and sand at the seashore will testify. This dialectic of opposites produces curious meanings that are as rich as they are puzzling, for each invades the province of the other, water, when frozen, becoming hard and rigid as stone[3] and evanescent as dust when vapor.

The association of stone and water has long attracted visual artists as well as travelers, for there is drama inherent in their juxtaposition. There is also poetry, as this passage by the poet Tam Lin Neville conveys:

> Yesterday, children were leaping rocks that surround a fountain in my neighborhood. These are real rocks brought in and placed here in the city, to gleam in the mist the jets of water create. The children, their bodies an inexpressible lightness, skip from rock to rock. In the gap between the

---

[2]   Water, no less than stone, is a social material. The meanings associated with bottled water, for example, are transformative. "[W]e can observe an extensive taxonomy and nomenclature emerging with the proliferation of technologically processed and purified bottled water that suggests the fluid is not an objective or singular thing-in-itself, but a physically and culturally mediated product — a conceptually contested substance with a plurality of forms and social associations involving status, health, safety, and a desire for the pristine." David Macauley, "The Domestication of Water: Filtering Nature through Technology", *Essays in Philosophy*, Vol. 67 No.1, January 2005, p. 13.

[3]   I am grateful to Riva Berleant for noting that old glacial ice is actually a changed substance and can be considered metamorphic rock.

unyielding medium of the rock and the elasticity and light-
ness of their bones something's hidden, waiting to be
found.[4]

What lies hidden here between the firm, the fragile, and
the flowing? Let me pursue this question from another
direction. For even more ubiquitous than its association
with water is stone rooted in the ground, softened or
obscured by plants and decorated by their blossoms, seen
under a vast sky or concealed from its eye, and sometimes
even in the most austere circumstances covered with the
delicate pastels and occasionally the intense color of lichen.
Perhaps most prevalent and powerful of these, though, is
the description of stone as bedrock, the association of stone
with its "mother earth". Actually this inverts the order, with
the earlier stage coming from the later. The converse,
"daughter", is more truly the case, for it is stone itself that is
the mother of earth. And an image waiting to be discovered
may be that of stone as nature's bones, the bones of the
earth. As with the children's bones, the bones of the natural
world constitute its skeleton, giving structure and support
to its flesh of soil, plants, and all living beings, including
humans. The sculptor Isamu Noguchi must have sensed
this by using stone as the backbone of the landscape in his
garden designs and landscape sculptures.[5]

Moreover, some of the sensory features of stone are dis-
closed only when stone is split into cross-sections and polished. I have already mentioned how this reveals its colors
and grain, but even dramatic qualities may emerge. The
hollow center of geodes is often jewel-like, dense with
multi-colored crystals, and exotic fossils are frequently
embalmed in limestone. The appearance of stone can
change under various kinds of light and when the light
comes from different directions.

---

[4]   Tam Lin Neville, "Early Mornings", *American Poetry Review*, 35/6
       (November/December 2006), 33. Used by kind permission of the au-
       thor.
[5]   Cf. Noguchi's UNESCO garden in Paris, Billy Rose Sculpture Garden
       in Jerusalem, and California Scenario.

In honor of its age and prevalence, stone exemplifies stability and permanence in the natural world (whether or not that is actually the case), and people have exploited these characteristics through many different uses. Stone may be gathered, quarried, and cut. As fieldstone or slate it may be carefully stacked into walls or embedded in the soil for walkways and roads, and it can be arranged into art objects, as in the work of Andy Goldsworthy.[6] Stone is one of the oldest building materials, used for support, for walls, as facing, and for floors. Nothing has a longer history than the use of stone for monuments and markers for the dead in the form of statues and gravestones, or using stone to construct an interior, sealing the body in a sarcophagus, stone crypt, dolmen, mausoleum, or pyramid.

The sense of permanence we assign to stone is, however, deceptive. Permanence is a cultural meaning, not a physical fact. Despite being used to symbolize a desire for stability and permanence, such meanings are thoroughly transformed and may be entirely disregarded by the social uses of stone. For stone reveals surprising malleability and transience. We could actually emphasize its impermanence by noting its cracking, breaking, and crumbling. Stone steps become deeply grooved from continued use, and parts of religious statues are worn smooth from the kisses of worshipping lips or the caress of fingers. Not only can stone be carved and pulverized; stone surfaces weather, inscriptions become illegible and even disappear;[7] vertical stones fall over and sculptures break. Sometimes one can experience the hardness and instability of stone simultaneously. The warning sign "Falling Rock Zone" recognizes the capacity of stone both to crumble and at the same time damage a vehicle or injure a person. Less destructive events may also befall stone. Its surfaces may be hidden by moss, lichen, or soil and buried by shifting earth surfaces or under profuse vegetation. Stone even has a kind of genesis as well as a

---

[6]   Andy Goldsworthy even gives stone biological properties when he says that the process of putting one stone on another is akin to the process of growth.

[7]   Shelley's "Ozymandias" gives poetic immortality to this transience.

demise, for the earth gives birth to stones that emerge from the soil from the action of winter freezing and thawing.

Stone possesses many possibilities for transformation: into jewelry, into sculpture, and into light and shadow in photographic art. Usually solid in the form of boulders, rocks, and small stones, stone emerges molten from the earth's core during volcanic eruptions and becomes gaseous in the intense temperature of stars. Solid as it usually is, stone is sometimes malleable, and sculptors have transformed its appearance into flowing garments and even into the soft surface of flesh. Stone may be molded as cement to simulate the appearance of natural rocks, emulated in stage sets, and turned into visual illusions in holograms. For a hard, solid substance, stone seems capable of unlimited alteration.

The Semiotics of Stone

Stone is, then, not as stable and permanent as one might at first suppose. Its many possible transformations suggest that stone possesses a certain fluidity of appearance and use. But when we move to the other side of the equation and shift our focus from the substance of stone to its meanings, their multiplicity is awesome. For meanings are cultural constructions, and rock and stone embody rich lodes of cultural meaning that range in many directions. Let us follow some of these and see where they lead.

A rich variety of metaphors is based on the perceived properties of stone. Perhaps the property most commonly appropriated for symbolic purposes is its stability, its presumed permanence. Stone, too, has a definite materiality as the bedrock of the earth, hard, unyielding, obdurate. This is what led Samuel Johnson to blithely dismiss Berkeley's claim that everything is ultimately a sensation in the mind by kicking a stone, exclaiming, "I refute it thus!"[8] He did

---

[8]   "After we came out of the church, we stood talking for some time together of Bishop Berkeley's ingenious sophistry to prove the nonexistence of matter, and that every thing in the universe is merely ideal. I observed, that though we are satisfied his doctrine is not true, it is impossible to refute it. I never shall forget the alacrity with which John-

indeed demonstrate that stone is unyielding while at the same time proving Berkeley right by the pain of a stubbed toe, ironically a sensation n the mind! Indeed, stone's durability is exemplified by diamonds, the jewel of choice for wedding rings. People have long used stone as a symbol of eternity. Gravestones and other memorials are nearly always made of stone, which perversely leads the curious visitor to old graveyards to read the weathered, often illegible inscriptions. Something that is decided irrevocably is "written in stone", probably not the best metaphor for an absolutely fixed decision.

Stones that dispense with carving altogether are more enduring memorials. Prehistoric standing stones: stone circles, henges, menhirs, and dolmens are human orderings of natural stone. Like pyramids, some are clearly burial crypts, but the purpose of others, such as those at Stonehenge, remains a matter of speculation, while the fields of standing stones on Easter Island and at Carnac have long outlasted the cultures that built them and their purposes remain hidden.

The omnipresence and availability of stone is probably the basis for such common expressions as "a stone's throw away" and "leaving no stone unturned". Metaphors derived from stone's hardness are probably the most frequent and have become trite. These evoke associations that are thoroughly social in meaning and use. Describing a person as stony-faced or flint-faced in contrast with being soft, warm, and loving, or as having a heart of stone have become embarrassing cliches. The durability of stone may be why it is used for names that hopefully will impart strength and stature to their bearers: "Flint" and "Rock" as given names, and "Diamond", "Stone", and the German "Stein" in surnames. Moreover, the beauty of stone is appropriated in women's names such as "Ruby", "Esmeralda", "Sapphira", "Opal", and "Jade", and in using rubies, emeralds, diamonds and other precious stones in crowns to bestow glory

---

son answered, striking his foot with mighty force against a large stone, till he rebounded from it — 'I refute it thus.' " James Boswell, *The Life of Samuel Johnson*, Part 2, Ch. 13.

as well as stature on a monarch, while the peasant May queen must be content with the transient beauty of a flower garland. On the darker side, stone may become a weapon, from the stone that David used to slay Goliath to throwing stones as a means of battle. When stoning is the punishment for transgressing the inviolability of social mores, who is innocent enough to throw the first stone? The cultural meanings of stone may be more durable than the material from which they are derived.

The mystery associated with stone and the magical properties ascribed to it may be the most fascinating of its cultural appropriations. What comes first to mind is the transformative power attributed to the philosopher's stone — the "holy grail" of alchemy. This is a substance, usually a powder made from a mythical philosopher's stone, that supposedly could turn inexpensive metals such as lead into gold or could create an elixir that would make people younger and so delay death. Philosophers have not been the only ones seeking gold in a stone. The pale, brass-yellow color and metallic sheen of iron pyrites, which, strictly speaking, are not stone at all but a mineral, have misled people into thinking they had discovered gold, whereas what they had actually collected was merely "fool's gold". Prospectors, it seems, may be no wiser than philosophers. The worship of gold has led to valuing still other stones. The meaning of a touchstone, originally a black siliceous stone similar to flint that was used to test the purity of gold and silver, has been elevated into a general criterion of genuineness.

Perhaps to compensate for the failure to find fortunes through its use, stone has been given other magical properties. Some believe that quartz crystals store natural energy and possess magical healing power. In fact, the study of this has been given the honorific name of 'crystalology,' and therapies have been devised to apply this power to different ailments. Stones have also had more rational applications to achieve therapeutic results: Many can attest to the calming effect of fingering worry beads, and physical tension can be dissipated by a hot stone massage. The strange ability of lodestones to determine direction has a scientific explanation from the fact that they have magnetic properties that exhibit polarity, whereas, as one journalist noted, the ability of a kidney-shaped stone to move every day may not.[9]

It is most common today for stone to exert its influence more in metaphor than in magic. Because stone has assumed many forms and acquired many uses, its characteristics have metamorphosed into many common expressions. Here is a sampling and one can easily think of more. From its weight, mass, durability and hardness, stone has been accorded special respect. It is used to confer security when "The Lord is my rock",[10] even though it is not eternal, for as Lucretius commented long ago, "Continual dropping wears away a stone." [11] The strength and power of rock and stone are respected in a "monumental" boulder, and its durability is acknowledged in describing a rocky coastline as rugged. "You can't get blood out of a stone" is an acknowledgement of stone's hardness and intransigence, as is its implicit violence in "killing two birds with one stone."

It is no surprise that the uses and meanings that rock and stone have acquired owe their origin to cultural needs and practices. Although these will vary with the culture, some of the usages I've mentioned occur in numerous cultures, such as having a heart of stone, leaving no stone unturned, and being a stone's throw away.

The Soft Side of Stone

It is now time to consolidate what we have discovered about stone and draw what conclusions we may. Few will dispute the claim that stone, as we know it, displays perceptual features directly and indirectly, and that it has been taken up for various uses and found in many different settings. And few can fail to be impressed by the imaginative meanings that center around rock and stone. We have seen here only a sample of the different appearances, forms, and images that

---

[9]   Haruki, Murakami. "The Kidney-Shaped Stone That Moves Everyday", *The New Yorker*, September 26, 2005.

[10]   *Samuel II, 22.2, 3.*

[11]   Lucretius, *De Rerum Natura*, I, 313.

rock and stone assume, but even these are powerful evidence of the important place that stone occupies in understanding and enriching our experience.

From all this it would seem that stone has two sides. One is the object that stands before us, the stubborn reality on which Sam Johnson bruised his toe, the rigid substance that enters into our ordinary experience, the stone that we seem to perceive. This is the hard side of stone: the stone of the geologist who, hammer and chisel in hand, studies the distribution, the types, and the history of the rock and stone that constitute the solid outer layer of the Earth. It is the stone of the builder, who lays a foundation of stone to support structures both small and large, and may raise that material high above the ground. It is the stone of the sculptor who, with care and discernment, transforms a coarse and stolid material into wondrous shapes with varied sensory qualities. And it is the age-old impediment of the farmer, who dulls his plow blade on it. The other side of stone is the rich range of meanings that stone holds for us, the values we find in it, the metaphors by which stone figures in our understanding, its influence on our imagination, and the powers we attribute to it. This is its soft side.

But now we come to a curious observation and the principal significance of this discussion. From all these uses and usages it is clear that stone is perhaps almost entirely a human, cultural artifact. The references of its meanings are in large part to the language, values, conventions, and practices of a culture. Moreover, it is still more important to recognize that our descriptive accounts of stone rest on perception that is distinctively human. The range and acuity of our perceptual experience are limited and directed by the biological structures and capabilities of our sensory organs. To add still more to the human factor, perception itself is not a purely organic event. As I have already noted, all perceptual experience is screened through many layers of cultural values, taboos, and traditions, as well as through those personal filters that we acquire from our individual experience, habits, and conditioning. The perception of color is typical. Studies of cultures that use stone tools show that color categories are not universal. In fact, studies of color perception offer considerable evidence of the social origin of color boundaries. "Sociohistorical psychology emphasizes the fact that sensory information is selected, interpreted, and organized by a social consciousness. Perception is not reducible to, or explainable by, sensory mechanisms, *per se*."[12]

This leads us to a curious conclusion: If both the entire range of human perception and the rich repertory of social appropriation of rock and stone are not only informed, influenced, and even constituted by our biological capacities but are perceived, shaped, and understood through the social and cultural layers that enfold us, then it turns out that stone does not have two sides. The world in which we live is necessarily a *human* world, a world we cannot avoid or evade. We are led to conclude, therefore, that stone has only one side, a soft side. It is not surprising that a poet can say it all, succinctly but cogently:

---

[12] "[P]ossession of linguistic color categories facilitates recognition and influences perceptual judgements, even in a language whose terms are less abstract than English." Roberson, D., Davies, I. & Davidoff, J. (2000) "Color categories are not universal: replications and new evidence from a Stone-Age culture." *Journal of Experimental Psychology: General*, 2000 Sept., Vol. 129(3), 369–98. Much research supports the hypothesis that the categories of the language we use influence the way we perceive the world. Among the ways in which culture influences perception are by addition, omission, organization, sharpening, and transformation.

Carl Ratner cites the seminal work of Sapir, Whorf, Vygotsky, and Luria, all of whom maintained that "sensory processes are subordinated to and subsumed within 'higher' social psychological functions." He argues that not only are color boundaries and focal points socially mediated but psychological functions in general are. Carl Ratner, " A Sociohistorical Critique of Naturalistic Theories of Color Perception", *Journal of Mind and Behavior*, 1989, 10, 361.

See also Dedrick, Don, Naming the Rainbow: Colour Language, Colour Science, and Culture (Dordrecht: Kluwer, 1998). This is a history of studies of color terminology, both universalist and relativist, and of theories in anthropology, linguistics, psychology, etc. The author takes a modified universalist view that a basic biological color perception exists in all human groups, with divergent cultural emphases. However, the question is not settled.

Aesthetics of Stone

The gods take stone
And turn it into men and women;
Men and women take gods
And turn them into stone.[13]

Stone is left, then, with only a soft side, a seemingly odd state of affairs and one that common sense finds most improbable. Doesn't stone ultimately stand free of our meanings and uses? But to posit an entity independent of our perception, which we seem to do so readily, is just that — pure assumption. Recognizing that our transactions with stone show us something not dependent on our will or our perception does not establish that they are *independent* of them. The first of these, the obstinacy of things, is part of all experience in the world of everyday life; the second is purely an assumption, more often, perhaps, a myth. Like many other myths, it may serve to make our lives more stable and so more comfortable. But like myths that we take at face value, it does this at the cost of delusion.

The most significant issue yet remains, and it is one for which the aesthetics of stone is only an instance. And it is actually an ontological more than an aesthetic question: If all that can be said about stone is not about stone *simpliciter* but ultimately only an aesthetics of the uses and meanings that accrue to it, have we gained the whole world but lost its reality?[14]

This is an issue only if we insist on the unfounded "truth" of common sense, more accurately on what is known as

---

[13]   Kenneth Koch, "On Aesthetics", from *One Train* (Knopf, 1994).
[14]   "What shall it profit a man if he gains the whole world and loses his own soul?" (*Matthew* 16:26). "The theoretical formulations of reality, whether they be scientific or philosophical or even mythological, do not exhaust what is 'real' for the members of a society. Since this is so, the sociology of knowledge must first of all concern itself with what people know as reality in their everyday, non- or pre–theoretical lives. In other words, commonsense 'knowledge', rather than 'ideas' must be the central focus for the sociology of knowledge. It is precisely this 'knowledge' that constitutes the fabric of meanings without which no society could exist." Peter L. Berger and Thomas Luckmann, *The Social Construction of Reality* (1966) (Doubleday, Anchor ed., 1967),

"common sense realism", namely that there is stone, itself, not dependent on human experience at all. For philosophers it is the "form" of stone, its noumenon. Stone here is on the level of similar positings, philosophical and religious, in the form of an Absolute, a divine Creator, substance, the soul, and gods. We "take gods and turn them into stone", and we take stone and turn it into gods. Hume realized this long ago:

> I would fain ask those philosophers ... whether the idea of substance be derived from the impressions of sensation or of reflection? If it be conveyed to us by our senses, I ask, which of them; and after what manner? If it be perceived by the eyes, it must be a colour; if by the ears, a sound; if by the palate, a taste; and so of the other senses. But I believe none will assert, that substance is either a colour, or sound, or a taste. The idea, of substance must therefore be derived from an impression of reflection, if it really exist. But the impressions of reflection resolve themselves into our passions and emotions: none of which can possibly represent a substance. We have therefore no idea of substance, distinct from that of a collection of particular qualities, nor have we any other meaning when we either talk or reason concerning it.[15]

[15] Other relevant texts by Hume include: "Where then is the power, of which we pretend to be conscious? Is there not here, either in a spiritual or material substance, or both, some secret mechanism or structure of parts, upon which the effect depends, and which, being entirely unknown to us, renders the power or energy of the will equally unknown and incomprehensible?" David Hume, *An Enquiry Concerning Human Understanding*, Section VII, Pt. I.

"Thus neither by considering the first origin of ideas, nor by means of a definition are we able to arrive at any satisfactory notion of substance; which seems to me a sufficient reason for abandoning utterly that dispute concerning the materiality and immateriality of the soul, and makes me absolutely condemn even the question itself. We have no perfect idea of any thing but of a perception. A substance is entirely different from a perception. We have, therefore, no idea of a substance." *Treatise of Human Nature*, Sect. V.

"The idea of a substance as well as that of a mode, is nothing but a collection of Simple ideas, that are united by the imagination, and have a particular name assigned them, by which we are able to recall, either to ourselves or others, that collection. But the difference betwixt these ideas consists in this, that the particular qualities, which form a substance, are commonly referred to an unknown something, in which they are supposed to inhere; or granting this fiction should not take place, are at least supposed to be closely and inseparably

We seem to have ended rather far from where we began, for it turns out that the underlying issue is ontological, not aesthetic. But perhaps these are never far apart. And for the resolution of this ontological problem aesthetics may be the key and display the need for a new philosopher's stone. In *The Rules of Sociological Method* Durkheim stated that "the first and most fundamental rule is: *Consider social facts as things.*"[16] A comparable philosophical rule would be, *Consider things as social facts.*

---

connected by the relations of contiguity and causation. The effect of this is, that whatever new simple quality we discover to have the same connexion with the rest, we immediately comprehend it among them, even though it did not enter into the first conception of the substance." *Treatise of Human Nature*, Section VI.

[16]   Emile Durkheim, *The Rules of Sociological Method* (The Free Press, 1938), p.14.

Chapter Seven

An Aesthetics of Urbanism

Ecology and its Significance

Our understanding of ecology has gone through several stages from its original biological meaning denoting the interdependency of all the biota and physical components that make up an environment to its extension as a concept about the relation of humans to their physical and cultural environment. Many factors besides physical conditions affect this complex interrelationship, factors such as social, cultural, political, legal, and economic ones, and the study of human and cultural ecology has emerged to accommodate these. The special importance of expanding the ecological standpoint lies in recognizing that humans do not stand outside nature, contemplating, using, and exploiting it. Humans are seen here as an integral part of the natural world and, as such, fully encompassed in ecosystems, from particular, local ones ultimately to the planetary. This transformation has constituted a scientific revolution comparable in importance to the Copernican Revolution and similar to it, for an ecosystemic approach removes humans from a favored place in the terrestrial world, just as the Copernican Revolution removed the sun from the center of the celestial universe.

Acceptance of this idea — the understanding of environment as an all-inclusive context in which humans are wholly interdependent with natural forces and other organic and inorganic objects — is slow. The concept applies, moreover, not just to rural peoples and environments, the number of which continues to shrink rapidly; it applies equally to urban environments where most of the world's population lives. For we face the reality of predominant urbanism and the emerging understanding of the urban region as an ecosystem with similar interdependencies of objects and organisms, from the most simple to the most complex.

The ecological model in biology thus has universal implications, for no organism can be understood apart from the system in which it functions. This principle applies to the dominant human organism as much as to any other. It proposes understanding humans as natural beings in continuity with the rest of nature, a conception that initially received powerful support from Darwinian evolution and to which ecological theory adds corroboration and sophistication. We humans, perhaps more than any other species, survive and prosper through our social organization and cultural practices. These are integral parts of the human ecosystem, and the rich field of cultural ecology explores how social and cultural conditions affect human well-being and influence survival.[1]

Indeed, we are at a stage in cultural evolution when this ecological understanding finds itself in competition with pre-scientific, sometimes indeed neolithic world views, just as Copernican astronomical theory once did and Darwinian evolutionary theory still does in some benighted places. At its heart this is a conceptual revolution for, if we carry an ecological understanding through to the very idea of environment, we find that we, as humans, are not only fully

[1]   The classic early statement on cultural ecology is anthropologist Julian Steward's "The Concept and Method of Cultural Ecology", originally published in 1950 and reprinted in 1955 in his *Theory of Culture Change* (Urbana: University of Illinois Press), pp. 30–42.
    For cultural ecology in the discipline of geography, see Karl Butzer, "Cultural Ecology", in Gary L. Gaile and Cort J. Willmott. eds., *Geography in America* (Columbus OH: Merrill Publ. Co., 1989), pp. 192–208. Two summary articles with bibliographies are Larry Grossman, "Man-Environment Relationships in Anthropology and Geography", *Annals of the Association of American Geographers* 1977, 67:126–44; and Ben Orlove, "Ecological Anthropology", *Annual Review of Anthropology* 1980, 9:235–73.

enclosed within an environmental complex but are an inseparable part it. We must, therefore, think of environment and of human life, in particular, in vastly different ways from before.[2]

Cultural ecology thus denotes an all-embracing environmental context in which each of its constituents, whether organic, inorganic, or social, is interdependent as well as interrelated with the others. And each factor, in pervasive reciprocity, contributes to an ongoing balance that promotes the well-being of the participating organisms. This ecological model goes far beyond the biologically unfounded paradigm of separate, individual organisms competing against one another for survival, a view that was never part of Darwinian evolutionary theory. By identifying these contrasting patterns — the individualistic and the ecological, their striking differences emerge clearly.[3]

Aesthetic Ecology

The meaning of environment has thus changed dramatically. It can no longer be thought of as surroundings but more as a fluid medium, a kind of four-dimensional global fluid of varying densities and forms in which humans swim along with everything else. In order to function in such an environment we are thrown on our own capacities, and these rely strongly on perception. Since the source and character of our capabilities lie in sense perception, the fluid medium of environment is a condition in which there are no sharp separations. It is important to recognize that, from the standpoint of sense perception, we experience environment

[2] Ecological and evolutionary thought in anthropology have long been entwined.

[3] An ecological model does not commit one unqualifiedly to homeostasis. While homeostatic factors are at work attempting to maintain a healthy balance in the ecosystem, this is not an equilibrium, for environmental changes occur constantly and, for humans, social environmental changes as well as changes in the individuals are frequent and ongoing. There is no ultimate stable ideal order; adjustment to changes is constantly necessary. For a comprehensive discussion of urban aesthetics, see Nathalie Blanc, *Vers une Esthétique environnementale* (Paris: Éditions Quae, 2008).

continuously and in continuity. This is a condition Kant called "pure sensation", wholly unformed and grasped in "pure intuition" and William James described it famously as "one great blooming, buzzing confusion."[4] At the same time as it lies at the origin of the aesthetic, the idea of sensory perception helps us grasp more fully the experience and meaning of environment.[5]

Perception, however, is not simple sensation for, as I noted earlier, sensation is never pure. Pure sensation is more an idea than an experience, for in itself sensation is entirely a physiological event. Even then it is not entirely a direct sensory experience. Sensation is unavoidably colored by the perceptual process, a process that embodies gestalt qualities and cultural conditioning, and it is apprehended through the conceptual and emotional filters humans acquire through the socializing process. Sense perception, then, involves not only surface qualities but every dimension of our sensory, our sensuous awareness. When we experience environment in a manner that is fully aware of its perceptual richness and in which immediate, qualitative perception dominates, we are in an aesthetic realm. We can say, in fact, that environmental perception originates as aesthetic perception.[6]

Not only is environmental perception fundamentally aesthetic but perception contributes significantly to our understanding of environment, underlining the fact that environment is undivided. The continuity of perception means that all the factors and features of environmental experience, including those that humans contribute, are bound together as a continuity. When we do not regard our-

[4]　Immanuel Kant, *Critique of Pure Reason* (1787), trans. N.K. Smith (London: Macmillan, 1956). First Part, §1 (A 20–1, B 34–5). William James, *Principles of Psychology* \ (Henry Holt, 1890), Vol. 1, pp. 461–3.

[5]　This allusion to Maurice Merleau-Ponty is deliberate. See Maurice Merleau-Ponty, "The Primacy of Perception", in *The Primacy of Perception and Other Essays on Phenomenological Psychology, the Philosophy of Art, History and Politics*, ed. James M. Edie (Northwestern University Press, 1964).

[6]　Much of this account of perception draws on earlier discussions. See especially the Introduction and Chapter Two.

selves as standing outside of experience, objectifying and conceptualizing its objects, then we come to recognize the initially undivided character of all experience. This inclusiveness is another way of approaching a central feature of aesthetic appreciation that I have called, especially in the context of the appreciation of art and nature, 'aesthetic engagement'.[7] Indeed, this same character of the experience of artistic and natural beauty is found in all environmental experience, and our encounter with the arts helps us grasp this key dimension of environment. In fact, what we learn from aesthetic appreciation can illuminate all environmental experience.

Relating aesthetic considerations to cultural ecology might seem fanciful, but the two are actually closely connected. Although the word 'aesthetic' is commonly used to refer to the value found in appreciating art, its fundamental, etymological meaning as perception by the senses enables us to consider all experience fundamentally aesthetic. And as the direct and immediate experience of any contextual order is perceptual, the perceptual experience of environmental contextuality can be understood as aesthetic. Further, aesthetic appreciation, like every activity understood from the standpoint of cultural ecology, is reciprocal. Appreciation is not only receptive; it is equally active, requiring the contribution of the appreciator of art or nature in discerning qualities, order, and structure and in adding the resonance of meanings to that experience. In this respect, the appreciator, by an analogous activity, joins in the creative constitution of art and environment in bringing to fruition an experience of appreciation.

Understood in this way, aesthetic appreciation is as context-dependent as any other experience, perhaps more so, inasmuch as appreciative experience is intensely and continuously perceptual. Another way of stating its contextual character is to describe appreciative experience as percep-

[7] 'Aesthetic engagement' is central to my account of the experience of aesthetic appreciation, whether of the arts or of nature. I first developed it at length in *Art and Engagement* (Philadelphia: Temple University Press, 1991).

tual engagement and, since as appreciative it is deter-
minedly aesthetic, as aesthetic engagement. Engaging with
an object of art or an environment, then, can be thought of as
an ecological event, as a cultural ecological occurrence. Stating this conversely, going from the concept of an ecosystem,
which is a cognitive idea, to its exemplification in aesthetic
engagement reflects the ecological model of perceptual
experience. In the one case we go from ecology to experience,
and in the other from perceptual experience to aesthetic
engagement, which is ecological in character. This reciprocity can be summarized by saying that the ecological concept
of an all-inclusive, interdependent environmental system
has an experiential analogue in aesthetic engagement.

This collaboration of sensory perception and sensory
meanings in an aesthetic-artistic activity is, then, the expression of a cultural ecological process. We can think of aesthetic engagement, in fact, as an aesthetic ecology. It is the
joining together in aesthetic appreciation of the viewer and
the painting, of the listener and the music, of the dancer, the
dance, and the onlooker. It is the repatriation of the inhabit-
ant with his or her environment. Aesthetic engagement is
thus the perceptual experience of a cultural ecological process. Once we grasp that all experience in its primary, direct,
and immediate form is perceptual, we begin to recognize
the intimate place that the aesthetic has in human experience. It becomes a key to revealing and evaluating cultural
experiences. How can we apply this key to the environments, the landscapes of everyday urban life?

Understanding the Urban Landscape

For most people an urban complex is coterminous with the
human environment; indeed, it identifies the context of
more than half the world's population. In most developed
countries, ninety per cent of the population lives in urban
centers, and the proportion in second and third world countries is increasing rapidly. Like all key concepts, urbanism
can be defined in different ways. How, then, to understand
it? For my purposes here, I shall construe it most broadly as

human organization on a large scale as part of an extended environmental complex largely shaped by human agency. The urban landscape covers a wide range. At one extreme stands the megalopolis, an urbanized region that incorporates several large cities with their industrial and commercial appendages into a continuous band or spread of built landscape. At other points on the scale we can identify the industrial park, the commercial strip, the shopping mall, and the town. Urbanism does not apply to the village, whose small scale, low density, and open space exclude the features commonly associated with the urban environment. These include a concentrated residential population, the satellite residential clusters housing a commuter population; large-scale industrial or other productive activities together with their effects on circulation patterns; support services in the form of utilities, hospitals, business and commercial services; and research, educational, and cultural centers.[8]

Now while urbanism constitutes the human environment for much of the world's population, it is a condition that has come about, with a few notable exceptions, not by deliberate choice or design but from the demands of a rapidly increasing population, commerce, industrial production, central governance, defense, cultural interests in the form of museums, libraries, arts centers, educational and

[8]   An enormous literature addresses the urban environment. A classic study is Jane Jacobs, *The Death and Life of Great American Cities* (New York: Random House, 1961). See also Paul L. Knox, "The Restless Urban Landscape: Economic and Sociocultural Change and the Transformation of Metropolitan Washington, DC", *Annals of the Association of American Geographers* 81:2 (June); Sharon Zukin, *Landscapes of Power: From Detroit to Disney World* (Berkeley and Los Angeles, University of California Press: 1991); James Howard Kunstler, *The Geography of Nowhere: The Rise and Decline of America's Man-Made Landscape* (New York, Simon and Schuster: 1993); Kevin Lynch, *The Image of the City* (Cambridge, MA: MIT Press, 1960); Alison & Peter Smithson, *Urban Structuring* (New York: Reinhold, 1967). For a recent treatment from an ecological orientation see Nathalie Blanc, *Vers une Esthétique environnementale* (Paris: Éditions Quae, 2008). See also my "Aesthetic Paradigms for an Urban Ecology", Diogenes 103, reprinted in *The Aesthetics of Environment* (Philadelphia: Temple University Press, 1992), and "Cultivating an Urban Aesthetic", also reprinted in *The Aesthetics of Environment*.

research institutions, and, of course, the emergence of nationalism and the thirst for political hegemony. To these we can add today the influence of global capitalism. We now see clearly how the exploitation and commodification of natural resources and the industrialization of the countryside have dispossessed masses of people, who are then driven to settle in or near metropolitan regions in order to scrape for survival.

Thus urban landscapes have developed and continue to expand, landscapes that offer amenities for the rich and, for the remainder of the population, a place in which to attempt to live and work, and to survive. The forms, characteristics, and ambience of this environment are rarely chosen but are shaped by geographical, political and economic forces. Instances of large-scale urban planning are rare: L'Enfant in Washington, D.C. in the late eighteenth century, Haussmann in nineteenth-century metropolitan Paris, Costa in Brasília in the twentieth. Most large cities consist in a center nucleus with historic origins and character, surrounded by successive generations of residential and industrial development. These began as the work of people who migrated there from the countryside and then constructed dwellings, commercial, community, and municipal structures where space was available and land values cheaper, while independent entrepreneurs later defined whole neighborhoods and industrial sites. There was little or no coordination among any of these decisions. Urban forms, then, that are shaped by given, independent conditions — geographical, climatic, political, economic, social — are largely the result of chance and circumstance. We can call this the historical, aleatoric urban model and it should be distinguished from prevalent ideal images of the city.

"The house is a machine for living", Le Corbusier announced. As does the house, so should the building and the city embody the values of order, harmony, uniformity and especially smooth, oiled functioning. This *mechanical model* is an ideal beloved of the culture that developed societies see themselves embodying. It envisions the quintessential virtues of an industrial order: efficiency, cleanliness, impersonality, uniformity, interchangeable modular units, expendability, and a social order of the sort that Charlie Chaplin caricatured in *Modern Times* which subjugates the human to the ethos of the machine. More recently, this industrialized social order was encased as a specimen of bourgeois culture in the opening tracking shot of Jean-Luc Godard's *Week-End*, which displayed an endless line of automobiles slowly moving, bumper to bumper, as if on an assembly line, as they conveyed their passengers steadily out into the countryside. It is an image of humans who, under the delusion of independence, are pressed into helpless uniformity.

Urbanism has now moved beyond these rather simplistic models to a more sophisticated stage as an ecosystem. This leaves behind the mechanical ideal of uniform, replaceable parts and adopts an organic vision. In sharp contrast to the mechanical, the biological ecosystemic model recognizes the urban region as a complex unity of many different but interdependent components, each preoccupied with its own purposes but at the same time contributing to and depending on a context that embraces them all.[9]

The ecosystem thus becomes an imaginative model of the urban environment. At the magnitude and complexity of mass industrial societies, the uncoordinated activities that characterize the aleatoric model produce disorder and inefficiency and easily lead to chaos and breakdown. The mechanical model is also inadequate, for it is at the root of the impersonality, anomie, and inhospitable character of industrialized urban regions. The biological concept of an ecosystem seems better able to compensate for the inadequacies of the earlier guiding principles. It can be more responsive to the workings and needs of human social life than the aleatoric model, more true to the human condition

[9]   These three models, the aleatoric, the mechanical, and the ecosystemic, are generalizations of common practices and ideals and are not intended to designate specific cities. Particular cities may exemplify some or all of the models at different times in their history and at different locations in the urban complex.

than the mechanical, and more resilient and responsive than both to the variety of human social forms and activities. Open-ended yet coherent, flexible yet efficient, independent yet balanced, the ecosystemic model appears to offer a truer vision for living in an urbanized environment.

How can we guide social activity by an ecological model? What sort of vision can lead us toward a more humanly successful social order? We need an incentive that is imaginative and enticing. Here, I think, is where the artistic-aesthetic mode of engaged experience can prove an invaluable guide, and the arts can be a guide in helping us identify and understand the perceptual dynamics of urban environments.

The Contribution of the Arts

Consider first what the arts do. The arts reveal aspects of our perceptual world, of our sensory environment. Each art sensitizes us to different perceptual modalities and the nuances of sensory qualities, and together the arts can educate us to the richness and depth of environmental experience. Painting, for example, can enhance our capacity for environmental perception, as well as making more apparent the visual qualities of color, shape, texture, light and shadow, mass, and composition. Painterly perception is not a matter of seeing the city *as* a painting but rather through the eyes of a painter and with the painter's sensibility. This comes not only from visual qualities of art but from grasping how these qualities can be applied to environmental experience. Thus we can think of a zoning plan as composing areas and their relationships; building codes as influencing mass and shape; constraints on lot coverage as the arrangement of volume and space; and patterns of distribution, density and activity as texture.

The other arts offer their own distinctive contributions to perceptual awareness. Music translates into environmental perception as a soundscape: ambient sounds and their timbres, textures, and volumes as generated by the multifarious activities of urban life, such as traffic, commerce, and human action. Amplified sounds, canned music, engines, electronic sounds, and human voices all contribute to the soundscape of a place.

It is not difficult to apply the three-dimensional arts to environmental aesthetic ecology. Sculpture translates into the arrangement of masses and space in relation to the human body. A sculptural sensibility develops not only from walk-around sculptures but also from walk-in sculpture, which turns mass and volume into ambient qualities. Architecture can help us experience the urban landscape as a deliberately constructed environment, deploying mass, volume, and the movement of human bodies, not as a static array, but as intimate interrelationships in a dynamic experience of constant change.

Architectural dynamics lead easily to the distinctive dances that emerge from the human activities that go on in every environment. To grasp the city as a mobile environment involving the interplay of bodies and other objects in various patterns of movement is to see the urban dynamic as an endless, complex array moving from one transformation to another. Indeed, the forms of urban mobility display characteristics of various dance forms. Circulation patterns of cars, trucks, buses, and trams in relation to the movement of people are choreographed by planners and traffic engineers into a complex modern dance. The fact that these are not random movements but reflect shifting patterns of interrelationships transforms the environmental dynamic into a formal ballet of social living. Since such movement is not erratic but coordinated or at least directed, we can perhaps grasp the interrelations of these patterns of movement as an elaborate tango. And when such movements respond to one another in active interplay, a dramatic element appears and the human landscape then becomes a kind of dance theater with staged movements and sequences. We can even extend the artistic metaphor and think of urban life as complex improvisational theater in which the dramas of human life constitute the plot lines. Humans are thus both the creative artists, the actors, and the participatory audience in an environmental drama.

In such ways, the arts as creative making and aesthetics as active perception combine to enlarge, illuminate, and enrich environmental experience. What can these modalities contribute to our experience and understanding of human life wherever it is lived? As I noted earlier, both the artistic and the aesthetic are inherent in environmental experience, the first in fashioning such experience and the second in bringing aspects of that dense perceptual experience into awareness. Humans, as part of the complex environmental dynamic, do not and can not stand back to contemplate the prospect. We must enter into it as artists through our activities and at the same time participate both actively and receptively in an appreciative mode. Thus do both the artistic and the aesthetic combine in our vital engagement with environment. What does this mean for living as part of our environment? What is its significance for creative aesthetic engagement?

An Aesthetic Urban Ecology

Developing *an aesthetic ecological model* from a basis in artistic-aesthetic engagement has profound implications for building environments that promote rich and satisfying lives. If we are unaware of the presence of the aesthetic and its implications, we are likely to become helpless, alienated perceptual pawns in the hands of impersonal forces. Unless we move to deliberately incorporate the aesthetic in building human environments, we must abandon all hope for the survival of a civilization that is not just human but humane. Can we go beyond bare survival to fulfillment? How, then, can we envision an urban ecology guided by aesthetic values? This is our central question.

An aesthetic ecology is an experiential ecology. Instead of denoting interconnected and interdependent *objects* in a particular region, it takes a human perspective and turns to the *experiential* dimension of environment. Further, an aesthetic ecology encompasses humans as interdependent as well as interrelated. With aesthetic engagement as an ecological model for environment, events are translated into experiences that combine to form the living world we inhabit. Aesthetic engagement is an effective touchstone in building environments that promote experience that is satisfying and rich.

What can an aesthetic ecology offer in helping us understand our habitations and shape them so that they contribute to personal and social fulfillment? This is the practical question that follows from my theoretical analysis. So, in good pragmatic fashion, let us turn to its implications for practice and ask what an aesthetic ecology offers for understanding and directing the urban landscape.

By focusing on sensory perception and sensory meanings as integral to the human environment, aesthetic ecology becomes experiential; it is an ecology of experience. And because it is all-inclusive, it is an engaged ecology, one that exemplifies aesthetic engagement. We have, then, at the very least, an ecosystemic model in which aesthetic considerations are considered not just significant but critical. Perceptual experience becomes the central feature in the interrelations of the people, objects, and activities comprising an ecosystem. Thus an aesthetic urban ecology denotes an integrated region with distinctive perceptual features: sounds, smells, textures, movement, rhythm, color; the magnitude and distribution of volumes and masses in relation to the body; light, shadow and darkness, temperature.

Such an ecology of experience is not a fully controlled order, an aesthetic environment on a large scale within which our perceptual experiences are programmed in a complex system. Rather a perceptual ecology identifies an ecosystem, such as an urban landscape, whose aesthetic features are significant factors in environmental design, so that we can eliminate or reduce negative perceptual experience and encourage experience that enhances human life. What negative perceptual conditions does ecosystemic perception lead us to try to guide and control? Many of these are obvious, such as reducing or eliminating air and water pollution, noise pollution, and noxious and offensive odors. To these we can add controlling extremes of heat and cold, strong winds, and excessive illumination, all of which are common conditions in large, barren, paved plazas and parking areas and amid the concrete structures and pavement of the urban core. To specify these even more, one need only mention characteristic offenders in the urban landscape: traffic noise and exhaust fumes, construction sounds and dirt, refuse, canned "music" in nearly every public and quasi-public place, vehicles hurtling from unexpected directions. These just begin the list.

Yet at the same time, sensory relief and aesthetic enhancement are possible. Some of these are localized and obvious, such as public buildings of architectural distinction and residential districts that reflect regional and cultural design features. Monuments at significant points in the urban texture capture attention and instruct as well as commemorate. Fountains are a distinctive urban aesthetic amenity that combines sculpture with the multi-sensory qualities of water in motion. These call attention to the aesthetic importance of public spaces.

Tiny "pocket" parks can function as oases of green, quiet, and clear air, places of safety and repose within the frenetic concrete jungle of commercial and industrial districts. Large urban parks provide an opportunity for creative and imaginative works of landscape architecture to provide experiences of cultivated nature. Public gardens are another urban amenity, and sensitive landscaping in highway design and parking fields can do much to ameliorate mechanical, drab circumstances. When present, water can be used to enhance the urban soundscape, not only by the soothing sounds of fountains, but by taking advantage of unchannelled urban streams and rivers to introduce refreshing irregularity on the grid pattern of streets and to offer visual relief from concrete and asphalt. Where cities are built on a harbor or waterway, the shorefront can become a recreation area, providing open space and contrasting sounds and vistas, opportunities enhanced with walkways, benches, and picnicking and bathing areas. Industrial shorefront offers another opportunity for a unique experience of urban commercial activity as a process of generating and receiving the shipment of goods and materials and exhibiting the functional beauty of the industrial and commercial process.[10]

Commercial districts can incorporate pedestrian streets and walkways, with arcades offering vendors and shoppers protection from sun and rain, and covered or enclosed walkways and pedestrian bridges providing relief in regions of extreme climate or heavy traffic. And on a minimal level, anti-noise ordinances and anti-pollution requirements can help protect pedestrians from high, offensive, and harmful sensory input.

All these perceptual considerations have implications, not only for comfort, pleasure, and stimulation, but for health and safety as well. They can contribute to creating an urban landscape that is understood ecosystemically and that, instead of oppressing its inhabitants, engages them aesthetically in ways that enhance and enlarge their lives. An aesthetic ecology that encourages aesthetic engagement offers a direction for constructing environments that promote rich and satisfying lives and that lead beyond mere survival toward human fulfillment. This direction has been marked by artist-designers who have demonstrated in practice the extraordinary capabilities of aesthetic ecological design. Patricia Johanson's environmental designs, such as *Fair Park Lagoon* in Dallas, Texas and *Petaluma Wetlands Park and Water Recycling Facility* in Petaluma, California, are exemplary projects that promote functional ecological processes infused with a keen artistic sensibility. The designs of the Brazilian environmental designer Fernando Chacel, such as *Marapendi Municipal Ecological Park* and *The Ecological Walkway at Rio Office Park*, similarly fuse an aesthetic sensitivity to landscape with an ecological vision that Chacel calls "ecogenesis".[11]

[10]   In *Functional Beauty* (Oxford: Oxford University Press, 2009) Glenn Parsons and Allen Carlson offer a comprehensive case for the aesthetic relevance of function, a quality especially applicable to the urban process.

[11]   See Caffyn Kelley, *Art and Survival; Patricia Johanson's Environmental Projects* (Islands Institute, 2006), with an Introduction by Lucy R. Lippard; and Xin Wu, *Patricia Johanson's House and Garden*

An aesthetically positive urban ecosystem can enhance public spaces and recognize how each neighborhood — commercial, industrial, residential, or recreational — has an individual character and yet affects the others in shaping perceptual experience. In a humanly functional aesthetic ecosystem, the urban landscape is not an external environment but an inclusive one that integrates its inhabitants, who participate actively and contribute to its functioning. Taking aesthetic engagement as a normative goal can be a powerful guideline in humanizing the urban landscape.

The Aesthetic-Ecological City

Applying the aesthetic-ecosystemic model is revealing and offers a touchstone in efforts to humanize urban life. It is comprehensive and coherent. The complexity of its components adds to the ecological challenge, for an urban region typically includes an industrial domain producing basic materials and equipment, such as steel, oil, and machinery; another manufacturing consumer industrial products, perhaps including airplanes, automobiles, computers, elevators, air conditioners; and the production of consumer goods in the form of clothing, books and newspapers, prepared foods, furniture and the many other kinds of objects and services that fulfill the city dweller's needs and desires and occupy his or her time and attention. The ecological model urges that these various domains be kept in balance and that they be of a proportion that no one of them dwarfs the capability of the others or overwhelms the urban dweller.

It is important to embrace under the rubric of the ecosystem social and cultural institutions and organizations: libraries, museums, schools and universities, houses of worship, research institutes, laboratories, and the like, the multiple institutions that constitute the social fabric. Critical among these institutions are the political and govern-

Commission; Re-construction of Modernity (Harvard University Press, 2008), 2 vols. Fernando Chacel, *Paisagismo e ecogênese/Landscaping and ecogenesis* (Rio de Janeiro: Fraiha, 2001).

mental ones: the bodies that constitute the city government, the legal system and the courts, the law enforcement agencies, and the social service agencies. It might seem strange to include these bodies in an ecological inventory. They are, however, of central importance. An ecological city must integrate political and cultural functions along with physical and biological ones.

A comprehensive urban ecosystem, then, when functioning as an integral whole, has no hard divisions between its physical structures, its social and political organizations, and the activities associated with them. For an urban ecosystem is comprised of more than physical components. It includes in equal importance the immaterial elements of social relations, behavior patterns, and customs and traditions. Indeed, these cannot be separated, since architecture and mechanical technology are bound up with language and culture, forces that shape decision, choice, and behavior. Moreover, the ecological city is a dynamic whole. It is a seething process of altering, tearing down, building, adjusting, revising, and constructing, always trying to adapt to changed social, economic, and technological conditions.

As an entirety the ecological city embodies a distinctive aesthetic of multiple dimensions, in large part an aesthetic of function where its efficiency constitutes its beauty. Function, of course, introduces a utilitarian factor, long excluded from traditional aesthetic theory, but present, in fact, in numerous contexts other than the arts and the natural world to which the traditional account of aesthetic appreciation has been unduly restricted. I have long argued for a more inclusive account of appreciation as aesthetic engagement that includes smooth, efficient functioning appreciated for its intrinsic beauty. The inclusion of function as a mode of beauty is part of a growing recognition of the expanded scope of aesthetic appreciation that includes the objects, activities, and experiences of everyday life.[12]

---

[12] See A. Berleant, "Aesthetic Function", in *Phenomenology and Natural Existence*, ed. D. Riepe (State University of New York Press, 1973), pp. 183–93. Reprinted in A. Berleant, *Living in the Landscape: Toward an*

It is sometimes questioned whether ecological concerns and aesthetic interests are compatible.[13] Different environments raise different considerations. Issues at stake in forest management or agricultural policy may have little bearing on urban policy. It is easy to see where these interests may conflict in the process of urbanization. To take one example, filling in wetlands for a housing development built to a prize-winning design is not uncommon. In fact, it is estimated that in the United States over fifty per-cent of the wetlands that existed in the 1780s were lost by the 1980s. In some countries, such as Canada, the percentage is even greater, in others it is less, but the issue is a global one. The loss of wetlands is a problem because wetlands are a crucial component in the propagation and maintenance of numerous species and are essential for maintaining biodiversity, and they also are a resource for many needs and activities of human populations.[14] Some might argue that wetlands do not represent environmental beauty and that filling them in for agricultural or housing improves appearances. This seems to be a clear case of ecological and aesthetic incompatibility.

Several aspects of such a situation require clarification and ordering. One is the matter of ecosystemic scale. It is important to recognize that no significant local change has exclusively local effects. Draining a wetland affects more than the local ecosystem. Patterns of wetland reclamation

Aesthetics of Environment (Lawrence: University Press of Kansas, 1997). See also Glenn Parsons and Allen Carlson, *Functional Beauty, op. cit.* Chapter Nine, below, "The Negative Aesthetics of Everyday Life", explores this enlargement of the scope of aesthetic appreciation.

[13] These issues are clearly and comprehensively discussed in Paul H. Gobster, Joan I. Nassauer, Terry C. Daniel, Gary Fry, "The shared landscape: what does aesthetics have to do with ecology?", *Landscape Ecology* (2007) 22:959–72.

[14] See Michael Moser, Crawford Prentice, and Scott Frazier, "A Global Overview of Wetland Loss and Degradation", a paper prepared for Wetlands International. Available in the Proceedings of the Conference of the Contracting Parties in Brisbane, Australia, March 1996 and published in vol. 10 of the Conference *Proceedings*. Available online at http://www.wetlands.org/inventory&/growi.html.

have regional effects and contribute to global consequences in species diversity and climate. By our actions we humans make ourselves part of the ecosphere and our actions may not have desirable consequences. Uses that are guided by considerations of sustainability and amelioration may meet human needs without causing permanent damage. Short-term goals must be balanced by considering long-term effects. Here an ecosystemic approach must be spatio-temporal and include the effects over time as well as the immediate physical results of an action.

But how does this mesh with aesthetic interests? Factors of design are involved in creating perceptual interest in every project: visual design; spatial design; dramatic, temporal factors in the sequence of experience. Cities encourage sensory engagement, and sensitivity to unplanned, gratuitous features and presences can be part of a comprehensive aesthetic presence. Also to be included are the multitude of fine perceptual details that are present in every environment, details of texture, plant and animal structures, light, color, and shape. Of course, all these include people's actions as participants in ecosystemic continuity and change. Moreover, it is essential to realize that an urban aesthetics must reflect the full range of aesthetic values, and that recognizing the aesthetic dimension of an urban ecosystem acknowledges nothing about the kind or multiplicity of its normative character. A wide variety of aesthetically negative characteristics may be present, ranging from perceptual intrusiveness and offensiveness to the repugnant, disgusting, repulsive, or loathsome.[15] The urban environment offers probably the fullest range of aesthetic value, from the sublime to the sordid. In the final analysis there is no incompatibility between the aesthetic and the ecological.

The relationship between the ecological and aesthetic dimensions of urban experience is a complex one. At the same time it is possible to show how these interests may be compatible. Central to understanding the values involved

[15] Chapter Nine develops this idea at length.

is recognizing the misleading and false separations with which such issues as this are usually structured, separations that turn situations into problems. In the wetlands example these would be the developers and investors with their private needs and interests, on one side, and the social and ecological values present in a wetlands environment, on the other. This places the issue in the form of conflict. How would this be seen differently if we adopted the idea developed throughout this book that continuity, not division, marks the human world, both ontologically and experientially?

The challenge is to afford such full consideration to all the relevant factors in the complex context within which human direction and decision-making take place in order to discover their interrelations and interdependence. In place of hardening presumed incompatibilities into conflicts, we can strive to recognize areas of mutual support and enhancement that more truly reflect what is actually present in such situations. This possibility is difficult to grasp in a culture that is so thoroughly indoctrinated with an ideology of small private interests in perpetual opposition with wider, environmental ones in a turbulent sea of conflicting desires.

Aesthetic engagement can provide a valuable criterion for an urban aesthetic ecology, offering an experiential model and a guide for shaping and humanizing the urban landscape. It becomes a kind of appreciative, normative process that can be recognized and incorporated into environmental experience. And as we shall see later, aesthetic engagement provides a basis for the aesthetic criticism of negative perception and a standard in developing positive experiences.[16]

Centering these considerations on the aesthetic-ecological city understood in this way adds yet another normative dimension, the ethical, for the ultimate criterion in assessing any human environment is how it contributes to the fulfill-

---

[16]   Aesthetics as a basis for critical judgment is the theme of Part Three and is developed at length in Chapter Nine.

ment of the people who are an inseparable part of it. Because ethical values are not a separate feature but suffuse the urban aesthetic ecosystem, they need to be integrated with the social and aesthetic values from which they are inseparable in living practice to achieve what Dufrenne called "aesthetic sociability".[17] If a disparity between ecology and ethics seems to appear, it is likely the result of seeing particular interests as separate and self-contained instead of as part of a common human spectrum of values. We introduce an ethical note here not as a casual addition but as a factor that broadens our vision by recognizing the presence of yet another dimension of experience. Its ramifications are vast and we shall pursue some of them in the chapters that follow.

[17] Dufrenne considers aesthetic sociability the true heart of aesthetics. Mikel Dufrenne, *Phénoménologie de l'expérience esthétique*, PUF 1953, p. 107 ; English trans. E. S. Casey et al, *The Phenomenology of Aesthetic Experience*, (Evanston: Northwestern University Press, 1973). Maryvonne Saison develops this idea in "The People Are Missing", *Contemporary Aesthetics* (www.contempaesthetics.org), 6 (2008), Section 1.

Chapter Eight

Celestial Aesthetics

Celestial Aesthetics

In no direction but skyward do we apprehend limitless space. Ocean vistas may be vast but there is always a horizon line to give them a boundary. The prospect from a mountain top may spread across vast domains but it is still bounded by the horizon. What we know about distances in outer space confirms their apparent infinitude. The Moon is a mean distance of 238,607 miles (384,400 km) from the Earth; the Sun, 91 million miles (146 million km). Stellar distances make the figures of high finance seem simple. Light travels at 186,282 miles (299,792,458 meters) per second, and the nearest star, Alpha Centauri, is about four and a quarter light years distant. Facing that infinite space can be disconcerting: we may feel at once both speechless and overwrought with ideas and associations.

Yet even in sky gazing there appears to be a limit that we call the celestial sphere. Leo Tolstoy recognized this:

> Lying on his back, he was now looking at the high, cloudless sky. 'Don't I know that it is infinite space and not a round vault? But no matter how I squint and strain my sight, I cannot help seeing it as round and limited, and despite my knowledge of infinite space, I am undoubtedly right when I see a firm blue vault, more right than when I strain to see beyond it.'[1]

Well, then, is the sky, limited or limitless? Does the answer depend on what we see or on what we know? And does it depend on where we stand or lie when gazing into the sky: on a boat? on a mountain height? from an airplane?

[1] *Anna Karenina*, Leo Tolstoy (New York, NY: Penguin Books, 2000), p. 800.

on a street in Manhattan? Much obviously depends on our vantage point, for we no longer need to experience space from the surface of the Earth. Some of the imaginative flights of early science fiction have become real, and space photography has filled our vision with images of the Earth as viewed from outer space, as well as of other planets, stars, and galaxies. From outer space, distances on the Earth's surface that seem endless in relation to the human body are miniaturized and bounded by the contours of continents and the planetary sphere.

Even the permanent spatial orientation of common sense is no longer credible. We may slip into speaking of having a standpoint, for example, but can no longer literally mean "standpoint" since our position on the rotating sphere of the Earth is changing in space at a speed of about 1,038 miles (107,218 km) an hour while we are moving around the sun at about 66,660 miles (105,000 km) per hour or 18½ miles (almost 30 km) a second. This may lead us to consider renaming our rapidly moving "standpoint" something like a "transitpoint". We might also consider regarding the Earth from the sky, except that from the vantage of space there is no sky. To see the sky you have to be on the Earth's surface. Considering the Earth from outer space we could call "celestial geography".

In his essay "Fluid Geography", Buckminster Fuller described the transformation that the landscape undergoes when regarded from the water instead of from the more usual viewpoint of the land itself.[2] This simple change of location constitutes not merely a physical alteration of position but also an inversion of the primary condition for orientation from a fixed and stable location to one that is continually in motion, always shifting position. For water is constantly moving, its surface broken by wind ripples, patterned in waves of varying sizes, undulating with swells, and moving sporadically from wind drift, while its underbody may be carried more steadily by the cyclical movement of tidal currents and the more regular action of ocean

[2]   Buckminster Fuller, *Ideas and Integrities,* ed. Robert W. Marks (New York: Collier Books, 1963), pp. 119–41.

currents. All these forces make a fixed position a geometrical, cartographic fiction, useful for navigation as so many other constructs are for their own conveniences.

The constant changes in location that prevail in a fluid environment actually change all the parameters that ordinarily delimit one's terrestrial existence and, on a larger scale, even our understanding of metaphysical being. For this change of location actually constitutes a change in reality. It is instructive for showing how ephemeral is the very notion of objectivity itself. The world, in which the human is the zero point from which everything is experienced, is, like water, fluid. For as the locus of experience, the individual person is necessarily the point from which and in relation to which distance is grasped and known perceptually. This turns absolute objectivity into a scientific fiction.

Motility does not characterize water only. The littoral is an ever-changing relationship between water and land. And the land itself undergoes continuous change, usually slow, to be sure, but nevertheless incessant. Like window glass, its fluidity is usually unnoticed, save during dramatic incidents like floods and earthquakes, and the slower but still detectable alterations caused by weather, climate change, physical disruption, and especially human action. Fluidity, however, does not end with the water or even with the land. The atmosphere is itself a fluid medium. Less dense and more elusive than water, its buoyancy can nevertheless support objects of great size and weight, such as balloons, parachutes, gliders, and airplanes. Of course air is not distributed throughout interstellar space but occupies layers (troposphere, stratosphere, mesosphere, ionosphere) totalling about 400 km, and becoming more and more rarified until it is entirely dissipated.

But let me speak not about Earth as if it were a self-sufficient body with which we must come to terms. Nor need we deal with the full reach of outer space, as if it, too, were indifferently present. Our concern is rightly with the human world and it is important to include in our understanding of "earthly" existence what we can learn from a vantage above the Earth's surface. Something of this changed perspective is now common among air travelers and it has been extended from the effects of reports by space explorers and satellite photographs. Antoine de Saint-Exupéry, one of the first to exult in air travel, gloried in the sense of boundless freedom he experienced when flying. "The aeroplane has unveiled for us the true face of the earth", he once wrote.

For many of us the view of the surface of the earth from the window of an airplane is a common experience. For me that experience retains a touch of wonder, because of both the physical experience of being airborne and the aerodynamic phenomenon, itself. This is enhanced by the awareness of going through a vaporous cloud layer and viewing the cloudscape from above, so different from the vantage of Earth. Gazing at the configurations of the Earth's landscapes from the air, landscape and cloudscape can easily be conflated, as in seeing a cloud bank above the ocean as the bank of a shoreline with the water below. Actual terrestrial shapes are much easier to discern from the air than on land. Hills and mountains become miniaturized, easily surmountable from the air instead of on foot. The hidden patterns of agriculture appear different above the various regions and national landscapes of the Earth's surface. And, of course, the view from the air also exposes the layout of industrial and urban landscapes with their suburban extensions imposed across the Earth's surface.

Is it necessary to ask which is the real world, that encountered on foot or that gazed on from terrestrial or outer space? We can easily give a commonplace answer: it depends on the location from which you regard the world. Or we could invoke a version of Russell's theory of types and say that both are real, each in its own order. Further, we could say, with Buchler's concept of ontological parity, that all such realities are equally real and that there is no hierarchy that elevates some as really real and others as illusory.[3]

---

[3]   Justus Buchler, *The Metaphysics of Natural Complexes* (New York: Columbia University Press, 1966). 2nd edition (State University of New York Press, 1990). Buchler states the principle of ontological parity (in contrast with ontological priority): thus: "Whatever is dis-

And we could certainly throw the astronomical universe, in which our planet is an insignificant speck, into the mix and consider whether, in fact, that universe is what is really real, since it is all-inclusive and can be measured and calculated. Here, too, however, stability and objectivity are greatly wanting, for distance and location are variously determinable, relative, as Einstein showed, to the position of the observer. Do we inhabit a cloud-like world, different when viewed from below, from within, or from above, and, like clouds, always moving and changing? Which, we may ask again, is the real world? What makes it "real?"

Myths and Metaphors

The celestial universe thus raises metaphysical issues and provides evidence for some answers and against others. And as our understanding of the universe has become transformed through astrophysics and space travel, the celestial universe is no longer a safe repository for the mythologies with which many religions and cultures have peopled the heavens. For our knowledge of that universe presumably dispels mythological explanations. No space explorer has yet reported seeing wingèd anthropoids playing harps and singing in celestial choirs. No key-jangling saint guards admission through any gates nor has any throne, occupied or not, been spotted within. Even Kant urged against such thinking, preserving aesthetic value yet at some sacrifice of rationality:

> If, then, we call the sight of the starry heaven *sublime*, we must not place at the basis of our judgment concepts of worlds inhabited by rational beings and regard the right points, with which we seen the space above us filled, as their suns moving in circles purposively fixed with reference to them; but we must regard it, just as we see it, as a distant, all-embracing, vault. Only under such a represen-

criminated in any way (whether it is 'encountered' or produced or otherwise related to) is a natural complex, and no complex is more 'real', more 'natural', more 'genuine', or more 'ultimate' than any other. There is no ground, except perhaps a short-range rhetorical one, for a distinction between the real and the 'really real', between being and 'true being'." p. 31.

tation can we range that sublimity which a pure aesthetical judgment ascribes to this object.[4]

What was open territory subject to inventive peopling with fanciful superior beings and animals is now inhabited only by mundane matter of varying densities in the form of meteorites, planets, stars, and galaxies. The heavens are also home to a much lower order of occupants. Astronauts encounter not only the space rubble of asteroids; they face the additional hazard of space refuse, ranging from defunct satellites and disused rocket stages and motors, to small particles like paint flakes, dust, needles, and explosion fragments. Still, imagination refuses to rest and space scientists have constructed their own fanciful and mysterious imagery of black holes, the big bang, dark matter, dark energy, and a population of stars, some termed giants and others brown, red, white, and black dwarfs.[5]

Mythical imagination also populates the night sky with constellations and extrapolates them into a mythical astronomy in the signs of the zodiac. We seem to find solace in order and unease in confusion, and so it is common to construct order out of chaos, constituting our own myth of cre-

---

[4] Immanuel Kant, *Critique of Judgment*, trans. J.H. Bernard (New York: Hafner, 1951), p. 110 (§ 29).

[5] According to Wikipedia (29 January 2009), *dark matter* is hypothetical matter that does not interact with the electromagnetic force, but whose presence can be inferred from gravitational effects on visible matter. *Dark energy* is a hypothetical form of energy that permeates all of space and tends to increase the rate of expansion of the universe. Dark matter and dark energy account for the vast majority of the mass in the observable universe; dark energy currently accounts for 74% of the total mass-energy of the universe. *Brown dwarfs* are sub-stellar objects with a mass below that necessary to maintain hydrogen-burning nuclear fusion reactions in their cores but which have fully convective surfaces and interiors with no chemical differentiation by depth. *Red dwarfs* are very low mass stars with no more than 40% of the mass of the Sun. A *white dwarf* is a small star composed mostly of electron-degenerate matter. A *black dwarf* is a hypothetical stellar remnant, created when a white dwarf becomes sufficiently cool to no longer emit significant heat or light. A *giant* star is a star with substantially larger radius and luminosity than a main sequence star of the same surface temperature. There are also *supergiant* and *hypergiant* stars, as well as bright *giants* and *subgiants*.

ation. There is insight in the naïve musings of a child's mind in this fictional account:

> Between the roof of the shed and the big plant that hangs over the fence from the house next door, I could see the constellation Orion. People say that Orion is called Orion because Orion was a hunter, and the constellation looks like a hunter with a club and a bow and arrow. But this is really silly because it's just stars and you could join up the dots in any way you wanted. And you could make it look like a lady with an umbrella who's waving, or the coffeemaker which Mrs. Sheers has, which is from Italy with a handle and steam coming out, or a dinosaur.
>
> And there aren't any lines in space, so you could join bits of Orion to bits of Lepus or Taurus or Gemini and say that they were a constellation called The Bunch of Grapes or Jesus or The Bicycle, except that they didn't have bicycles in Roman or Greek times, which was when they called Orion Orion. And anyway, Orion is not a hunter or a coffeemaker or a dinosaur. It's just Betelgeuse and Bellatrix, Alnilam and Rigel and seventeen other stars I don't know the names of. And they're nuclear explosions billions of miles away. And <u>that</u> is the truth.[6]

Of part of it, anyway, for, of course, the names of stars only substitute a lesser fiction for a greater one.

Gazing into the sky is probably one of the most common occasions on which many people are struck with a sense of wonder. Ronald Hepburn recognized its importance for aesthetics:

> [T]he presence of wonder marks a distinctive and high-ranking mode of aesthetic, or aesthetic-religious, experience characterizable by that duality of dread and delight. So conceived, sublimity is essentially concerned with transformation of the merely threatening and daunting into what is aesthetically manageable, even contemplated with joy: and this achieved through the agency of wonder.[7]

There may be more immediately dramatic sights in nature than gazing into the sky, such as facing a great water-

---

[6]   Mark Haddon, *The Curious Incident of the Dog in the Night-Time* (New York : Doubleday, 2003), ch. 173.

[7]   R.W. Hepburn, *'Wonder' and Other Essays. Eight Studies in Aesthetics and Neighbouring Fields* (Edinburgh: Edinburgh University Press, 1984), p. 152.

fall, viewing the landscape from atop a high hill or a mountain, witnessing storm waves crashing on an ocean shore. But the sky is immediately present in all our outdoor activities and it is the direction to which we appeal from indetermination, religious practice, habit, or cultural belief. And the heavens are a willing collaborator. They offer occasions for mystical experience and provide many with an experience of religiosity. But for others, viewing the heavens evokes a sense of the immensity of the earth and the cosmos, and evokes a feeling of awe and a sense of humility. Few experiences of nature are so freely available and yet so profound. But this direct and pure pleasure is easily corrupted, if not by physical obstructions blocking the gaze of the city dweller, then from imaginative constructions clouding our vision.

Celestial experiences, if one may call them that, do seem to have a special, indeed unique status for people of different times and cultures. Readily available and frequently powerful, it is not hard to see why the heavens have been so closely associated with myth and religion, fixed so strongly that the association is hardly dispelled by the airplane, not to mention space travel. At the same time, these experiences are just that, experiences, and, as such, are neither evidence nor proof of anything. The differences between religious experience and religious doctrine or belief are profound. We may cherish the first while maintaining scepticism of the second. Such differences, while clearly drawn and powerfully important, have still not penetrated popular consciousness.

The impulse to mythologize has led people to construct multiple universes, and mythologies have peopled the heavens. We might even complain that, with such an array of unworldly creatures and celestial domiciles, the heavens must suffer severely from overpopulation. But is there another use to which our imaginative impulses can be put? Is there a vision of the universe that is humanistic without being anthropomorphic, and that is compatible with science yet still poetic and imaginative?

Once myths served as causal and other sorts of explanations of the events in nature and the actions of humans. Then they responded to unanswered and unanswerable questions. Now, perhaps, we may think of myths mostly as fanciful, as imaginative discernments of similarities and relationships that can illuminate nature and humans. They range from romantic superstition to outright falsehoods; at their best they can capture imaginative insights. They may use perception as a springboard to fancy and fancy as grounds for understanding. At their most pernicious, myths can quell curiosity with fabrications and discourage the pursuit of knowledge.

Let me consider whether the impulse to mythologize might take a different form from fabricated explanations and still enable the heavens to offer space for imagination to soar. One possibility is to replace myth with metaphor, explanation with suggestion, perhaps even religion with poetry. As one might expect, the celestial universe has been a powerful stimulus to the poetic impulse and, as one might further expect, the quality of its art spans stellar space. Some of the best space poetry avoids the temptation to find profundity in infinity and stays with simple perceptions and direct responses, like this poem by Sara Teasdale:

The Falling Star
I saw a star slide down the sky,
Blinding the north as it went by,
Too burning and too quick to hold,
Too lovely to be bought or sold,
Good only to make wishes on
And then forever to be gone.

And space can even become the source of a prosaic observation, as in this poem by Robert Frost:

But outer Space,
At least this far,
For all the fuss
Of the populace
Stays more popular
Than populous.

But let me move from the lyrical and matter-of-fact in poetry to a different kind of metaphor, one put to different use. The first use of which I have been speaking goes from the literal to the metaphoric; the second, to which I now turn, goes from the metaphoric to the literal, or rather the presumably literal.

The Celestial Sublime

The very magnitude of spatial objects and distances is, as I noted earlier, difficult to conceive. Perhaps, indeed, it is inconceivable. There is, nevertheless, a concept in aesthetics that helps us grapple with the experience of unimaginable magnitude. The enormity of the sizes, distances, quantities, forces, and events in our present knowledge of the astronomical universe calls for the aesthetic concept of the sublime. Unlike the experience of beauty that, Kant claimed, is bound up with an object and can be apprehended by a concept of the understanding, the feeling of the sublime is evoked by boundlessness and conveys a negative pleasure. Is there a celestial sublime?

Like Burke, Kant identified an element of pain that accompanies the experience of the sublime. Unlike the sense of beauty, in which there is a harmony between the image of nature and the concept it engenders, the sublime produces a negative pleasure. This pleasurable pain rises from the overwhelming magnitude of the object, such as a desert, a mountain, or a pyramid; or from its illimitable power, as in a storm at sea or an erupting volcano. We can have an abstract idea of such magnitude, but the imagination cannot provide a representation that corresponds to that idea, and this produces a painful pleasure. This "negative sign of the immense power of ideas" produces what Kant called agitation, in contrast to the calm feeling of beauty,[8] and he considered it a negative presentation or a non-presentation.

Jean-François Lyotard, who has written so tellingly in our own time of the sublime, accepted Kant's account of this

---

[8] This is Lyotard's account of Kant's view. See Jean-François Lyotard, "The Sublime and the Avant-Garde", in *The Lyotard Reader*, ed. A. Benjamin (Oxford: Blackwell, 1989), pp. 203–4.

non-presentation. He agreed that, unlike the experience of beauty, "the imagination fails to provide a representation corresponding to the idea."[9] In fact, Lyotard finds in Kant's aesthetic of the sublime the germ of the avant-garde in the development toward abstract and minimal art.

> The avant-gardist attempt inscribes the occurrence of a sensory now as what cannot be presented and which remains to be presented in the decline of great representational painting.[10]

Ideas that exceed our comprehension have become ever more insistent during the course of the twentieth century. Concepts of destruction, cruelty, and death, of power and helplessness, of devastation and tragedy, concepts that reflect conditions often present in human experience, have grown to such proportions that it is no longer possible to encompass them by reason. Examples proliferate uncontrollably: the calculated policies of genocide that devastated the Tutsi in Rwanda in 1994 and are now directed at the Darfur in Somalia echo the Nazi policies toward the Jews in the late 1930s and early '40s; the continuing threat of a nuclear holocaust and its consequences — these illustrations only begin a horrifying litany.

Representational painting strove to approach the incomprehensible in human experience directly in the shocking expressionism of artists like Soutine, less directly in Dada, even less in Surrealism, until the representational image was abandoned entirely and painting became wholly abstract. The work of Anselm Kiefer, with its sense of unutterable devastation, is one such response to present-day conditions. Certainly not all abstract art encounters the sublime, and the range of inarticulable and inconceivable apprehension is broad. Abstract art does not always evoke intimidation or terror; a sense of mystery and awe may also occur in the inarticulable experience of the sublime. Feelings of the metaphysical sublime emerge in the late paintings of Mark Rothko. In many of these, two rectangles

---

[9]   Lyotard, *op. cit.*, p. 203; Immanuel Kant, *Critique of Judgment*, trans. J.H. Bernard (New York: Hafner, 1951), p. 108.

[10] Lyotard, *op. cit.*, pp. 204, 208.

extend to the edges of the canvas, dark above pale, conveying an eerie sense of empty space leading to the abyss.

Much art, representational or abstract, uses images as a kind of visual synecdoche, implying an entirety by presenting a part of it. Van Gogh's celebrated painting of peasant shoes is an unforgettable instance; Cézanne's images of Mt. Saint Victoire and Monet's of the Houses of Parliament do this repeatedly and cumulatively. One might even speculate that landscape paintings work in this way, suggestively, leading us, by representing one scene, to grasp what might be called the sacred beauty of the natural environment, an idea that becomes trite when spoken but perhaps sublime when experienced.

These examples of ways in which art strives to apprehend the inconceivable offer a key to the celestial sublime. The image of a region of the cosmos in a photograph taken in outer space is a direct representation but it is necessarily only of a small part of the whole. Our discussion of metaphor earlier is useful here, because such a photograph may be considered a synecdoche, representing the unimagible whole by an imagible part. Viewing a fragment of the heavens acts metaphorically to lead us to an imaginative grasp of the enormity of the whole, the unpresentable whole in a presentable part, the celestial sublime.

The case of the planet Earth is different. We can in fact have an image of the whole, or of as much of the whole as we can have of any three-dimensional object. We could say that the idea to which such an image corresponds is that of an ecosystem, not merely a three-dimensional object but of the planet as Gaia, including with its physical processes the human activities that are an integral part of that system. In Kant's terms the Earth could then be considered beautiful, since we can have an idea of reason equal to its object. Unlike the cosmos, our experience of the Earth as an ecosystem can be grasped by reason. So the Earth retains its beauty, the heavens their sublimity.

Global Ecology

We must acknowledge that the valuable concept of an eco-system, both as descriptive and as explanatory, is really metaphorical. This fact does not detract from its value but encourages us to recognize, here again, the importance of not confusing an image with a thing, imagination with sub-stance, metaphor with reality. The central notion in ecology is of a complex system of interrelated and interdependent organisms and their environment. The cumulative evidence for systemic intradependence has become so great that the concept of ecology has widened far beyond its original biological meaning.[11] It is now applied freely to the entire biosphere and extended anthropologically to cultural ecology, philosophically and socially to social ecology and deep ecology, and critically by eco-feminists. There seems no limit to the scope and applicability of the idea. In all these applications of the concept of ecology, it is the systemic nature of the relationships, not the relationships themselves, that can be considered its metaphorical core.

Space exploration has given ecology enhanced significance. Viewing the Earth from outer space through the lens of a camera puts things, we might say, into greater perspective. With difficulty we can locate the small planet Earth revolving around a third degree star, one of 200 to perhaps 400 billion or more stars on the edge of the Milky Way, itself one of billions of galaxies in the observable universe. This array is obviously impossible to grasp as a visible totality but its magnitude can be roughly imagined from space photos of the Milky Way and other galaxies. But what of our planet in this cosmic array? It is now possible to grasp the Earth as a spatio-temporal totality by imaginatively combining the images of different hemispheric views, much as we infer the volume of a box or a building by joining multiple perspectives. Our understanding of Earth has been transformed.

---

[11] The German biologist Ernst Haeckel coined the term 'ecology' or *oekologie* in 1866 as "the comprehensive science of the relationship of the organism to the environment." Frodin, D.G., *Guide to Standard Floras of the World* (Cambridge: Cambridge University Press, 2001), p. 72.

It seems that a global awareness is growing, reluctantly and painfully, as widespread industrial and individual activities produce global effects, some of which are building to crisis proportions, the most conspicuous example being climate change. We are beginning to grasp such elementary causal relationships, indeed to feel them somatically as we suffer the early effects of climate change. The idea of a global ecosystem would encompass the complete range of human actions and consequences.

Living intelligently as part of such an ecosystem would lead us to anticipate the effects of proposed actions and to strive for balance within the narrow margin of play in a field on a universal scale. The significance of a global ecosystem is not a matter of biological interest only; one can also find aesthetic properties present. Like any ecosystem but on the all-inclusive scale of the whole, a global ecosystem can exemplify the formal aesthetic features of harmony, proportion, and unity in variety, as well as a range of enhanced perceptual pleasures emerging from an enlarged repertoire of styles, traditions, and media.

It would be interesting to pursue the aesthetics of a global ecosystem and see to what degree its aesthetic features could serve as pragmatic criteria, as well. How successful in promoting human well-being would a global ecosystem be that was guided by aesthetic principles and values? Harmony, for example, would include social relationships, and proportion would affect economic and commercial activities of production and consumption. Unity in variety has international implications as well as domestic social application. These aesthetic features are not the only ones nor are they universal or necessary. However, they do characterize much art and appreciative experience and have significant implications for practice.

The critical components in the global ecosystem are many and complex. They include both human and non-human elements, and both catastrophic and gradual changes. Major change in the non-human world may proceed slowly on an evolutionary scale that is difficult to observe as it goes on. Much biological species evolution, for example, must be inferred from the evidence it leaves behind, even though some evolution, such as that of the HIV, is observable. Many evolutionary processes in geology are also slow, such as the uplift of mountains and the formation of stream valleys. Both the physical surface of the earth and the biota that live on it undergo gradual but cumulative and observable change together in erosion, weathering, soil change, and plant and animal succession. And of course there is catastrophic change: earthquakes, floods, fires, volcanic eruptions, tidal waves, and rapid species extinction.

But all of these changes go on in a world that human beings inhabit. Humans, as central participants, are clearly the major factor on both the local and immediate scale of change and on the global. No human actions can be excluded from being considered part of the ecosystem. Moreover, humans in a global ecosystem are implicated in changes determined by yet another order — changes that are deliberate, planned, and goal-directed. From an ecological perspective, human action must be compatible with concurrent interactions and processes in the global environment. Human participation may also add another aesthetic factor. This would be the case only if the participation exemplified aesthetic engagement, if it were not entirely goal-directed but included sensory satisfaction in the perceptual process and integration in the ecosystemic process.

Can we move from the concept of Earth as an ecosystem to an ecosystemic view of a larger realm of which Earth is a part? Is it possible to envision a still larger systemic order? Can there be a celestial ecology? Is there a celestial ecosystem? Given the rather vague and indeterminate meaning of 'celestial' as "the sky" and "the heavens", these questions are actually meaningless.[12] Considering what to call a celestial perspective, then, is puzzling. We could speak of it as a universe. The universe is sometimes identified with the cosmos, but this identification is presumptive, for these words mean rather different things. The universe, following its <u>etymology</u>, includes the Earth, the solar system, the galax-

[12] 'Celestial' is derived from the Latin *caelum,* sky, and is associated with heaven, divinity, the sky, and the visible heavens.

ies and the contents of intergalactic space. To speak of the
universe as a cosmos introduces a somewhat different connotation, for a cosmos would regard the universe as an
orderly, harmonious whole (κόσμος, order, orderly arrangement). The Greeks contrasted cosmos with chaos or unpre-
dictability (Χάος, the primal emptiness, space, in Classical
Greece; later the meaning changed to "disorder"), and
inherent disorder can easily be understood as a feature of
the universe, as it has been in chaos theory.[13]

To consider the celestial world as a whole, as a universe,
thus does not prove or settle anything, for 'universe' is a collective noun and we don't exactly know what it collects.
Our knowledge of much about the universe is vastly incomplete and unsettled. The spatial geometry of the universe is
the subject of various and competing theories that must
accommodate the fact that the universe is expanding.
Whether the universe is finite or infinite is debated, its size
is ambiguous, and we have little detailed information,
together with some major mysteries, about the motions on
various scales of its different constituents—planets, stars,
and galaxies. It's unlikely that anything that we do or that
happens on this planet would have any cosmic effects
(except, metaphorically speaking, for humans). It would be
presumptuous, then, to speak of the universe as a cosmos,
since we do not know what it encompasses and, hence,
whether the universe is indeed ordered. And consequently,
we cannot claim that the universe, indeterminate as that
concept is, is an ecosystem.[14]

We have cast doubts on the possibility of describing or
even divining a celestial ecology. But as we have seen, it is
not absurd to consider ecosystemic status for the planet
Earth. Perhaps we can best conceive of a global ecosystem
from a celestial perspective. But can we do the converse?
Can we apply what we know of the global ecosystem

---

[13] Chaos theory, interestingly, is more a mathematical theory of order
       than of chaos, for it discovers that a rational pattern emerges when
       chaos is pushed to the extreme.
[14] I am grateful for the advice of the astronomer Prof. David Batuski on
       this account.

metonymically to the universe? Here our understanding cannot proceed or it will carry us back to the ungrounded realm of mythology. We must remain content with an earthly perspective in which we can still feel delight and wonder at celestial phenomena, even if they are unpeopled by a mythological imagination. Since we do not have a concept of the cosmos that is detailed and specific but can only infer it metonymically, it is not meaningful to acknowledge Kant's criterion and use an "idea of reason" to speak of a celestial or a cosmic ecology. Might not the "sublime" be a more appropriate concept than beauty in our apprehension and appreciation of celestial phenomena? It would also remind us of the necessity for humility in the true face of human inadequacy.

We can, however, adopt a celestial perspective on a global ecosystem. It is satisfying enough to occupy ourselves with engaging and nurturing the beauty of Earth and appreciating the sublimity of the heavens. We might see this by walking along with Thoreau: "How few are aware that in winter, when the earth is covered with snow and ice … the sunset is double. The winter is coming when I shall *walk the sky*."[15]

---

[15] Thoreau, "Walking", quoted in David Macauley, "Walking the Elemental Earth", *Analecta Husserliana LXXI*, A.-T. Tymieniecka, ed. (Kluwer, 2001), p. 18.

Chapter Nine

The Negative Aesthetics of Everyday Life

In beginning this new phase of our inquiry, we cannot help reminding ourselves of the limitations to the common association of aesthetics with art and its connotation of art that is good or great. What that value is and how to assess it are central questions for aesthetic theory, and these questions have become increasingly difficult as the boundaries of art have expanded beyond recognition and aesthetic values have become more diverse. We have seen that the word 'aesthetic' is no longer synonymous with 'beauty' and has applications far wider than to art alone. We have noted that the etymology of 'aesthetic' identifies sense perception as central to its meaning, and we have emphasized that core meaning. And we have gone so far as to call aesthetics the theory of sensibility.

Sensory experience, however, is not always positive, and when it offends, distresses, or has harmful or damaging consequences, the aesthetic lands us in the realm of the negative. In this chapter I want to identify some of the conditions where aesthetic value is present but in unsatisfying, painful, perverse, or even destructive ways. I shall focus on the human environment, where the aesthetic and the moral are difficult to disentangle and are often fused. We can give a name to sensory experience that has no clear positive value, the underside of beauty, so to say, and call it negative aesthetics.

It may seem strange to speak of the negative in a discipline so closely associated with the treasured values of art and beauty. But aesthetic values are no longer confined to the museum and the scenic drive where they are honored but kept isolated and innocuous. They have become increasingly prominent in conflicts with values in morality, religion, economics, environment, and social life. And we have also come to recognize that aesthetic values live below the surface of conscious perception in everyday life. It will be illuminating to discover to what distant shores the winds of negativity can carry us.

Aesthetic Value

Because the scope of aesthetics radiates far beyond its historical focus on artistic and natural beauty, appraising aesthetic value has become increasingly complex. Critical judgment rests on normative experience: how well a performance succeeds, how effectively a novel or a painting holds us, how well an art object magnetizes our attention, how breathtaking is the view of a landscape. All such judgments assume that there are differences of aesthetic value, differences that range from utter failure to our magical absorption and illumination by masterworks.

It is important to recognize that acknowledging differences in value does not mean that they can be measured by a graduated scale. Values are often designated as "higher" or "lower", "better" or "worse", but grading them in such ways does not necessarily require quantitative differences or designate them. Even identifying a range of aesthetic value between positive and negative poles greatly oversimplifies the normative range and complexity of these values. The situation is comparable to the presumptive poles of beauty and ugliness: beauty can be discerned in many of the forms of ugliness since these are not unequivocal concepts or opposites but only salient points of a nuanced, non-sequential, and complex range of aesthetic values that includes, for example, the bizarre, erotic, repugnant, and kitsch, along with the pleasant, the beautiful, and the sublime.

Nor are aesthetic values singular or homogeneous. A situation may possess complex and even incompatible values. A dramatic situation, for example, may be at the same time bizarre, ludicrous, pathetic, and perhaps even tragic, combinations of the sort that Harold Pinter was a master at evoking. Moreover, in considering aesthetic value we need not be committed to seeking a quality or feature inhering in an object, as if beauty were simply one factor added to others. We might prefer, as Gilles Deleuze does, to consider it a force in art that is exerted on the body and manifested in sensation.[1] On the view taken here, value is inherent in an aesthetic field or situation and is not a feature or quality of any particular part of it, such as the object or the appreciator.

What makes something aesthetically negative? This question introduces further complexity. One might say at first that it occurs when an aesthetic situation has a predominately negative character that outweighs the positive, for example by being trite, perceptually shallow, offensive, demeaning, or even harmful. For value here designates a character of experience. What that character is and how to assess it are not obvious but are nonetheless key questions for aesthetics.

Because aesthetic value rests on the centrality of sense perception, it involves experience that is somatic and not exclusively psychological. It engages the entire human organism in a cultural modality that is as integral to the organism as its biological features. And since aesthetics starts with sense experience understood as a human capacity that, like all other human traits, is molded by shared historical, cultural, and material conditions, we have a basis for judgment that is not, as often assumed, purely arbitrary, personal, or subjective. Because sensory experiences that are shared are not always equally rewarding and, in fact, not always positive, we have empirical grounds for recog-

[1]   Cf. Gilles Deleuze, *Francis Bacon. Logique de la sensation* (Paris: Éd. de la Différence, 1981, reed. Éd. du Seuil, 2002), pp. 54, 57.

nizing and assessing the full range of aesthetic value and, in addition, the diversity of normative experience.

Critical as well as popular discussion tends to center around questions of aesthetic merit, and disagreement about value forms the basis of much of the theoretical as well as the critical response to such experience. Logically speaking, however, this judgment should come not at the outset but only after a theoretical view is developed and the relevant data identified. For how can the judgment of such a value be reasonably made without first coming to an understanding of what is meant by 'aesthetic' and the value associated with it?

Aesthetics and Negativity

When we come to critical aesthetic judgment, then, we are led to its grounding in shared experience construed organically and culturally and under common material and geographical conditions. When evaluation becomes so severe that there is little or nothing that can be said in defense of an aesthetic experience; that is, when an aesthetic occasion is perceptually distressing, repellent, or painful, or has effects that are harmful or destructive, then understanding the aesthetic obliges us to acknowledge negativity. So we can speak of negative aesthetic values, of negative aesthetics when, in the primacy of perceptual experience, the experience as a whole is in some sense unsatisfying, distressing, or harmful. Aesthetic experience is not always benign.

It will be illuminating to identify some of the many ways in which the negative occurs in aesthetics, but it would be misleading to attempt to classify distinct modes of aesthetic negativity. Indeed, it is often difficult to distinguish aesthetic negativity clearly from the aesthetically positive, as well as from the different forms that it takes and from moral considerations. The very complexity of the aesthetic contributes to obscuring the negative, but once we recognize its presence in aesthetic experience, we can begin to explore this often unacknowledged value. And when such a study is undertaken for its own sake and not merely to provide logical symmetry to positive aesthetics, we can recognize the significance and substance of a negative aesthetic domain.

It is important not to equate negative aesthetics with negative criticism. The unfavorable critical assessment of art works and landscape design is a familiar practice. Such judgments are part of the practice of art and environmental criticism. To identify inadequacies in the dynamic development of experience, unrealized possibilities of perceptual expansion associated with unskillful workmanship, unsubtle performance that fails to realize the possibilities of the score or the script, or perceptual blocs that inhibit appreciation is to make a critical assessment. Such an assessment is the normative function of art criticism. It recognizes that aesthetic value is present but incompletely fulfilled: art that could be better, design that could be more successful, landscape that could hold more charm or be more accommodating, music that could engage us more fully, an audience that might more imaginative and open to new dimensions of aesthetic experience. Criticism may find some value intended that is not fully realized or some feature present in an art object that is not apprehended by the onlooker or the audience. This deficiency is a common condition and one for which the critic urges improvement. Criticism may also take a positive direction and identify artistic successes in fresh insights, nuances and, best and rarest of all, occasions of aesthetic transport.[2]

Negative criticism thus does not necessarily exclude positive values but may find that they are in some way unfulfilled or unrealized. Negative aesthetics is distinguished by its scope. There are circumstances, though, where no positive value is present or intended or where the merit of an entire object or situation is entirely obscured by negative factors. What I want to call negative aesthetics refers to

[2]   I have written more extensively on the aesthetics of criticism in *The Aesthetic Field: A Phenomenology of Aesthetic Experience* (Springfield, Ill.: C.C. Thomas 1970). 2nd edn. (Cybereditions (www.cybereditions.com) 2001. I develop the idea of environmental criticism in *The Aesthetics of Environment* (Philadelphia: Temple University Press, 1992. Paperback edition, 1994).

whole domains of sensibility suffused with negative value. Works with no redeeming qualities, from those that are trite, baldly unsubtle, overly sentimental or maudlin to those that are sadistic, degrading, or damaging. There is plain bad art just as there are situations that are aesthetically offensive or painful. And, moreover, because aesthetic perception is direct and immediate, not always intense or associated with art, and often common and even commonplace, the aesthetically negative often slips by unnoticed and eludes critical scrutiny, settling into vague discomfiture. Part of this discomfort, as we shall see, may result from the subtle presence of negativity or from the very failure to recognize that aesthetic negativity is indeed present. The difference, then, between defective art and negative aesthetic value is that between a deficiency in aesthetic merit and cases in which negative value is actively present.

Negative aesthetics has a far broader range of application than the criticism of art. It takes many forms and instances of it are common. One species of such negative value is what is usually called bad taste, such as kitsch and sentimentality. Objects so described emulate or parody positive aesthetic value and may, indeed, themselves form cultural criticism. Examples of negative aesthetic value include clichés, jargon, and all such formulaic writing. While most widely visible in journalism, it is also common in scientific research papers and scholarly writing. Negative value also occurs in lauding the trivial or the mediocre where there is little that is aesthetically positive, as in some bathetic pop tunes and television soap operas. All these inhabit the negative side of the ledger of aesthetic value and represent its failure, even its degeneration. Negative aesthetics may also become a surrogate for the moral and be applied to social matters. This occurs when aesthetic language is used to condemn practices that are unacceptable or thought to go over the line, as when a person's reprehensible action or a manifestly unfair governmental policy is called 'ugly' or an offensive personality 'unattractive'. The difference, then, between defective art and aesthetic value with no redeeming characteristic is that between a deficiency that reduces aesthetic value and cases in which little or no positive value can be discerned at all.

Although such designations and distinctions as these can be useful for identifying various forms of aesthetic negativity, it would be mistaken to think that modes of negativity can be arranged in neat categories and that each instance must clearly exemplify one form or another. Fine categorial discriminations are not needed since individual instances involve subtle distinctions and require fluid categories that alter with the circumstances. Cases will also differ in intensity and extent, but this need not affect their negativity, only their degree of negativity. The touchstone is the experience, not the category.

Aesthetic negativity may apply to entire works of fine or popular art. Instances of aesthetic negativity are so prevalent that we are insensible to most of them since they have become invisible from endless repetition. Relatively mild negative occurrences may be called "aesthetically offensive", and may go beyond being merely another expression for bad taste and can apply to art objects and artistic practices. The case of art that people find deeply offensive is difficult to adjudicate. It is important to separate personal feelings from those that are shared by virtually all those in a society who experience that art. And even common distaste does not itself invalidate an art work. Some artists deliberately press against the limits of perceptual and moral comfort. This may, in fact, be a social benefit by extending the range of endurable experience, as in scatological art, erotic art, pornographic art, and profanatory art. Even though some may find such work deeply troubling and even painful, it may perform a social function by accustoming people to face experiences that they consider unmentionable or anathema. Apart from any aesthetic value such art may possess, it may have value in enlarging our intellectual and physical awareness as well as our emotional capacities. Art that is deeply disturbing to moral or religious feelings can, in fact, be artistically strong, as evidenced in work by Courbet and Dali. It may be difficult to adjudicate between art that deliberately transgresses the limits of propriety to explore untrod regions of aesthetic sensibility and art that cynically contrives to be offensive merely to achieve notoriety.

My discussion here largely concerns art works that are judged to possess no positive aesthetic value, and there is much here that lies beyond the offensive. What of art that hovers on the border of masochism and sadism, such as body art, ranging from tattoos and body piercing to disfiguring plastic surgery and self-inflicted violence? It is probable that no general guide can be given and that the possible negativity of each instance and type of aesthetic experience needs to be examined and analyzed individually through its own features by identifying and evaluating aesthetic, cultural, and moral considerations.

Perhaps more prevalent are forms of aesthetic negativity not directly associated with art objects but present in situations that are not ordinarily considered aesthetically: urban environments, cultural practices such as ceremonies and rituals, and the functioning of an organization. These are practices of aesthetic import that may have no recognizable compensating features and may be perpetrated through ignorance, insensibility, or callousness, or from motives of enhancing power.

While explicit violence is relatively easy to recognize, more insidious are forms of covert violence. Violence to human sensibility is sometimes difficult to detect but nonetheless frequently profound and even devastating. Like the permanent physical damage caused by persistent malnutrition, habitual drug use, or extremely loud sound, the damage to both perception and health may be deep and lasting. Here one can count things that may not be directly apparent and dramatic but are pervasive and damaging, such as the many forms of environmental pollution, among them smog, noise, water, and space pollution. It is worth noting that although pollution is rightly condemned on ethical grounds for its adverse effects on health and well-being, every form of pollution also includes perceptual insult and causes aesthetic damage, as well. High levels of sound or noise, bad air, excessive visual stimulation, and overcrowding are aesthetically as well as physically damaging.

Most of these have been widely discussed, but not usually related to their negative aesthetic effects. Spatial pollution may need some explanation because space is not ordinarily considered something capable of pollution. Yet spatial pollution nonetheless does take various forms, such as overcrowding in vehicles, in classrooms, in auditoria, on airplanes, in public spaces of all kinds. It is the consequence of overly dense construction: private houses packed so tightly that they have inadequate outside private space for light and air, apartment districts that compress people in both inside and outside spaces, impeding movement and even constricting breathing. Space pollution can take a vertical dimension, as in apartment buildings so high that people can be trapped on the upper floors by insufficient or inoperative elevators and stairways too long to descend in an emergency. Such conditions produce bodily experience that is oppressive and claustrophobic, as well as physically exhausting. We might even include here the cooptation of air space by multi-story structures, filling that space with oppressive masses. Space may also be abused by disuse. Commercial districts and public plazas in large urban areas are lifeless at night because no one chooses voluntarily to be there. Deserted, they become threatening to a lone pedestrian.

Signage on the common commercial strip is another example of spatial pollution. Gaudy colors, oversize panels, exaggerated features of all kinds thrust themselves on our sensibility. Not only is there generally little positive that can be said about the sensory experience; such signage also affects driver safety by distracting attention away from operating the vehicle. Even granting that we can become inured to such common cultural practices, the range of physical and psychological resiliency and toleration is not infinitely expandable.

The aesthetics of negativity, then, is not a simple designation. Some mild instances of aesthetic offense are "artless", we may say, as in children's or amateur painting or a beginner's playing a musical instrument. And there are cases when aesthetic value is deliberately attempted but fails badly, as in the clichés of suburban landscaping or front lawns decorated with plastic ornaments, or perhaps when aesthetic value is deliberately parodied as camp. Many instances of aesthetic offense display great differences of intensity and extent from the innocently negative. They may be perpetrated deliberately through callous disregard or by intention and produce extreme perceptual discomfort. It would not be difficult to make a long list of these, but two examples will indicate their prevalence. These are the vulgar co-optation and commercialization of the natural landscape by billboards and other signage, and of public pedestrian space by canned music or private mobile phone conversation. Not only are these negative aesthetically but morally, as well, by designedly imposing private or commercial interests on a vulnerable public. Their moral dimension comes not only from their negative consequences but because they are perpetrated deliberately.

The negation of aesthetic values, then, clearly exceeds the realm of the arts to become a common condition of the human environment, indeed what we might call a pathological social condition. The forms of such negativity may differ in intensity and in the kind and character of their effects. We can speak of social and physical environmental situations so thoroughly bland that they dull our sensibilities as *aesthetic deprivation*: tract housing, big box stores, and ritual conversation. Deprivation can become so complete that it actually extinguishes our capacity for sensory experience. Conditions of such deprivation may be harmful and produce aesthetic damage either through the loss of the capacity for perceptual satisfaction or by withholding aesthetic occasions. We can undoubtedly distinguish other modes of aesthetic negativity, and aesthetic criticism can make an important contribution by identifying and exposing their occurrences and their effects.

Aesthetics and Social Function

Now I want to apply a moral overlay to the aesthetic by identifying *situations* where a moral dimension, often negative but sometimes positive, cannot be separated from the aesthetic. A moral factor is not only present in oppressive signage; it is also inherent in the omnipresence of advertising, itself, that practice of commercial manipulation that rests on creating interests not intended to promote well-being but to stimulate often false or harmful desires. Indeed, commercial environments are gardens of aesthetic and moral symbiosis. The ubiquity of canned music in public spaces is a particularly flagrant aesthetic-moral intrusion, the former by attempting seduction by perceptual techniques and the latter by psychologically manipulating moods to promote vulnerability. It is hard to participate in the life of Western society without having to endure continuous perceptual, that is, aesthetic offense, from billboards decorating highways and sports fields to advertising posters confronting the eye on the inside and now commonly on the outside surfaces of buses, trolleys, and subway cars, and especially along the roadside. Indeed, any large or small publicly visible surface becomes an opportunity for advertising display. What makes these practices morally culpable is the fact that they are perpetrated intentionally, their motive being to impinge on passersby for the purposes of influence and profit. Such practices extend to television, film, and the Internet, not to mention their long history in the print media, all of these being public surfaces. At times the aesthetically positive and the morally negative may coincide, as they do when fine graphic design used for the purposes of advertising. These introduce another moral dimension in the commercial exploitation of art.

Furthermore, the effects of commercially motivated persuasion are frequently deleterious to the recipient, sometimes to a relatively mild degree by encouraging unaffordable expenses or imprudent behavior, sometimes flagrantly by enticing the victim into unhealthful or dangerous activities. The moral dimension of such intentionally negative aesthetic practices is especially vile when extended to subliminal television advertising and advertising directed at children. And this negative aesthetic is even more vicious in encouraging the abuse of health by presenting the practice of smoking, drinking alcohol, or drug-taking as hip or cool, not only openly through advertising but by using covert persuasive techniques such as television and film drama, employing techniques from a commercial motive that deliberately ignores the effects of such behavior. The skillful employment of such practices by political operatives may be considered devious. Indeed, commercial, social, and political motives underlie much aesthetic negativity. Using aesthetic techniques in the service of the morally negative carries a long history and widening usage. The complex and subtle interpenetration of the aesthetic and the moral has central importance in charting the domain of the aesthetically negative, and this will become increasingly apparent as we proceed.

In the technologically-oriented social world that has developed since the industrial transformations in the dominant technology, the aesthetically negative is represented in the many "quick and dirty" solutions that disregard both their environmental and human consequences in the interests of speed, convenience, and profit. The list here is endless, from the polluting runoff from the hills of slag that accompany mining operations and the utility poles disfiguring and obstructing the streetscape, to roadways that blast a straight course through every geographical configuration in the name of efficiency. In its extreme form the aesthetics of negativity includes actual physical pain that follows the massive abuse of human sensibility. It may appear bizarre to construe all of these as in part aesthetic, but insofar as their impact lies in their perceptual force, they have as much a claim on the aesthetic as a good work of art whose effectiveness likewise resides in its perceptual force.

What we have discovered so far is the need to recognize the facts of aesthetic negativity and also to acknowledge negative situations in which there is an inherent moral presence. From a traditional standpoint, negative aesthetics would seem to be an oxymoron. How can the values of beauty and art be negative? Yet it is necessary to acknowledge the factual presence of such work, of such events, of such conditions as I have identified. Rather than dismissing them as aberrant or ignoring their aesthetic dimension, it is essential to view these occurrences clearly and to ask what they represent. For we have here a different category, a different condition: aesthetic negativity in the interpenetration of art and the aesthetic throughout the human world. Often it is art-making that becomes the vehicle of the negative. On a different tack, art and aesthetic experience can have a compensatory social role in *revealing* the morally negative. And conversely with the convergence of moral values and aesthetic ones, the question may be asked whether ethical grounds may sometimes be an appropriate basis for judging art. The unavoidable questions are "Why?" and "How?"

It is increasingly clear that moral considerations often intrude into the aesthetic situation and that it is difficult to keep them apart. Can we even compare and judge such different kinds of value? Although there have been times when aesthetic and moral values were considered exclusive, each in its own separate place, the fact is that they are perhaps often fused in the same situation and that their inseparability demands recognition and adjudication. Occasions where both aesthetic and moral values are conjoined may take different forms and it can be useful to consider their possible combinations. These include situations where both aesthetic and moral value are positive, situations where both are negative, and situations where one is negative and the other positive. And of course the positive and negative may not be univocal and can occur with different intensities.

The argument that aesthetic values should outweigh moral ones has been familiar since the aestheticism of the late nineteenth century. Other Victorians maintained the converse, that moral considerations must take precedence over aesthetic ones. There may also be cases where both aesthetic and moral values are negative. And there are often times when the moral and the aesthetic cannot be considered separately, when the force of the one lies in the force of the other. It could sometimes be claimed that a social ethic underlies the morally negative. It will be illuminating to approach these possible relationships but they are only the more salient of the many forms these interrelations may take, and the considerations I shall mention do not exhaust their possibilities.

When both aesthetic and moral factors are in play, does the aesthetic ever take precedence? A positive answer recalls "the aesthetic movement," where *art pour l'art* was held to override all other considerations. Consequences be damned! This view has generally been put aside as unduly romantic in eulogizing aesthetic values at the cost of all else. Given the suffusion of the fine and applied arts throughout modern industrial societies, it would be blindness to deny the profound influence of the arts on the environments of daily life, not only in industrial and environmental design but on behavior and on awareness in general. Indeed, popular culture has become a fashionable academic subject and nearly always exemplifies ways in which artistic and aesthetic interests, coupled with commercial and political ones, pervade and affect modern social life. The moral factor cannot be suppressed.

Since art and the aesthetic embody perceptual interests, it might be argued that expanding perceptual possibilities and capacities is most important, and that repugnant objects and malevolent actions presented in an artistic context need to be tolerated for their overall benefit in enlarging the scope of our awareness. Isn't expanded consciousness inherently valuable? Sounds once considered noise may become music: dissonance consonance, cacaphony harmony. Writing deemed incoherent or incomprehensible may later be venerated as high literary achievement. Painting called banal or child's play may come to be admired for its skill and subtlety; erotic images may become artistically acceptable. Indeed, can even bad taste harbor good?

Then there are cases where modest practical advantages seem to compete with aesthetic ones. Does the safety presumably provided by the increased visibility of the bright yellow covers of cables securing utility poles compensate for the aesthetic affront to the landscape from the ubiquitous yellow slashes that line city streets and country roads in many parts of the U.S.? Does the opportunity for advertising along highways justify co-opting scenic vistas in rural surroundings by turning them into backdrops for huge splashes of commercialization and forcing drivers into becoming an involuntary audience? There is also the opposite situation where, instead of sacrificing aesthetic values to commercial ones, significant harm may be produced by preserving aesthetic advantages. Doesn't the discomfort in breathing the air or the increase of asthma and lung cancer among city residents outweigh the enhanced color of the sunset or the moonrise viewed through the atmospheric miasma?

Moreover, perceptual experience itself can be harmful and even damaging, as in the effects on health from the prevalence of garbage on city streets or exhaust fumes suffusing pedestrian walkways and filtering into dwellings. Just as pleasant, delightful, or beautiful surroundings can shorten medical recovery time, we should recognize the depressing emotional effects of ugly or oppressive environments. Here, too, our terminology must expand beyond aesthetic deprivation to include aesthetic harm. Many kinds of competing values do not directly involve the aesthetic, such as economic, political, social, religious, and legal ones. But this makes it all the more important to recognize the aesthetic consequences they introduce. The rehabilitation of historic districts, for example, can often be justified on aesthetic as well as historical, cultural, and economic grounds.

Considerations of this sort lead to cases in which negative moral factors may outweigh positive aesthetic ones. How should we adjudicate situations where grave social ills accompany the production of great art, as in the princely courts of the Renaissance, or those in which an artist's work is carried on at the expense of the welfare of his or her associates? Do the pyramids vindicate the enormous human cost involved in constructing them or the great medieval cathedrals outweigh the sacrificial poverty of generations?

And is the displacement of the residents of poor neighborhoods of urban districts, neighborhoods that may possess a
distinctive identity and character, a just sacrifice in order to
clear land for clean and orderly redevelopment? Is it better
to retain the narrow, twisting pedestrian lanes of medieval
towns and old districts in modern cities in order to preserve
their history and distinctive ambience or to sacrifice them to
real estate and other commercial interests served by
improved automobile accessibility and traffic flow? Obviously no general answer can be given to whether aesthetic
or moral values should take precedence, and the complexity of factors makes each case unique. It is essential, however, to recognize the aesthetic values that are involved and
to give them significant weight in decision-making.

Conflicting aesthetic and moral values are often obscured
by conflicts between economic interests and social justice.
Values of freedom and human rights seem to chafe against
political concerns for safety and security, but the requirement to choose between them is often misrepresented. Like
such false alternatives, moral and aesthetic values are not
always in conflict and can, in fact, enhance each other. Comfortable, pleasant, harmonious working conditions are not
an unnecessary amenity for the workplace but are actually
conducive to greater productivity and social harmony.
Humane personnel policies not only embody a social aesthetic in the intrinsic satisfactions of harmonious social relations but promote moral and economic values, as well, in
greater job satisfaction, less inefficiency and wastage, and
the social stability that comes from feelings of loyalty.
Humane vision and humanitarian policies may be both aesthetic and moral.

Instances where both aesthetic and moral values are negative might seem to be the least controversial. It is unlikely
that negative aesthetic concerns would come under discussion if the negative moral judgment had overwhelming
force. But this happens more rarely than one might think.
Few would object to tearing down slums and replacing
them with comfortable, healthful, and attractive housing.
But what if this utterly destroyed the cultural fabric of the

neighborhood or if the housing proposed were economically segregated high-rises or closely-packed, uniformly designed tract housing? Here the aesthetic and the moral are inseparable.

Negative aesthetic values may be the compelling reason for rejecting a practice in which the moral objection may not be strenuous or when the choices that are proposed are not necessary or the only ones. Must inexpensive clothing necessarily be ill-cut or decorated with banal print designs? Could not the aesthetically negative be at the same time morally negative? Similarly, bad art involving negative moral values, such as much pornography, by enhancing their visibility, might contribute to re-making the world into one that is more just and humane. Art can thus have a social or political agenda, and recognizing negativity in the interconnection of the aesthetic and the moral could serve a positive function.

But when moral and aesthetic negativity coincide, the instances are more extreme and the issues become more complex. Nazi and Soviet propaganda art force us to ask further questions about the relationship between the aesthetic and the moral, and the complexity of their relations needs to be uncovered. Art that embodies social criticism is not by that fact negative art. It may actually have a social function in revealing moral negativity, and the more perceptible its revelations, the more aesthetically positive it may become. Marcuse's observation is apposite: "The truth of art lies in this: that the world really is as it appears in the work of art."[3] Can we ignore de Kooning's women or Kiefer's landscapes?

It is crucial to distinguish between art that is itself aesthetically negative and art that *exposes* negativity. The art in the last of these need not itself be negative; indeed, if it were, it would be ineffectual. One could actually argue that art revealing or portraying moral negativity dominates the aesthetic of our time. In various forms, from expressionism and Dada to Pop Art, both personal anguish and social criticism

---

[3]   Herbert Marcuse, *The Aesthetic Dimension*, xii.

are dominant. Moral negativity is embedded in Zola's and Steinbeck's novels. It is portrayed in the condemning images that populate the work of artists of the Weimar Republic such as George Grosz, Käthe Kollwitz, and Otto Dix. It is dramatized vividly in *Guernica's* visual condemnation of the savagery of the Spanish Civil War. Many artists at work today devote themselves to documenting a century of the greatest atrocities perpetrated thus far in human history. Such art is not itself morally negative; it is the iniquity it reveals that is. Clearly, the interrelations of the morally and aesthetically negative and positive are manifold. Delineating their presence in particular situations and in careful detail is necessary before just judgment is possible. "Cruelty is not only a moral category but an aesthetic one: it always targets sensibility." [4]

Another mode of negativity, as important as it is often unnoticed, must be mentioned. This is art or art-like actions that are aesthetically positive and directly embody moral negativity in order to expose social negativity, that is, the presence of the morally negative on a social scale, as in exploitation, oppression, and war. The Mexican muralists Diego Rivera, José Clemente Orozco, and David Alfaro Siqueiros exhibited this in striking ways. Work of the sort I have just mentioned may evoke a sense of moral negativity but that does not turn it into negative art. Social negativity frequently calls for the honesty of art to expose it. Judged on aesthetic grounds, such art may actually attain its heights

---

[4]   Katya Mandoki observes, "That someone can watch death, pain, or a conflagration as a spectacle and feel pleasure is, unfortunately, a fact. The proof is their repeated display in films and television. This attraction to the tragic in real life explains the crowds that gather at traffic accidents or similar events, the repeated transmission of tragic and violent images in the mass media and even the existence of something as monstrous as snuff. This attraction, perverse or not, amoral or immoral, is aesthetic, embarrassing as it may be." She also identifies "aesthetic poisoning" and the aesthetics of the immoral, noting that "Cruelty is not only a moral category but an aesthetic one: it always targets sensibility." *Cf.* pp. 38, 40–42. Katya Mandoki, Everyday Aesthetics: Prosaics, the Plan of Culture and Social Identities (Ashgate, 2007. See also her "Terror and Aesthetics; Nazi Strategies for Mass Organization", in Critical Concepts in Political Science, ed. Roger Griffin and Matthew Feldman (Routledge, 2003).

on the shoulders of negativity as, to take an entirely different example, Bach's *St. Matthew Passion* transfigures the agony of Jesus.

Socially generated violence does not lie outside the purview of the arts. Art works depicting military brutality and massacres have a long history, from the chilling literary descriptions in Biblical accounts of battles and the even more graphic descriptions in the *Iliad*, to the bitter harvest of novels and films about modern warfare. Painters have often glorified military actions but they have also exposed their brutality in such unforgettable works as Goya's "The Third of May 1808" and Delacroix's "Massacre at Chios". And poets are no exception. War elegies abound, such as Wilfred Owen's "Spring Offensive", and even massacres are memorialized in John Milton's "On the Late Massacre in Piemont" and Y.A. Yevtushenko's "Babi Yar". Dmitri Shostakovich's Thirteenth Symphony was inspired by this last poem and led him to observe, "People knew about Babi Yar before Yevtushenko's poem, but they were silent. And when they read the poem, the silence was broken. Art destroys silence."

At the same time it is ironic to consider how readily art has been made to fire up the engines of war. The arts have been freely employed for this purpose, from marches and songs of battle to the glorification of "victories" in monuments, paintings, patriotic songs, photographs, films, and national holidays. Theatrical metaphors, curiously enough, have even become part of the vocabulary for describing military procedures: areas of military action are called war "theaters"; plans of attack, "scenarios"; even the deployment of troops or matériel is termed "staging". The image at work here seems to be that of the theater director devising how best to achieve a desired effect on the audience, while the practices to which these figures refer are, in fact, deliberately planned acts of human, social, and even environmental violence. But more of this in the next chapter.

The verbal picture I have painted may not be attractive but it has the intellectual virtue of truth and the moral virtue of truthfulness.[5] It opens a field of investigation in which much more needs to be said. Yet to recognize a need is a precondition to fulfilling it. I hope that the complexity of this portrait does not obscure its principal figures and that it also reveals alternative ones. Being prepared to recognize and to identify clearly the forms of negativity and their actual presence is a prerequisite to positive change. Here aesthetics can be a major player.

---

[5]   Aristotle, *Nicomachean Ethics*, Bks. 4 (1127) and 6 (1141). Moral virtue is concerned with choice while intellectual virtue concerns demonstration.

Chapter Ten

Art, Terrorism, and the Negative Sublime

In due time, the theory of aesthetics will have to account not only for the delight in Kantian beauty and the sublime, but for the phenomena like aesthetic violence and the aestheticization of violence, of aesthetic abuse and intrusion, the blunting of sensibility, its perversion, and its poisoning.[1]

Terrorism and Aesthetics

It has become increasingly clear that the arts, and the aesthetic, more generally, occupy no hallowed ground but live on the everyday earth of our lives. Recognition is growing that the aesthetic is a pervasive dimension of the objects and activities of daily life.[2] Perceptual experiences that possess the characteristics of aesthetic appreciation are marked by an intense, focused sensibility we enjoy for its intrinsic perceptual satisfaction. We typically have such experiences with works of art and with nature, but they are equally possible in other occasions and with other kinds of objects. Such experiences engage us in an intensely sensory field in which we participate wholly and without reservation, as we customarily do with works of art. The objects and occasions, however, may be ordinary ones, such as eating, hanging

---

[1] Katya Mandoki, *Everyday Aesthetics: Prosaics, the Plan of Culture and Social Identities* (Ashgate, 2007), p. 42.

[2] Recent work includes Katya Mandoki, *op. cit.*, Yuriko Saito, *Everyday Aesthetics* (Oxford: Oxford University Press, 2007), *The Aesthetics of Everyday Life*, ed. Andrew Light and Jonathan M. Smith (New York: Columbia University Press, 2005).

laundry, engaging in social relations, or operating a perfectly functioning automobile or other mechanism. The range of such occasions is limitless, and this adds to the significance of the aesthetics of the everyday.

Such an expansion of the aesthetic has important consequences. Perhaps the most striking is the need to acknowledge that the range of aesthetic experience includes more than the appreciative engagement with art and nature. But not only does the aesthetic extend to the uncustomary but it encompasses the full range of human normative experience. Experiences of the aesthetic include not only the elevated and noble but the reprehensible, degrading, and destructive. This is so not as the result of an arbitrary decision to include them but from actual experience and practice. The aesthetic offers a full and direct grasp of the human world. That it may include violence and depravity is not the fault of aesthetics but of that world.

A salient symptom of that world is terrorism. Its wanton violence and uncontrolled destruction are appalling. But easy moral outrage offers no understanding, and only by grasping the meanings and significance of terrorism can we hope to deal with it effectively. Let me begin with the Happening, for the Happening can provide a forceful illumination of the aesthetic of terrorism.

Not that Happenings took negative form. A syncretic, visual-theatrical artistic development of the1960s, Happenings were a deliberate artistic innovation intent on transgressing all the hard boundaries that protected the arts and made them safe. In Happenings audiences became the performers, no clearly circumscribed object could be identified as the work of art, aesthetic distance was relinquished to the active engagement of the audience, artistic genres were fused into unrecognizable combinations and, most significantly, the boundary between art and life disappeared. Happenings were often playful, even festive occasions that danced over the pieties of conventional artistic axioms.

Some commentators quickly recognized that the importance of the Happening lay beyond its iconoclasm and entertainment value. One of them was Regis Debray, a young French radical intellectual, who "regarded a revolution as a coordinated series of guerrilla Happenings. Some of his admirers, in fact, took part in Happenings as training for future Happenings when they would use guns and grenades."[3] What many had considered a bizarre exaggeration following the dismissal of traditional artistic forms turns out to have been an uncanny pre-vision of the world half a century later. The net of terrorism in which the world is now enmeshed is all-enclosing. But how can terrorism be considered in the same sense as art? The question itself seems outrageous.

Happenings made a radical break from the aesthetic tradition by denying that art occupies its own exclusive realm separate from the world outside. Yet it was not only Happenings that rejected this tradition; many other artistic developments in the twentieth century deliberately crossed that boundary. The presumptive difference between the world of art and the world of daily life lies at the source of such perennial problems in aesthetics as the status of truth and illusion in art, the moral effects of art works, and the nature of artistic representation. Such continuing issues, all of which can be traced back to Plato, find in artistic autonomy the domain of human freedom, as Kant had claimed.[4] Yet at the same time it is an autonomy that, by philosophic decree, vitiates the force of the arts and ignores their power.

The tradition of restricting and removing art from the world of daily life dates from Plato's suspicion that the arts can have a morally degenerating influence. Expressed most famously in *The Republic*, it led him to advocate strict controls on the use of the arts in education and to propose censorship.[5] This, of course, was related to Plato's mistrust of sense experience, which he considered the source of illusion

---

[3] Arnold Berleant, *Art and Engagement* (Philadelphia: Temple, 1992), p. 40.
[4] Immanuel Kant, *Critique of Judgment*, (J.H. Bernard (New York: Hafner, 1951) §4. See A. Berleant, "Aesthetics and the Contemporary Arts", *The Journal of Aesthetics and Art Criticism*, XXIX, 2 (Winter 1970), 155-168. Reprinted in Arnold Berleant, *Re-thinking Aesthetics, Rogue Essays on Aesthetics and the Arts* (Aldershot: Ashgate, 2004), ch. 4.
[5] *The Republic* Bk. II, 377A-382; Bk. III, 376E-403B.

and false belief. These views were reinforced and enlarged by Kant, who claimed early in the modern period that the autonomy of judgments of taste is entirely independent of the existence of the object of our satisfaction and is not bound up with practical interest.[6]

The effect of these ideas on the history of philosophy has been profound. Plato's mistrust of the senses and artistic independence and his failure to recognize the imaginative contribution that the arts can make to education and moral development joined with Kant's denial of full aesthetic satisfaction to the interests of daily life. Together they functioned effectively to muzzle the power of the arts. Yet once we recognize the active interplay that occurs between art objects and activities and the world in which they exist, we find vast new opportunities for power and influence.

The force inherent in this relation has not been lost on the modern state. For philosophical aesthetics deliberately to ignore the political potential and use of the arts is to hand that power over to others whose values, standards, and behavior are often ignorant, manipulative, and self-aggrandizing. The traditional separation of aesthetics from daily life has freely allowed the political appropriation, often the misappropriation, of the arts. That is why governments practice "news management" and other forms of censorship, why they "stage" conferences, rallies, and other political events, why they promote "official" art, and why they persecute artists who do not conform to their purposes and destroy their works. Art is dangerous, and Kant got it backwards when he placed morality and art in separate domains.

In the interpenetration of art and the human world are the grounds for a new aesthetic vision and the need to articulate it.[7] When Happenings fused art with the everyday world, they did so as art. But what about presumably non-art

---

[6]   Immanuel Kant, *op. cit.* , First Book, §2-5.
[7]   Developing such an aesthetic has been the incentive of most of my
       previous work. See especially *Re-thinking Aesthetics, Rogue Essays on
       Aesthetics and the Arts* (Aldershot: Ashgate, 2004), *Art and Engagement*
       (Philadelphia: Temple University Press, 1991), and *The Aesthetic*

objects that are directly perceived as art? There is, of course, "found art", where an object is extrapolated from the everyday world, segregated, and framed: a piece of driftwood, a bouquet of field flowers, and, of course, the perennial urinal. Art is claimed where none was intended. Some instances of found art are benign, some provocative, others deliberately inflammatory. They say nothing about the motives of those who did the making and for whom the idea of art was probably far from mind. What found art does do is center our attention on an object or event in a way that resembles the intense focus we give to things designated *as* art by an artist, an institution, or the art world. Like Happenings, found art places art squarely in the ordinary world. Can this apply to acts of terrorism?

Some of the most striking claims of art for things outside the art world were responses to the terrorist attacks of 9/11. The avant-garde composer Karlheinz Stockhausen called them "the greatest work of art ever ... the greatest work of art for the whole cosmos", "a jump out of security, the everyday". And the British artist Damien Hirst excluded art from all moral judgment, arguing that the violence, horror, and death associated with Ground Zero (the name given to the site of the demolished New York World Trade Center) do not rule out the possibility that film footage of the attack could be "visually stunning" and resemble works of art.[8] Indeed, perceiving that footage as art may be the ultimate

---

Field: A Phenomenology of Aesthetic Experience (Springfield, Ill.: C.C. Thomas 1970). Second (electronic) edition, with a new Preface) 2000).

[8] Stockhausen, cited in Emmanouil Aretoulakis, "Aesthetic Appreciation, Ethics, and 9/11", *Contemporary Aesthetics* Vol. 6 (2008), sect. 1. Hirst, a British artist, called the September 11th terrorist attacks "a visually stunning artwork." *Loc.cit.*. Aretoulakis argues that "there is a need for aesthetic appreciation when contemplating a violent event such as the 9/11 terrorist attacks. What is more, appreciation of the beautiful, even in case of a 9/11, seems necessary because it is a key to establishing an ethical stance towards terror, life, and art. It should be stressed that independent aesthetic experience is not important in itself but as a means to cultivating an authentic moral and ethical judgment." My discussion of terrorism was stimulated by Aretoulakis's thoughtful and balanced consideration of the aesthetic significance of the 9/11 attacks.

act of framing. Whether these events can be considered found art can be debated but the label we give them is incidental. Of more concern here is the claim that they *are* art or *like* art.

Attributing artistic achievement to the perpetrators may seem revolting, but it would be arrogant and myopic to blithely dismiss statements like Hirst's and Stockhausen's. For we must take care not to confound the aesthetic with art or to consider either of these necessarily positive. To call the film footage of the attack visually stunning acknowledges their aesthetic impact. Many art works could be described in similar terms but yet reflect different content and moral meaning. Frederick Edwin Church's "The Icebergs" (1861) is visually stunning; so are Turner's "The Burning of the Houses of Lords and Commons" (1834) and Mathias Grünewald's "Crucifixion" (1515).

But so also are many natural events: sunsets, the full moon in the night sky, the sea in a great storm. But perceptual force alone, while aesthetic, does not make art. It may lie in the subject-matter of an art work but as part of the whole it is something different. There is a sense in which Stockhausen's comment can be taken literally by regarding the 9/11 terrorist attacks as theater. Stockhausen himself composed musical works with dramatic venues and enormous scale, so his calling the attacks "the biggest work of art there has ever been" was not entirely unpredictable or out of character.

But how can we respond to these comments? Is it possible to disentangle the aesthetic from the moral in such a highly charged situation or does the moral issue entirely overpower the aesthetic one? There are no unequivocal answers and perhaps the consideration of Happenings, transgression, and violence can help us make these assertions understandable. They may suggest a way of grasping them that is not immediately obvious. But first, however, is the matter of terrorism, itself.

Simply to list the definitions of 'terrorism' would take pages. What they have in common is the use of violence or the threat of violence.[9] Most often added to the definition is that terrorism focuses on a civilian population with the intention of creating widespread fear, and that it is motivated by political or ideological objectives. Terrorism also carries an element of the unexpected. An element of chance enters into its choice (if we may call it that) of victims and sometimes in the determination of specific time and location, and this adds greatly to the fear that acts of terrorism evoke.

It is interesting to consider that this combination of elements that define terrorism—violence, civilian victims, fear—does not specify the perpetrators. These may be indifferently radical groups of the right or left, military, paramilitary, governmental, or non-governmental organizations. The media unquestionably play a central role in promoting such fear. When fear-mongering is deliberate, the media that practice it could themselves be considered terrorist organizations, just as could other fomenting organizations, such as government bureaus (what Badiou calls "bureaucratic terrorism"[10]) and *ad hoc* groups of individuals who may be the perpetrators, as in the Oklahoma City bombing. It is important to recognize the scope of terrorism, since labeling organizations as 'terrorist' because they use or threaten violence toward a civilian population, regardless of their place in the social order, is revealing and sobering: they are not necessarily marginal. Recognizing the wide range of sources of terrorism helps avoid self-righteous exclusions.

It is important to realize that the use of terror is not confined to Asia or the Middle East. Terror, in fact, has become a standard practice at the present stage of world history. Totalitarian states know well that terrorizing a population is the most effective way of controlling it, far more potent than overt force. We can recognize the climate of fear and terror that has spread not only throughout regions in the African, Asian, and South American continents; it is being

---

[9] See Walter Laqueur, *Origins of Terrorism: Psychologies, Ideologies, Theologies, States of Mind* (Woodrow Wilson Center Press, 1998).

[10] Alain Badiou, *The Meaning of Sarkozy* (London & New York: Verso, 2008), p. 92.

deliberately implemented in Western industrialized nations, as well, by the use of so-called national security measures. Indeed, if state terror were made visible, it would obscure the individual acts of terror that have achieved such notoriety today.[11]

Acts of terrorism are appallingly inventive and their range is extreme. They extend from suicide bombers in the Middle-East and the release of the nerve gas sarin in the Tokyo subway by the religious cult Aum Shinrikyo and its attempts at biological terrorism to the 9/11 suicide plane crashes perpetrated by Al Qaida. But we cannot exclude state terrorism in this portrayal: the use of overt police action and military force to control social activities, gangs dispatched to foment social violence, and secret police to instill fear. And there is also the increasingly sophisticated propagandistic use of the media — magazines and newspapers, TV talk shows and news broadcasts — to proliferate false information, obscure and distort current events, and instill insecurity. This is no reign of terror; we are living in an age of terror.

Can Terrorism be Justified?

The scope of terrorism is, then, surprisingly large and its definition surprisingly inclusive. At the same time it is important to recognize the difference between terrorism and terror and not to confuse the two. Terrorism is, as we have seen, the calculated use of violence or threat of violence against a civilian population with the intent of causing widespread fear for political purposes. Terror, on the other hand, is the overpowering *emotion* of intense fear. More about this later. What I am concerned with just now is terrorism, not terror, as such.

Can terrorism ever be justified? What makes terrorism so morally appalling is that its victims are circumstantial,

---

[11] One is reminded of Hobbes' characterization of the nature of war as not actual fighting but "in the known disposition thereto," a description that applies not only to what has been called a "cold war" but equally to a society in a state of continual fear and thus easily moved to violence. See Thomas Hobbes, *Leviathan* (1660), ch. 13.

uninvolved, and oblivious of what is happening. It is a vicious lottery with equal opportunity to lose. The devastating results of terrorist acts are not much different from the so-called "collateral damage" suffered by civilian populations throughout the whole history of warfare. Violence visited deliberately on an innocent, circumstantial population condemns it as one of the most heinous social wrongs, irrespective of any self-justifying motives. For this reason terrorism can never be vindicated, and terrorism practiced by a state is no more exempt from moral condemnation than when used as a tactic by a political or religious group.

But apart from the question of whether terrorism is ever justifiable, it must nonetheless be recognized and understood. Visible and bold acts of terrorism force us to acknowledge that such acts of violence are not aberrations committed by deluded individuals but social actions deliberately perpetrated by groups and for clear reasons. They may be the arms of state oppression or they may represent political opposition to what is perceived as correlative injustice. Terrorist acts are often committed in response to the social violence of exploitation or oppression of one population group by another. Yet one form of violence cannot be selectively justified over against another. By being directed against unwitting victims, all such actions are morally flawed. A violent act committed in response to other acts of violence is not thereby exonerated: both are equally condemnable. Can terrorism be considered morally justifiable when it is the only available means to a political or ideological end, when there is no alternative way to redress an injustice? This is the critical moral question and central to understanding terrorism.

The question of the justifiability of terrorism does not, however, answer the *aesthetic* question: are aesthetic values present in terrorist acts? Is there an aesthetics of terrorism? What, indeed, has terrorism to do with aesthetics at all? It is necessary to confront these questions because acts of terrorism make effective use of the techniques and skills of art and possess aesthetic force. Yet how can we speak of political acts such as terrorism in the same breath as art and the aesthetic? Must art that uses violence to convey a moral message and make a moral judgment be condemned when that message could not be made in any other way? We arrive again at the same moral dilemma. This is a question that must be faced by any argument for true democracy, the political form that claims to provide means for peaceful social change.[12] Democracy or terrorism?

The use of terrorism as a political act thus raises difficult aesthetic as well as moral issues, and it is important to understand terrorism, not just to condemn it. Indeed, considering terrorism from an aesthetic vantage point can cast considerable light on such acts. For these events are perceptually powerful, engaging not only the visual but all the senses. They are aesthetic because of their sensory force. These are desperate acts committed in order to make a moral and political statement through their aesthetic, that is, their sensory impact. Moreover, their inherent political import is a dramatic rejection of the traditional difference between art and reality, a feature they have in common with the modern arts.

Since aesthetics centers on direct sensory perception, it is clear that acts of terrorism have powerful aesthetic force. All those who experience the effects of terrorism—its chance victims, their relatives and associates, the organizations and institutions that are damaged, the general public, the social order—all can attest to its aesthetic impact. Human values—and the value of humans—are at stake, but we cannot measure such value quantitatively. How is it possible to compare or judge experience? Is a physical act of terrorism such as a suicide bombing worse than the repression of a whole population by a government policy instituted in the name of security, causing widespread fear and requiring overt acts of brutality to enforce it? Is a deliberately planned riot designed to manipulate a population less terrifying than, say, an attempt to poison a public water supply? Here,

---

[12] This is a problem that stands apart from the aesthetic questions I am dealing with here and clearly requires its own separate treatment. As a version of the means-end problem, it has long history of philosophical debate.

I think, differences in conditions, means, and consequences need to be identified and each situation appraised on its own terms and not by some general formula. At the same time and more important, such alternatives are morally unacceptable as well as rationally irresolvable. There is no choice between Hitler and Pol Pot.

Unlike acts of sabotage, acts of terrorism have no direct military target. Perhaps it can be said that in this respect they mirror the largely self-contained character of art. And what sort of aesthetic value can terrorism have? "[T]he tragic in real life will necessarily have an aesthetic dimension as long as the sensibility of the subject comes into play by judging something as being 'tragic'."[13] Is there art in terrorism? It cannot be denied that much of the political effectiveness of terrorist acts comes from their carefully planned aesthetic impact. Indeed, their effect is primarily, often spectacularly theatrical. We can in fact say that such actions are deliberately designed to be high drama. In this sense, then, is theater any less appropriate a way to describe a spectacular act of terrorism than it is to designate military activities? Perhaps it now becomes understandable how an artist could consider a terrorist act a work of art.

Can terrorism have positive moral value? Simple ascriptions of positive and negative value no longer fit. Such morally complex situations demand a different kind of analysis. If a terrorist act contributes to achieving social justice, can we even ask whether it is morally positive or negative? A Kantian analysis would find it negative, for such actions cannot be universalized. A utilitarian analysis would find it positive to the extent it contributes to political or social reform, if it does indeed have that consequence, rather than the redoubled use of state terror. But can we even presume to balance immediate pain, death, and destruction against future benefits?

Neither of these analyses resolves the issue. Universalizability is an ethical principle and a logical desideratum but it is not axiomatic and exempt from critical

---

[13] Mandoki, *loc. cit.*

reflection. And to consider consequences only selectively is effectively to disregard terrorism's wide-ranging fallout. Moreover, failing to acknowledge the full scope of consequences continues the common practice of hiding behind moral principles at human cost. Most important is the further consideration that means and ends are never separable. What kind of society can emerge from terror-induced change? Though the intent of terrorist action may be the goal of human liberation, the short-term effects are unavoidably negative. And its long-term effects?

It is clear that the moral issues terrorism raises are complex. In traditional terms the judgment may seem clear, but under full consideration it becomes ambiguous. As in warfare where everyone claims right, justice is on every side—and so, too, is injustice. The pain of an enemy is no less great than one's own. Life lost is a lost life, no matter whose life it is.

Is a spectacular terrorist act aesthetically negative or positive? It must be considered positive because of its dramatic force. If, however, fear and terror overpower perceptual experience, not only in its unwilling "participants" but also in its larger "audience," so that they feel in actual danger, a terrorist act exceeds the possibility of rewarding aesthetic experience and so is aesthetically negative.[14] So aesthetically, too, is terrorism indeterminate. Such situations seem, then, to be ambiguous both morally and aesthetically.

How a terrorist act can be morally positive in any sense may be difficult to see. We must acknowledge that the strategy of the acts and the motives of the actors may be guided by the goals of liberation, of a more just social order, of an end to oppression and exploitation, and other humane objectives. But they may also be guided by the intent to preserve power and the social and economic privileges that accompany it. Do any ends ever justify terrorist means? Their morally reprehensible effects are so blatant that it seems inconceivable that any goal, however noble, could exonerate them. One cannot choose between two incom-

---

[14]   Both Burke and Kant noted the impossibility of experiencing the sublime when one's safety is at risk. *Cf.* Kant, *Critique of Judgment*, §28.

mensurable wrongs. At the same time, even if a terrorist act could claim to be morally positive — which I do not believe is possible, does this justify its aesthetic negativity? Morality and aesthetics are not easily distinguished here. Pain and delight are both inherently moral and aesthetic: The same act can be both morally and aesthetically positive or negative, for the moral and the aesthetic may be fully interdependent, inseparably fused. The very perpetration of a terrorist act is at the same time both aesthetic and moral, spectacularly destructive.

Generalities pale before the intense particularity of terrorist acts. Every incident has its unique conditions and no logical decision procedure seems possible. Does the sheer scope and force of a terrorist act place it in a new and different category? Just as we cannot measure aesthetic pleasure or grade works of art, fear and terror are not truly quantifiable. Nor are consequences fully determinable. And because both their scope and their intensity cannot be specified precisely, they are truly inconceivable. There is a concept in aesthetics that denotes experience so overwhelming that it exceeds comprehension — the sublime, and it is worth considering whether the sublime could conceivably be applied to acts of terrorism.

The Negative Sublime

The sublime is a theory that reflects with great discernment on a distinctive kind of aesthetic experience. While the sublime became prominent in the eighteenth century as a key dimension in the development of aesthetic theory, it has become increasingly important in recent aesthetic discourse. The starting point is usually Kant's account, although Kant was not the first to elaborate a theory of this distinctive mode of aesthetic apprehension. Burke's discussion of the sublime had come half a century before,[15] and

[15] Edmund Burke, *Philosophical Inquiry into the Origin of our Ideas of the Sublime and Beautiful* (1757) (Oxford: Oxford University Press, 1990). Burke did not originate the concept; a treatise *On the Sublime* is attributed to Longinus, in the third century CE, although its authorship and date of composition have been contested.

while Kant's formulation has dominated subsequent discussions, Burke's observations are particularly germane to the present one. For according to Burke, the central feature of the sublime is terror. The most powerful passion caused by the sublime in nature, he states, is astonishment, a state of mind with an element of horror in which all other thoughts are suspended. Fear at the prospect of pain or danger freezes the capacity to reason and act and evokes the overpowering feeling of terror. As "the strongest emotion which the mind is capable of feeling", Burke maintained that the feeling of terror is a principal source of the sublime: "[W]hatever is qualified to cause terror, is a foundation capable of the sublime...." [16] And, "Indeed, terror is in all cases whatsoever, either more openly or latently the ruling principle of the sublime."[17] Burke described many emotions associated with the sublime and the conditions under which the sublime may be experienced, and he cited many instances of terror incited by fear. His analysis, however, did not proceed beyond such descriptions.

Kant, too, recognized fear as a feature of the (dynamical) sublime.[18] In contrast with Burke, Kant developed an elaborate theory illuminated by a distinction between the mathematical and the dynamical sublime. In the first, the magnitude of the absolutely great is a measure that the mind cannot wholly encompass.[19] Applied to a terrorist act, its effects and consequences cannot be fully described or even mentally encompassed and are incommensurable. Its material consequences in the form of physical destruction and social disruption, the scope of the human anguish inflicted, and the protective measures and reciprocal violence wreaked upon society in reaction can never be fully enumerated. Its human consequences are immeasurable because they are incalculable. We may indeed say that we

---

[16]   Burke, *ibid.*, Part One, Section VII; Part Two, Sections I and II; Part IV, Section III; pp. 36, 53-54, 119.
[17]   *Ibid.*, Part Two, Section II, p. 54.
[18]   *Critique of Judgment*, §28.
[19]   *Ibid.*, §27.

cannot quantify the destructive force of a terrorist attack: it evokes the mathematical sublime.

The second, Kant's dynamical sublime, concerns the fear we feel in response to the enormous might of nature, although we must nonetheless feel secure and unthreatened, able to rise above that fear and not be subject to it. Ironically, even war, Kant avers, has something sublime in it if carried on with order and respect for citizens' rights,[20] presumably by protecting non-combatants. In the place of might in Kant's dynamical sublime, the sublime in terrorism is present in the intensity of physical force, in its engulfing emotional power, in the overwhelming psychological pressure of the situation.

Like Kant's dynamical sublime, the effectiveness of terrorism lies in its potential threat to safety and in the very insecurity and social instability that result. In terrorism safety is especially equivocal: while there may be non-combatants, everyone is vulnerable. The actual victims are but sacrificial lambs for its effect on the larger population. Another important difference is in the fact that, unlike the quantitative forms of the Kantian sublime in which both magnitude and force seem to be immeasurable, the intensity of the terrorist sublime is also immeasurable and its dimensions indeterminate. And it rests on consequences that are qualitatively indeterminable and thus incomparable. Only in their circumstances and means are the acts and effects of terrorism distinguishable. Since both the scope and the intensity of terrorist attacks are beyond conception, both morally and aesthetically, we need a new concept, the "negative sublime", as their truest and most eloquent identification.

Because acts of terrorism elude meaningful quantitative determination, we must further acknowledge their *moral* and *aesthetic* incommensurability, indeed, their very

---

[20]   *Ibid.*, §28. "War itself, if it is carried on with order and with a sacred respect for the rights of citizens, has something sublime in it, and makes the disposition of the people who carry it on thus only the more sublime, the more numerous are the dangers to which they are exposed and in respect of which they behave with courage." p. 102.

inconceivability. Perhaps the only concept that can fully categorize them is the negative sublime. Like the aesthetic, the sublime is not necessarily a positive determination but a mode of experience. Hence to call such acts of terrorism the negative sublime is not an oxymoron but the recognition of negativity whose enormity cannot be encompassed in either magnitude or force. The uniqueness of such extreme actions renders them capable of description only. One might claim that an act of terrorism exemplifies the post-modern sublime as Lyotard described it, in making the unpresentable perceptible.[21] And because the moral and the aesthetic are inseparable here, the negative sublime incurs equivalent aesthetic and moral value. That the moral is also aesthetic makes it even more intolerable. Death is the ultimate human loss, and body counts and statistics are deceptively specific and impersonal. Such qualitative consequences as the human suffering from extreme acts of terrorism are beyond measure. "After the first death, there is no other". [22]

Acknowledging that there may be an aesthetic in acts of terrorism, even a positive aesthetic, does not condone or justify such action, for in terrorism the aesthetic never stands alone. Recognizing its presence may help us understand the peculiar fascination that the public has with such events of world theater. These are indeed acts of high drama that fascinate us by their very sublimity.[23] But the theatrical

---

[21] There is a resemblance here to Lyotard's characterization of the sublime as making `the unpresentable perceptible. "The art object no longer bends itself to models, but tries to present the fact that there is an unpresentable... ." *Cf.* Jean-François Lyotard, *The Postmodern Condition: A Report on Knowledge* (1979) (Minneapolis: University of Minnesota Press, 1984), p. 81; "The sublime and the avant-garde," in *The Lyotard Reader*, ed. Andrew Benjamin (Blackwell: Cambridge, MA, 1989), p. 207.

[22] "A Refusal to Mourn the Death, by Fire, of a Child in London," in *The Collected Poems of Dylan Thomas* (New York: New Directions, 1957), p. 112.

[23] "...far from articulating the need of personal expression on the artistic level, art becomes fully politicized as an agency that acts on its own in the social sphere, thus enabling itself to interact with and affect the world directly." Artetoulakis, *op. cit.*, sect. 4. Again, "If we do not merely settle into thinking of art as personal expression within

forcefulness that impresses us with their image is indissolubly bound up with their moral negativity, and identifying them as the negative sublime is to condemn them beyond all measure. As an agent here in the social sphere, art affects the world directly. Indeed, "by attacking reality, art *becomes* reality".[24]

Terrorism dramatically exposes the inseparability of the moral and the aesthetic, yet it is an extreme form of what is always the case. Utopian thought, to turn to the other side of the normative ledger, also has a strong aesthetic component. Utopianism is pervaded by moral values of social and environmental harmony and fulfillment. Its goal of facilitating living that is deeply satisfying through the fruitful exercise of human capacities is as aesthetic as it is moral.[25] To conform to the tradition that separates the aesthetic from the moral mirrors its segregation from everyday life and constricts its force. Let us see the picture whole and not in parts.

---

the canonically bounded domain of the aesthetic, and we ascribe to art an active involvement ... then we better be ready to come to terms with art as a realm in which humanity exercises its utmost creative/destructive potential, and not in the so-called (since Hegel) world of the spirit but in the world itself." Stathis Gourgouris, "Transformation, Not Transcendence," *Boundary 2* 31.2 (2004): 55-79. Quoted in Aretoulakis, *loc. cit.*

[24] Aretoulakis, *op. cit.*, sect. 5. Katya Mandoki saw it plainly: "What must be noted is that art and reality, like aesthetics and the everyday, are totally entwined, not because of the explicit will of the artist, but because there is nothing further, beneath or beyond reality. Even dreams are real, as dreams. The effort to unite art-reality is, therefore, unnecessary. Moreover, when art manifests itself as a mechanism for evasion or for emancipation ... [it is] fatally and irremediably immersed in reality, whether indexically pointing at it by the evasion itself (silence is very eloquent) or by assuming particular sides for criticism or emancipation. Mandoki, *op. cit.*, pp. 15-16.

[25] I have called such a joining of the aesthetic and the ethical "humanistic function." See my essay, "Aesthetic Function", in Arnold Berleant, *Living in the Landscape: Toward an Aesthetics of Environment* (Lawrence: University Press of Kansas, 1997).

Chapter Eleven

Perceptual Politics

Aesthetics and politics

It is clear that the critical power of the aesthetic makes it an effective instrument for social analysis, one that has not yet been adequately recognized and utilized. Its significance lies not only in the ability of the aesthetic to serve as a critical tool for probing social practice but as a beacon for illuminating the direction of social betterment. This may seem at first to be an outlandish claim but for the fact that the aesthetic has begun to emerge as a key factor in political theory, although its transformative implications have not been reckoned.

In recent years this connection between aesthetics and politics has become explicit. The literature is large, ranging from observations of an aesthetic politics that began with Nietzsche (although preceded by Kant and Hegel), moving through Heidegger, Benjamin, Blanchot, Adorno, Marcuse, Sartre, and Merleau-Ponty, and most recently to Derrida, Lyotard, Deleuze, and Rancière, to cite only some of the more prominent contributors.

Two principal features mark the discussions of the social relevance of the aesthetic in this body of literature. One is the focus of philosophical commentaries on what art and litera-ture signify and contribute to our understanding of truth and being. The other is their concern with the social relevance of the aesthetic in experience, politics, and the nature of society. For many of these thinkers the aesthetic is uttered in the same breath as art, and art is often seen through either a Marxist or a psychoanalytic lens, or through both.

We can take Herbert Marcuse as one example. Marcuse's views reflect the influence of both Marx and Freud. Art, he holds, has a liberating function: "it is committed to an emancipation of sensibility, imagination, and reason in all spheres of subjectivity and objectivity." Important as this emancipation is, it has its source, Marcuse argues, in "Eros, the deep affirmation of the Life Instincts in their fight against instinctual and social oppression." Art has an ideological function, as well, but Marcuse is critical of Marxist aesthetics for its class-based analysis of art, even though he acknowledges that there is always a social presence in art. Art, he holds, contributes to the political struggle by helping achieve a change of consciousness.[1]

Both of these influences, Marxism and psychoanalysis, characterize the writings of the Frankfurt School, with which Marcuse was associated, and are central in the work of Theodor Adorno and its other leading figures. Adorno's lengthy *Aesthetic Theory*, a representative example, deals almost exclusively with art. Without contesting Adorno's case for the significance of art in culture, society, and politics, I claim that art is not the most fundamental factor in aesthetic analysis.

We find the same identification of the aesthetic with the arts in theorists associated with post-structuralism and deconstruction. Jean-François Lyotard, for example, coupled aesthetics with the arts in his intense concern over their critical function. His belief in the "deep-seated exteriority of art" sees art as a political force and an alternative to theory, and aesthetics, he believed, shares this critical role. [2] Gilles Deleuze made a similar association where "the two senses of the aesthetic become one, to the point where the being of the sensible reveals itself in the work of art, while at the same time the work of art appears as experimentation." [3]

It is of basic import, however, to recognize the difference between art and the aesthetic and to separate the consider-

---

[1]   Herbert Marcuse, *The Aesthetic Dimension: Toward a Critique of Marxist Aesthetics* (Boston: Beacon Press, 1978), pp. 9–11, 16–18, 36 and Ch. V.

[2]   J.-F. Lyotard, *Discours, figure* and *Economie libidinale*. See David Carroll, *Paraesthetics: Foucault, Lyotard, Derrida* (New York: Methuen, 1987), pp. 28, 36, 51.

[3]   Gilles Deleuze, *Difference and Repetition* (1968), trans. Paul Patton (New York: Columbia University Press, 1993), p.68.

ation of each from that of the other. From all that has gone before in this book, it is clear that, even though intimately related, these terms have very different meanings and referents. I have maintained that the aesthetic is a mode of experience that rests on the directness and immediacy of sensuous perception, perception that is deeply influenced by the multitude of factors affecting all experience—cognitive, cultural, historical, personal. Art, on the other hand, denotes the multifarious ways in which people shape that experience. Traditionally this process of shaping direct experience has been done through artifacts, especially in painting and sculpture, poetry and fiction, and most of the other art forms. This fashioning of experience has gone on regardless of whether the arts are traditional or classical, contemporary or popular. Art has also been made by directly manipulating the perceptual materials of immediate experience, as in performance art and conceptual art, as well as in dance. Since perception as an experiential condition precedes the activities through which it is shaped, channeled, and ordered, it denotes the fundamental ground of all artistic activity. Aesthetic perception is thus the foundation of art, and aesthetic theory should deal with both art and perception.

Certainly the breadth of aesthetic perception invites pursuit in many directions. But here I focus on one that is especially important for its critical potential: the social. My intent in this book is to explore the foundational significance and social uses of aesthetic perception. And as neither perception nor cognition is self-contained, consideration of the one will illuminate the other. The appearance of the aesthetic as a prominent theme in political theory is one of its striking uses.

Moved by the pervasiveness and insistence of political forces in social life, many scholars have been drawn increasingly to recognize the strands of the aesthetic that are woven into its texture. They have gone beyond dealing with the ways that the arts are used in political propaganda and for arousing patriotic feeling. The aesthetic has come to be recognized as a perceptual domain of considerable power and influence, and some analysts have assigned it a crucial place in political theory. Making the aesthetic central in political theory may be surprising, for two such dissimilar domains of thought and experience might seem, at first, difficult to reconcile. Yet the association of aesthetics with politics has been made, and it will be illuminating to look at some applications that assign the aesthetic dimension a critical place in social and political thought. Let me then trace some of the appeals to the aesthetic in founding political theory, first considering Friedrich Schiller before moving into contemporary proposals.

Schiller's *Letters* and Beauty as a Condition of Humanity

This recent scholarly trend has its most direct source in Schiller's *Letters on the Aesthetic Education of Man* (1795).[4] This early work by the German romantic poet continues to radiate a benign influence despite profound changes in the intellectual climate. Schiller's detailed and eloquent study openly reflects the early influence of Kantian philosophy. At the same time, his own thinking developed over the several years during which the *Letters* were composed. We find in them, then, not so much a consistent philosophical exposition as an expanding understanding of the conditions of human fulfillment in what he called the aesthetic state.

Schiller went to eloquent lengths in recognizing and attempting to accommodate the different and sometimes conflicting aspects of human experience, principally the physical, sensory factors and the rational, cognitive ones. Following Kant, he found their reconciliation in a balance that allows absolute dominance to neither but rather integrates their forces in harmonious interplay. The 'disposition,' as he called it, that emerges in this process and makes

---

[4]   F.C.S. Schiller, *Letters on the Aesthetic Education of Man*, trans. Reginald Snell (New York: Ungar, 1965). See here especially the "Twentieth Letter," pp. 97–99. It should be clear that I am not presuming to offer a full historical account of the social aesthetic, which goes back at least to Plato, but the initial and continuing influence of Schiller's *Letters* places them at the head of this recent trend.

their resolution possible is the aesthetic. Humanity is most fulfilled, Schiller claimed, in the contemplation of beauty, and a genuine work of art, requiring both our sensuous and intellectual powers, creates in us the loftiness and strength of spirit that characterize freedom.

This brings us to the heart of our present concern for, Schiller argued, through beauty people acquire a social character, and taste makes social harmony possible by establishing harmony in the individual.[5] Thus a homology emerges between the fulfilled person and the aesthetic state that is reminiscent of Plato's theory of justice in *The Republic*. "Everything in the aesthetic State, even the subservient tool, is a free citizen having equal rights with the noblest...." In such a condition of aesthetic appearance the ideal of equality is fulfilled.[6]

For Schiller, then, the beautiful world exemplifies its moral standing and represents the freedom of the citizen in which every person is restored to a harmony of rational and sensory forces. "Beauty alone can confer on him [Man] a social character."[7] At the same time this is no private, individual affair but is social through and through, for an aesthetic sensibility promotes empathy and an awareness of others. Schiller thus brought together the aesthetic, the moral, and the social.[8] No one has united these strands of human value more explicitly or more eloquently.

---

[5]   *Ibid.*, p. 138. The full passage is, "The dynamic state can only make society possible, by curbing Nature through Nature; the ethical State can only make it (morally) necessary, by subjecting the individual to the general will; the aesthetic State alone can make it actual, since it carries out the will of the whole though the nature of the individual. Though need may drive Man into society, and Reason implant social principles in him, Beauty alone can confer on him a social character. Taste alone brings harmony into society, because it establishes harmony in the individual."

[6]   *Ibid.*, p. 140.

[7]   *Ibid.*, p. 138.

[8]   Here, in various translations, are passages from the Seventeenth and Twenty-seventh Letters that express these ideas: " 'The aesthetic life' will invariably restore [each specialized person] to himself as a rational-sensuous harmonic whole. Finally, by promoting empathy and awareness of others, aesthetic sensibility gives rise to the development of a society and state in which the individual becomes, as it

Finding a model of community in the aesthetic has become a recurrent theme in recent political philosophy. This shows not only the suggestiveness of the aesthetic but also displays the widely different interpretations it has received. Let me consider several representative examples here, not with the intent of developing a full-blown critique of each but rather of revealing some of the uses to which the aesthetic has been put in political theory.

Ankersmit on Aesthetic Politics

In his book *Aesthetic Politics,* F.R. Ankersmit uses the aesthetic in an original and provocative defense of democracy.[9] The core of his argument is based on an analogy between pictorial representation and that which is represented, on the one hand, and between the state and the citizen, on the other. It is mistaken, Ankersmit insists, to assume that there is some kind of unity between the work of art and the world. The separation between representation and represented is unbridgeable; moreover, this same "aesthetic barrier" exists between citizen and state. Ankersmit argues that this breach must be recognized as the foundation of the democratic model, for it is out of their conflict that political power and the proper forms of its disposition arise.

A democratic state, therefore, cannot develop by means of direct democracy or out of a common bond between citizen and state. Such attempts lead to bureaucratic social and political intermediaries that provide the basis for totalitari-

---

were, the state itself."

"The aesthetic state alone can make it real, because it carries out the will of all through the nature of the individual. If necessity alone forces man to enter into society, and if his reason engraves on his soul social principles, it is beauty only that can give him a social character; taste alone brings harmony into society, because it creates harmony in the individual."

"The beautiful world [is] the happiest symbol of how the moral should be, and each beautiful natural being [Naturwesen] outside of me [is] a happy citizen who calls out to me: 'Be free like me.' "

[9]   F.R. Ankersmit, *Aesthetic Politics, Political Philosophy Beyond Fact and Value* (Stanford: Stanford University Press, 1996).

anism.[10] Thus political differences about whether a state properly represents its people is like disagreeing over whether a painting represents reality properly. Such disputes can never be objectively resolved but reflect differences in taste or feeling that are similarly unresolvable. And, Ankersmit holds further, just as there are no fixed rules that tell painters how to go from the landscape to their picture of it, aesthetic political theory makes us aware of an aesthetic gap or void between the represented and the representative, between the state and society. Thus like the artist's picture, political theory ought to retain a prominent role for the state and we should focus on its enhanced position to better understand present-day democratic politics.

Ankersmit carries the aesthetic analogy further. Each artist and each distinctive style determines anew how to make the transition from the represented to its representation. This constant process of renewal is also why all works of art belong to a new or different world that cannot be reduced to the world that we experience.[11] Such an approach confirms the view that legitimate political power originates in this aesthetic difference between the individual citizen and his or her representative. Therefore, Ankersmit concludes, political power possesses an 'aesthetic' rather than an 'ethical' nature, and an ethical approach to politics should be replaced by an aesthetic one.[12]

Ankersmit's political argument is guided entirely by this underlying aesthetic analogy, and the scope and detail with which he develops it are impressive. It is all the more surprising that a case so inclusive and replete with historical and analytical detail should devote so little attention to establishing and justifying this reading of the aesthetic. For the claims on which his argument rests are not commonly acknowledged. Ankersmit's use of the aesthetic actually begs the question of the separation between the landscape and the painting of the landscape. While these may be different, their relationship can be explained in various ways,

---

[10] *Ibid.*, pp. 18–20.
[11] *Ibid.*, pp. 114, 101.
[12] *Ibid.*, pp. 23, 49.

not all of them by an unbridgeable gap. Some accounts emphasize their resemblance and stress the continuities between landscape and painting and between the experience of landscape and the experience of painting. Other accounts see painting as self-sufficient and find no need to reconcile or compare it with what might seem to be represented. What Ankersmit simply takes for granted as the unbridgeability of the representation and the represented treats one of the most obstinate and unresolved puzzles in aesthetics — the ontology of the work of art — as settled. Moreover, this issue is not generally considered to be the central concern of aesthetic theory.

The pertinence of Ankersmit's analysis, then, is highly questionable. For some theorists the illumination that art offers is accessible only when centered on the work of art alone and does not depend on a close relation with an external subject-matter. The subject of a portrait, for example, is not the person who sat for it but the person in the painting, itself. Museums are filled with portraits whose models, if known at all, are long gone. Such information, moreover, is generally considered as of historical interest only and aesthetically irrelevant. The painting is complete and self-sufficient and simply offers itself as such. Indeed, in the hands of a master, the brush can tell us more about the person than we may be able to articulate from knowledge of the actual individual. Furthermore, for many aestheticians the comparison is irrelevant. Much the same can be said of the landscape. The Platonic comparison of an image with its reality is beside the point: the only reality is the image.

This dualism of a painting and its subject, like so many other divisions of the world, creates other problems. For when we compare a painting with its subject, we are engaging cognitive concerns that obscure the painting that is before our eyes with the question, How close is the likeness or resemblance? Furthermore, this problem does not exist for abstract art, where there may be hardly a recognizable bond between the pictorial surface and the surface of the world. That is to say, art is about itself, and only in the illumination we gain by engaging with the work can we gain a resonant understanding that we can carry away. Much more can be said in response to this supposed problem, but it is sufficient here to recognize both the assumptiveness of Ankersmit's argument and its questionability.

But this is not the only difficulty with Ankersmit's case: its logic is seriously flawed. For even if his aesthetic claim were solid, it would provide only a flimsy base for his political analysis. Arguments from analogy have a weak logical status for they are suggestive rather than demonstrative. An analogy does not prove the parallel that is drawn; it only proposes a resemblance in the expectation that this will suggest how the parallel could be more complete. A purported resemblance between a painting and its subject-matter, on the one side, and an individual and the state, on the other, thus fails on logical as well as aesthetic grounds. For whether or not there is a disjunction inherent in the aesthetic relation proves nothing about the political one. More compelling reasons than an aesthetic parallel that is itself questionable must be given if Ankersmit wishes to reject any intermediary or continuity in the human-political relation. However, he simply assumes the separation and proceeds to utilize it as an explanatory principle.

What is perhaps most interesting here is that an appeal is made to aesthetics to justify a political theory. And just as the aesthetic involved is a particular feature or issue and not a theory, so, too, are the social meanings to which it is unquestioningly applied. For Ankersmit's view of the political problem lies in a disjunctive relation of the individual and the state, a relation and the conflict it engenders that stand, he asserts, as the basis for political democracy. This, however, is no statement of political or social fact but a problem that arises from the very way it is structured, a conceptual dilemma far more common than is usually recognized. The discussions earlier in this book have made the case that no entities are wholly discrete, yet it is an unquestioned axiom of liberal democracy that the difference between the individual and the state is fundamental and ineradicable: it is a distinction made into an opposition. Many of the various political theories and mechanisms that have been proposed are efforts not so much to reconcile as to balance these presumably opposed interests. This is what can be termed, following the phenomenologist Marvin Farber, a methodogenic problem, one that arises out of the adoption of a method, in this case, a methodology of division, and not from the substance of the situation.[13]

This political analysis, then, receives little support from what turns out to be a basic disanalogy with art. For whatever may be the case in aesthetics, art has little in common with political theory other than, in Ankersmit's analysis, a separation into pairs of irreconcilable parts. Can aesthetics contribute to politics anything more than an imaginative logical suggestion? That Ankersmit has recourse to the aesthetic suggests that a special value may reside there. His use, unfortunately, does little to identify or profit from it, but the value of aesthetics, heuristic or substantive, is something that others have nonetheless considered. Like the arts, aesthetics has been put to multiple purposes and it is instructive to continue to follow its uses in political theory, as distinct from its traditional role in a critical analysis of art.

Ferguson on Aesthetics and Community

Kennan Ferguson offers another such appropriation of the aesthetic by appealing to Kant's theory of judgment to provide the basis for community.[14] Kant's recourse to a *sensus communis,* the capacity for judging in a fashion that is common to human reason as a whole as the grounds for affirming a subjective universal, leads aesthetics, like morality, to the public sphere. Like others, Ferguson credits Kant with creating an ethical aesthetics, "a normative public sphere that directs, teaches, and demands communal standards."[15] It is by means of disinterestedness, he holds, that aesthetic judgment, like moral judgment, can overcome its subjective grounds and affirm its public setting.

---

[13]   Marvin Farber, *Naturalism and Subjectivism* (Albany: State University of New York Press, 1959), p. 8 and passim.

[14]   Kennan Ferguson, *The Politics of Judgment: Aesthetics, Identity, and Political Theory* (Lanham, MD: Lexington Books, 1999).

[15]   *Ibid.*, p. 11.

As he develops his case, Ferguson is rightly concerned to retain the integrity of those differences in identity that are invariably present among people and spawn social diversity, determinants that are variously ethnic, cultural, and gender-based. He thinks that, by recourse to the non-linguistic figuration of aesthetics, we can hope to grasp the complexities and ambiguities of political identity and communal understanding. "The potency of aesthetics is in its very flexibility and contingency."[16]

We find here the important recognition that the aesthetic, like the moral, involves an individual determination, yet one that is at the very same time a communal one. For judgments of taste carry a determination that is public as well as private and hence possess social significance. Ferguson's emendation of the Kantian universal so that it can accommodate fundamental social and cultural diversity is important and necessary. Yet significant as this is, to ground it on Kant's appeal to a *sensus communis* elevates a hypothetical construction to axiomatic status on a doubly weak underpinning. Kant's common sense is not an empirical truth; it is a metaphysical principle given logical status that is dictated by the necessity for universality by basing judgment on concepts and not feeling.[17]

A significant consideration in political theory Is thus grounded on aesthetics but at the cost of accepting the Kantian fiction of a *sensus communis*. Such an appeal to aesthetics in political theory gets its credibility from Kant but its aesthetic import is wholly casual. Is there something less assumptive than postulating a *sensus communis* that can bring aesthetic judgment to a common focus?[18]

Chytry on the Aesthetic State

The most extensive and intensive examination of the significance of aesthetics in cultural and social thought is

---

[16] *Ibid.*, pp. 43–44, 46.
[17] Kant, *Critique of Judgment*, § 20.
[18] Maryvonne Saison notes the central place Mikel Dufrenne gives the sensus communis as the ground of an "aesthetic sociability". See "The People Are Missing", *Contemporary Aesthetics*, Vol. 6 (2008), §1.

undoubtedly Josef Chytry's 1968 study, *The Aesthetic State*.[19] Focusing on the aesthetic impact on German thought from the mid-eighteenth century to the mid-twentieth, Chytry finds its origins in Greek culture, particularly in the Homeric model of aesthetic judgment exemplified in the Judgment of Paris and the Athenian polis. He regards the Greek amalgam of poetry and politics in rhetoric and persuasion as the theatricalizing of political life. Chytry sees this aestheticism as the guiding ideal of a tradition that runs through Florentine poetic humanism, with its courtly aestheticism and its model of the artist-magician-scientist, to the mid-eighteenth century in England and the Third Earl of Shaftesbury, who formalized aesthetics for modern thought.[20]

The main body of this extensive survey pursues the political ideal of the polis through a series of major German thinkers, from Winckelmann and Schiller to Heidegger and Marcuse. Chytry's careful scholarship is unnecessarily recondite, and it is further hampered by a style that layers classical, mythological, and historical allusions in language whose obscurity of expression magnifies its complexity. Nonetheless his study is a major effort to articulate the significance of the aesthetic in human moral and social life. For Chytry the aesthetic state is no simple condition but an expressive life that joins persuasion, loveliness, and fairness.[21] This amalgam of the moral, the social, and the aesthetic, rooted in classical thought, is a powerful ideal. It is a vision that achieves universality, he believes, in the tradition of the Kantian subjective universal of the *Third Critique*.

Chytry's notion of the aesthetic thus fuses Homeric poetry, the "tragedy" of Troy, and the theatricality of politicians' persuasive rhetoric in the Greek aesthetic state with the courtly splendor of the late Renaissance and early Baroque. And with these he joins Shaftesbury's endorsement of that Greek ideal, along with his elevation of the

[19]　Josef Chytry, *The Aesthetic State: A Quest in Modern German Thought* (Berkeley and Los Angeles: University of California Press, 1968).

[20]　Ibid., xxxi–lxxiv.

[21]　*Ibid.*, pp. 492–5.

enjoyment of beauty as the highest good.[22] All this Chytry transmutes into the ideal of an aesthetic state as the manifestation of beauty.[23]

In this way Chytry boldly amasses the cultural forces of the lengthy Western tradition in the fulfillment of a vision that is both beautiful and noble. At the same time he is bound by the dimensions of that tradition. While synthesizing the greatest and best of its humanistic understanding, his boundaries retain the Kantian frame of the subjectivity of freedom in a universe of rational objectivity, and his model remains the Athenian polis with its theatrical rhetoric of persuasion. Politically, too, he is tied to the Western tradition that preserves its faith in liberal individualism, a tradition epitomizing so much of the Western understanding of freedom. Chytry's aesthetic state thus possesses the warmth of the humanizing ideal without its creative illumination.

Rancière and the Politics of Sensibility

In recent political theory the most forthright use of the aesthetic in its etymological meaning as sense perception has undoubtedly been made by Jacques Rancière, principally in *The Politics of Aesthetics (Le partage du sensible: Esthétique et politique)*.[24] His identification of the aesthetic with perceptual experience is both distinctive and highly important. Raincière is one of the few since Schiller to recognize the political significance of the perceptual basis of the aesthetic.

---

[22] *Ibid.*, pp. lviii, lxx, lxxii.
[23] "Men and women who have gone so far as to make her [love's] presence criteria to their communal life know no sharp distinction between, at one end, her political manifestation as the voice, the chant and music, of persuasion, of those sweet winning words that beguile all to enjoy mutual toil and a mutual reward in the art of living together and creating things of beauty, and, at the other, a marveling at the reality of the universe as something wonderously fair, a veritable cosmos — to, at least, those 'in Love.' " *Ibid.*, p. 496.
[24] *Le partage du sensible: Esthétique et politique* (Paris: La Fabrique-éditions, 2000). English edition, *The Politics of Aesthetics*, trans. Gabriel Rockhill (London & New York: Continuum, 2004). References will be to the English edition with the corresponding page number in the French edition in parentheses.

He sees the revolutionary significance of Schiller's *Letters on the Aesthetic Education of Man* in placing thought and sensibility on an equal plane. For Schiller, Rancière holds, aesthetic education must develop the capacity to live in a sensible world of free play and appearance, and this capacity is the pre-condition of a free political community.[25]

Rancière makes the political implications of the aesthetic explicit from the outset: "I call the distribution of the sensible the system of self-evident facts of sense perception that simultaneously discloses the existence of something in common and the delimitations that define the respective parts and positions within it."[26] Explicating what is meant by *le commun*, Gabriel Rockhill, the translator, suggests "something in common" or "what is common to the community," which is "strictly speaking what makes or produces a community and not simply an attribute shared by all of its members."[27]

Rancière is at pains to distinguish this aesthetics from art and its domination of political thought. He reverts to the Kantian sense of the aesthetic, following Foucault's interpretation, as "the system of *a priori* forms determining what presents itself to sense experience. It is a delimitation of spaces and times, of the visible and the invisible, of speech and noise, that simultaneously determines the place and the stakes of politics as a form of experience.... It is on the basis of this primary aesthetics that it is possible to raise the question of 'aesthetic practices' as I understand them, that is, forms of visibility that disclose artistic practices, the place they occupy, what they 'do' or 'make' from the standpoint of what is common to the community."[28]

This last has special significance, for "The important thing is that the question of the relationship between aesthetics and politics be raised at this level, the level of the sensible delimitation of what is common to the community, the

---

[25]   *Op. cit.*, p. 21 (40–41).
[26]   *Op. cit.*, p. 12 (12).
[27]   *Op. cit.*, pp. 102–3.
[28]   *Op. cit.*, p. 13.

forms of its visibility and of its organization."[29] The common sensible is the context the arts serve, and they do so within what Rancière calls certain 'regimes': the regime of images, the poetic regime, and the aesthetic regime. This last refers to art that is based, not on ways of doing and making, but on a mode of thought, a regime of the sensible through which the artist renders sensible what has not been codified as knowledge. It is in this sense that art acquires its autonomy, operating independently of ordinary meanings and associations and fuelled by a form of thought that has not yet become knowledge.[30] Here is where Schiller's idea of aesthetic education has its place, leading people to recognize the sensible world in order to live in a free political community. "It is this paradigm of aesthetic autonomy that became the new paradigm for revolution...."[31] At the same time, art becomes the paradigm for work, re-shaping "the landscape of the visible" and re-structuring "the relationship between doing, making, being, seeing, and saying."[32]

The political implications of this redistribution of the sensible are momentous. They are a consequence of the ability of artists to recast the perceptual forms that have been received and accepted as commonplace. "The dream of a suitable political work of art is in fact the dream of disrupting the relationship between the visible, the sayable, and the thinkable" directly through perceptual means. "It is the dream of an art that would transmit meanings in the form of a rupture with the very logic of meaningful situations."[33] As Slavoj Žižek explains, Rancière asserts that "the aesthetic dimension [is] INHERENT in any radical emancipatory politics."[34]

---

[29] *Op. cit.*, p.18 (24). Maryvonne Saison identifies "the ambiguities of the ideal of aesthetic sociability in classical aesthetics" and their persistence in Rancière in "The People Are Missing", *op. cit.* , Sect. 1.
[30] *Op. cit.*, pp. 20–23.
[31] *Op. cit.*, p.27 (39–40).
[32] *Op. cit.*, p.45 (72–73).
[33] *Op. cit.*, p.63.
[34] "The Lesson of Rancière", Afterword to *The Politics of Aesthetics*, p. 76.

The Perceptual Commons and an Aesthetic Politics

The interest in aesthetics by political theorists is a signal development in philosophy. It is hardly an innovation,[35] but its emphatic recurrence in contemporary thought has far-reaching significance. It can mean several things. One is a desperate turn to the arts as a way of rejuvenating political theory, whose re-working of old ground has yielded meager results in tired reaffirmations of liberal democratic theory for an age so different from its Classical origins and eighteenth century revival. We might view the recourse to aesthetics as a way of bolstering that same ideology, for the recent theorists I have discussed, with the exception of Rancière, espouse what is essentially the same agenda. This apologetic use of philosophy has a long history,[36] a history shaken at its foundations by Marx and Nietzsche but not displaced. Let us consider where we now stand with the aesthetic.

The association of aesthetics with the social and the political is, as we have seen, neither far-fetched nor casual. We found in our review of aesthetic politics that Rancière's treatment of the sensible is distinctive in recognizing the political potential in the literal meaning of the aesthetic. He is not alone in following this usage: Wolfgang Welsch has made effective use of the force of *aisthēsis* as an instrument of cultural criticism.[37]

The implications for social and political philosophy of this transformation of the aesthetic are profound, for when the sensible is followed through on its own terms, the results are indeed metamorphic. I want to claim, further, that it fulfills part of what is implicit in the very meaning of perception. But to my knowledge there has not been any

---

[35] An aesthetic politics can be traced back at least to Kant and Hegel, not to mention classical Greece. See Josef Chytry, *Cytherica: Aesthetic-Political Essays in an Aphrodisian Key* (New York et al: Peter Lang, 2005), pp. 122 ff. This is traced out in some detail in Crispin Sartwell, *Political Aesthetics; Introduction to the Discipline*, unpublished ms., Ch. 1.

[36] I have exposed the apologetic tradition in moral philosophy in "The Social Postulate of Theoretical Ethics," *Journal of Value Inquiry*, IV, 1 (January 1970), 1–16.

[37] Wolfgang Welsch, *Undoing Aesthetics* (London et al: Sage, 1997).

attempt to carry through the transformative potential of *aisthēsis*: transformative politically, transformative culturally, transformative metaphysically. The groundwork for accomplishing this has occupied the previous chapters of this book. What remains is to pursue its social implications and political consequences.

The history of philosophical explanation notwithstanding, there is no ontology *a priori*. Ontology is itself a social as well as a philosophical construct. Can we begin, then, with the life-world, "that province of reality which the wide-awake and normal adult simply takes for granted in the attitude of common sense"?[38] The life-world can indeed be a sobering point of reference, for it situates us in the world we actually inhabit. At the same time, that world is the repository of all the effects of those processes by which humans come to consciousness. And so, together with philosophy, one of its products, it is heavily layered.

The idea of a "perceptual commons" offers a direction in groping through the many conceptual layers that form experience in the shape of a human world. Indeed, we may call the perceptual commons the most inclusive environmental condition of human life. By the simple fact of living we are embedded in a perceptual sphere, and it is from here that we must proceed in order to function in that world. This is the point from which we must endeavor to understand the conditions that precede all those acts of conceptual separation that divide the human world.

The perceptual commons is not private nor is it public. It is common. It is present with direct access, and any effort to constrain contact is a deviation from that condition— indeed, an imposition. This carries a heavy baggage of consequences. Environmental ones are obvious: Everyone has a claim to the free and ready enjoyment of pure air, and

---

[38] Alfred Schutz and Thomas Luckmann, *The Structures of the Life-World* (Evanston: Northwestern University Press, 1973), p. 3. "In the natural attitude, I always find myself in a world which is for me taken for granted as self-evidently "real." I was born into it and I assume that it existed before me. It is the unexamined ground of everything given in my experience, as it were, the taken-for-granted frame in which all the problems which I must overcome are placed." p. 4.

uses of air that load it with pollutants or smells, that affect its temperature, poison its character or quality, set it in violent motion or prevent its movement must compensate for those aberrances by restoring its neutrality. The same can be said about visual perception. Everyone has a stake in the visual environment, and this places a heavy social interest on architectural and urban design. It is appalling to recognize how freely and widely industries, groups, and individual people simply appropriate large portions of the perceptual commons for their private interests, entirely ignoring the social effects of their actions.

This raises the question of the relation of the social and the individual, one of the great themes in Western political theory. Indeed, from the vantage point of the perceptual commons, stating the issue as an opposition of the individual and the social rests on a presumptive and vastly misleading social ontology. The perceptual commons is neither social nor individual. One could liken it to a reservoir, except that it is not a reserve but the very substance of experience. And it is a key point at which the widespread oppositional contrast between individual and society displays its error. That idea is itself a social construct so deeply embedded in cultural consciousness in the West and for so long that it is difficult to recognize its social origins. As we have seen, a similar fate befalls the concept of subjectivity. Yet habit does not make ideas true, and hoary falsehoods are all the more pernicious for being sanctified.

It is revealing to consider how we might understand the human world from an ontology of continuity instead of division, separation, and opposition. Indeed, the perceptual commons is inherently undifferentiated and, from the standpoint of perceptual experience, continuity is its most salient characteristic. Things are not perceptually discrete even though some might appear distinct, but differences are nonetheless distinguishable. Aristotle's recognition of the difference between a distinction and a separation provides an underlying insight. Every object in the human world, however it be distinguished in different contexts, has its history and associations in relation to human uses.

Often this history is perceptually apparent if we are attentive to its signs: from worn stone steps to social practices of congregation and worship, from land and stone conformations on the earth's surface to geological processes, from human physiognomy to diet and health.

It would be fascinating to sketch the outlines of a human civilization based on the recognition of the continuities that draw things together. That would signify true civilization, that is, people living civilly, living in civil society, where the prevailing patterns of relations exemplify mutuality, support, and assistance, all the forms of enabling that promote human life and fulfillment. These are markedly in contrast with social relations based on opposition: competition, personal aggrandizement, conflict, power relations, subordination, subjugation, oppression, force, war — all of the many modes of conflictual interaction common to the world we humans have fashioned.

The political implications of an aesthetics based on recognizing humans' claim to the perceptual commons and to its equal enjoyment are world-shattering, for the perceptual commons can be construed as the basis for natural justice: it is an organic claim asserted and applied equally. The social values that would be embodied are humane and positive. Their fulfillment would serve the goals of the many existing social institutions and forces that have been striving, under oppressive circumstances, to create the conditions in which humans can achieve most fully their individual and collective potential.

Political forms need to be devised to reflect this transformation of social ontology, and social forms and institutions need to be developed to further those positive ends. These cannot be projected a priori but have to be fashioned as more humane conditions develop. Certainly they would be most unlike the hierarchical and oppositional political and social forms that prevail in the present world and that structurally preserve the framework of conflict: public vs. private, individual vs. state, right vs. left. Consider how the forms through which communication takes place and decisions are made embody opposition: debate, dialectic, criticism, argument. In contrast, open, fair, and equal discussion rarely occurs without being quickly pre-empted by conflictual patterns. In fact, the very concepts of morality itself embody an oppositional structure: good vs. evil, guilt and innocence, and in economics, scarcity vs. abundance.

As part of the moral rehabilitation of social life it is also necessary to expose the many myths that obstruct humane goals: self-justifying beliefs that block changes with barriers of negativity and drape humanity in a dark pall. Among the most pervasive and insidious are myths of human nature that ascribe inadequacies and failures to inherent defects in human being, such as original sin and ineradicable self-interest and selfishness. Other such myths include supernaturalistic superstitions that place human fate in the hands of inscrutable forces. These are part of a culture of negativity that delights in defaming all generous human motives by generalizing those that are self-gratifying. But there are other motives: sympathy as well as selfishness, generosity as well as greed, help and support as well as domination and exploitation. None of these traits and patterns is fixed, and a positive, humane world would encourage enabling traits and behaviors instead of preaching and ingraining the negative and oppositional. It will be difficult to displace this debilitating yet powerful tradition, yet intellectual maturity consists in seeing through the myths with which we all are clothed to the naked reality beneath. It is a process of divestment that we can only hope it is not too late to begin.

Chapter Twelve

The Aesthetics of Politics

The Aesthetic and the Political

It is one of the wonders of philosophy that an idea should persist despite all possible evidence for abandoning it. Of the many ideas in aesthetics to which this comment can apply, the one that is most pertinent here is the belief in the autonomy of art. One can understand why such a belief should take hold. Many factors connected with art suggest that much of its force and value lies in the relative independence of making and appreciating art. The creative impulse is always unbridled and unpredictable, and often it is coupled with the healthy influence of deliberate iconoclasm. Less obvious is the directness of aesthetic engagement in appreciation and its opportunity for original experience. But independence is a different matter from autonomy, and claims for absolute self-sufficiency in art, as in social life, are wishful but ungrounded.

Our reconsideration of the aesthetic and the artistic did not support the autonomy of the artistic enterprise but, on the contrary, demonstrated its responsiveness to the forces in the human world. Whether as subject-matter, referent, incentive, or motive, the larger and all-inclusive social world is immanent in art in diverse and often unpredictable ways.[1] And, conversely, aesthetic perception, which lies at

---

[1] These considerations say nothing about historical and social factors, such as the aesthetic movement, *art pour l'art*, and other expressions of romantic ideology.

the heart of art, is immanent and pervasive in the human world. Exposing the many strands and layers of the influence of the aesthetic, as I have tried to do, reveals as much about human sociality as about art.

It is not easy or simple to peer through the conceptual miasma that blankets perceptual experience. At the same time, a stunning revelation emerges as we begin to recognize the influences that inform it. I have already described how perception is never wholly private but is shrouded in multiple associations, structures, and assumptions through which it is shaped, directed, and interpreted. This has profound political implications. It means, in fact, that there is no clear beginning: no pure sensation, no guiding axiom, no original condition, no *sensus communis*. Nor can we begin with radical subjectivity, with consciousness, phenomenology notwithstanding. In fact, we must recognize the presumption rather than the priority of subjectivity, that storm anchor of the Western philosophical tradition.

Subjectivism, moreover, is not only a misleading idea and a dangerous illusion; it is also an obstacle to a transformative politics. Few commentators have been able to liberate themselves from its tenacious pull,[2] and this inability acts to impede and indeed prevent the re-founding of a politics of freedom. For freedom, as it is commonly understood, is bound up in the related tradition of individualism, yet we have seen that the assumptions underlying individualism can also be placed in serious question. Yet how else can we proceed? How else can we conceive of freedom, of the political sphere, of the human world if not in terms of subjectivity and individualism?

In its root meaning as sense perception, aesthetics, when pursued with an effort to set aside cognitive meaning and prejudgment, becomes a kind of radical phenomenology. Perception is never pure, never somatically direct, as

---

[2] Subjectivism is one of the most pervasive and powerful intellectual forces in modern Western thought, resembling in these respects Cartesian dualism, to which it is related, and almost equally ineradicable.

William James pointed out,[3] and we saw earlier how we invariably edit and add to sensation.[4] One of philosophy's unending tasks is to articulate and examine the grounds and significance of pre-cognitive processes and, perhaps we might add, post-cognitive processes, as well as cognitive ones. These processes are well-disguised behind multiple structures designed to hide or render them palatable, from the euphemisms of linguistic fig leaves to self-gratifying, pseudo-scientific cosmologies religious or ideological in origin. Burke saw the danger with admirable clarity: "When we go but one step beyond the immediately sensible qualities of things, we go out of our depth. All we do after, is but a faint struggle, that shews we are in an element which does not belong to us."[5]

Setting aside the natural attitude, the classic precondition of phenomenological description, is only one of philosophy's primary steps. To suspend the assumption of existence only begins Salome's dance by discarding the outermost of the many interpretive layers that veil sense perception. Indeed, the source of much of the continuing freshness and vitality of the arts lies in their uninhibited use of pre-cognitive perception, a force that persists despite every effort to capture and constrain art by reductive explanations.

Let me review briefly some of what we now understand about the multifarious influences on sense perception. We know, with all the qualifications that must be assigned to any knowledge claim, that social influences and pressures affect our apprehension of the very data of sensory perception. Social psychologists have amassed a large body of experimental evidence that documents the effects of such

---

[3]   "[T]he general law of perception, which is this: that *whilst part of what we perceive comes through our senses from the object before us, another part* (and it may be the larger part) *always comes out of our own mind."* William James, *Psychology* (Holt, 1892), p. 329.

[4]   See Part One, especially Chapter Four.

[5]   Edmund Burke, *Philosophical Inquiry into the Origin of our Ideas of the Sublime and Beautiful* (1757) (Oxford: Oxford University Press, 1990), Part Four, Section 1, pp.117–8.

influence.[6] We have also noted the powerful challenge to the presumed objectivity and independence of truth provided by the continuing work in the sociology of knowledge that began in the 1920s and '30s. This shows how our understanding of reality is socially constructed, and that "whatever passes for 'knowledge' in a society ... is developed, transmitted and maintained in social situations" and forms the reality that is taken for granted. [7] The very foundation of what is distinctively human in perception is its character as a socially and historically achieved and changing mode of action; and is thereby invested with a cognitive, affective and teleological character that exemplifies perception as a social and not merely a biological or neurophysiological activity. What is more, perception is not an activity of the perceptual system or of a specific sense-modality but an activity of the whole organism. Heidegger, too, recognized the powerful influence of cultural tradition. "All philosophical discussion, even the most radical attempt to begin all over again, is pervaded by tradi-

---

[6]   Among the classical experiments are Asch's studies on the influence of social pressure on visual perception and Hastorf and Cantril's study of the influence of motives on group perception. Studying the perception by the onlookers of a contentious football game, Hastorf and Cantril concluded that "out of all the occurrences going on in the environment, a person selects those that have some significance for him from his own egocentric position in the total matrix." The event they studied "actually was many different games" and the varying accounts observers gave of what took place were equally real to them. The study found that people's perceptions were influenced by what they wanted to see. The researchers concluded, "In brief, the data here indicate that there is no such 'thing' as a 'game' existing 'out there' in its own right which people merely 'observe'. The game 'exists' for a person and is experienced by him only insofar as certain happenings have significances in terms of his purpose." Albert Hastorf and Hadley Cantril, "They Saw a Game: A Case Study", *Journal of Abnormal and Social Psychology*, 1954.

[7]   Peter L. Berger and Thomas Luckmann, *The Social Construction of Reality, A Treatise in the Sociology of Knowledge* (Garden City, New York: Doubleday, 1966), p. 3. This book provides an excellent account of the field. Martin Heidegger, *Basic Problems of Phenomenology* (1954) (Bloomington, IN: Indiana University Press, 1975), p. 22.

tional concepts and thus by traditional horizons and traditional angles of approach."[8]

More recently, deconstruction has emerged as a methodology of critical analysis and argumentation for questioning underlying ideas and raising basic questions without limit or end, a kind of terminal yet productive incompleteness. We might even balance this by recognizing in the body of theoretical and practical certitude offered by the sciences the unavoidable but qualifying influence of the experimenter on every investigation. What well may be emerging here is a vastly different notion of human knowledge from the ideal of absolute certitude and completeness that has stood as the standard from classical times to the twentieth century. I do not mean to diverge into an epistemological study here, but it is necessary for our critical purposes to acknowledge these factors as the ground for any discussion of basics and beginnings and not to elevate consuetude beyond its proper measure.

This is not to psychologize or sociologize philosophy but to recognize that philosophy is not independent and that its claims for priority are inadequate if they do not take into account the psychological and social conditions that affect all inquiry. The attempt to find a true beginning in consciousness, whether perceptual or cognitive, cannot be sustained. At the same time, we need not wait for physiological psychology to explain what constitutes consciousness: brain functions can identify organic causal events but they do not dissolve their manifestations. Consciousness may be a question but it is not an answer.

Considerable illumination comes from the work of anthropologists, sociologists, and other behavioral scientists, all of whom have demonstrated in detail the formation of conscious thought in the human interactions through which cultural, linguistic, historical, and cognitive ideas and structures are shaped and absorbed. The body of evidence accrued by these sciences is overwhelming. What is needed is to acknowledge that evidence and incorporate it

---

[8]   Heidegger, *loc. cit.*.

into our philosophical deliberations. Putting aside traditions ignorant of such facts is the pre-condition of fresh and liberating understanding. This is hardly the final truth in such matters, for we cannot legislate future inquiry, but it enables us to dispense with whatever inherited doctrines cannot endure the light of the present.

Aesthetic Politics

To what kind of politics can an aesthetics of perception lead? Much of the history of Western political thought is mired in mythology, and one of the most persistent myths concerns the origin of the human community. Indeed, origins are one of the favored subjects of myth and the seventeenth century fiction of the state of nature incorporated many of the common explanatory features of such myths. I call this a fiction because it is an entirely imaginative construction that provides a presumably rational explanation of the formation of community out of a loose, inchoate collection of people who, in a correlative myth, contract with one another to establish political order. The presumptive conditions under which they do this vary with the version, such as the classic ones proposed by Hobbes, Locke, Rousseau, and Hume or, more recently, by Rawls's notion of the "original position." And just as varied are the political orders that they justify, from absolute monarchy to liberal democracy. One can understand the appeal to an age of reason of so rational a reconstruction, but this merely adds a second myth to the first, of a social contract to a state of nature, pandering to our present age of narrow calculation in the service of wider unreason. Still, the myth of a pre-social condition persists.

As we have seen throughout this book, an aesthetically-guided philosophical process can help identify and expose the multiple layers of assumptions, constructions, axiomatic presuppositions, and cultural teachings that obscure sense perception so thickly. Salome's dance never ends. Still, it is appropriate to ask if the landscape of an aesthetic politics begins to appear through the haze. Do we discern there the polis as the model of an aesthetic polity? Is it still useful as an ideal of human community, for with all its historical limitations and failings, the polis was, for a brief time, actual? Much of its appeal lies in the fact that the polis joined community with law and a participatory, self-determining socio-political process in which there was no alienation of citizen and state.[9]

And what of the perceptual commons? What can this contribute to an aesthetic politics? I believe there is much to be discovered here. The perceptual commons is a germinal idea that expands into a many-petalled bloom. It can contribute to dispelling the mists of myth before the direct force of experience. And still more important, it provides the basis for commonality and all the nurturing support this condition can provide.

Many features of a positive politics are implicit in the idea of a perceptual commons. The presence of such a commons entitles everyone who shares that experience to participate equally in its enhancements and possibilities. Entitlement without access is empty, and therefore conditions and facilities must be present that enable all people to make free and full use of the commons. Enabling, however, is not sufficient, for people have not only to be informed but induced to participate, and so the availability of the commons needs also to be promoted. From this emerges, not the familiar ethics of penury but an ethics of profusion. And from this we can generate an ethics of care, not conflict; of justice, not privilege.

To emphasize the aesthetic in experience is to engage in openness, cooperation, connectedness, vulnerability. Ken-ichi Sasaki observes that "When it was coming into existence, aesthetics was charged with the real and urgent philosophical problem of its time: how to construct a new

---

[9] Maryvonne Saison, in "The People Are Missing", *Contemporary Aesthetics*, Vol. 6 (2008), pursues the idea of an aesthetic sociability in the thought of Deleuze, Foucault and others with great sensitivity.

world."[10] This remains its continuing charge in the face of what stands as a perennial problem. Perhaps emancipation from a tradition of negative mythology and the practices of negative sociality will make it possible for a new aesthetics to provide a source of new patterns to develop and fresh models to emulate in the quest for positive culture.[11]

Conclusion

The task of constructing the outlines of a new world is, I believe, is the most urgent philosophical challenge of our time, and it is by starting with aesthetics that this can best be undertaken. To show why and how this reconstruction can proceed has been the intent of this book. Its breadth of inquiry has encompassed the major domains of philosophic thought: ontology and metaphysics, epistemology, ethics, social and political philosophy, all under the guidance of an aesthetics of perception. It has been necessary to cast the range of inquiry so broadly in order both to ground the aesthetic and to establish its proper context. But what I most hope to have done is clear the terrain of many of the conceptual and structural obstacles that confound our thought and occlude our understanding, difficulties for many of which philosophy is particularly responsible. And I hope to have established the conditions for the capacity of the aesthetic to

---

[10] Ken-ichi Sasaki, "The Politics of Beauty", paper delivered at the XXII World Congress of Philosophy, Seoul, Korea, August 2008, §0. See also Salim Kemal, "Nietzsche's Genealogy — Of Beauty and Community", *Journal of the British Society for Phenomenology*, 21/3 (October 1990), 234–49. Reprinted in *Nietzsche's On the Genealogy of Morals: Critical Essays*, ed. Christa Davis Acampora (Rowman & Littlefield, 2006).

[11] It is not in the spirit of these comments but nonetheless necessary to acknowledge that any and all of these features of a positive aesthetics can easily be subverted and turned into instruments of oppression, as human history so eloquently documents. But my purpose is not to safeguard aesthetics from sadistic misuses. There will always be those whose ingenuity can easily find ways to drag the banner of human ideals in the mud. If humans ever develop a civilized culture, such perverse efforts will wither on sterile soil and their perpetrators provided compensatory care.

illuminate and liberate our grasp of the world on which we have placed our indelible mark.

It may be that the perceptual commons we have been considering is another way of identifying the human environment, the human world, and that in re-shaping environment we are enhancing and making coherent its participating constituents. How this perceptual landscape is appropriated, designed, and populated concerns everyone, and it allows endless possibilities, both aesthetic and political. We cannot help but be affected by the crass and exploitative uses of the human environment in the political, military, industrial, and commercial co-optations of the perceptual conditions of human life. An aesthetics of perception offers an alternative, and this, in turn, can provide the means by which to transform the human world.

But even as the perceptual commons is environmental, it is first and foremost aesthetic. This is why the aesthetic verges on the political and where its unique social contribution lies. Such a perspective leads Sasaki to note

> What we learn from early modern aesthetics is that when basic values become suspect and or even invalid, aesthetic judgment is the only path towards the establishment of new values…. [M]easuring the goodness of a new world by its beauty can also be an important guide at a turning point in civilization. But consider this: there is beauty in the tracks of missiles flying against a dark sky, and sublimity in the collapse of a glacier. While beauty is the only direct mark of value, it is also involved in an undeniable ambiguity in our contemporary civilization. I am convinced that the most real and important task of aesthetics is to speculate on this ambiguity on the horizon of our global civilization. [12]

Sasaki echoes Schiller by introducing beauty in establishing new values. The aesthetics of politics is not about beauty in the conventional sense as commonly applied to art and nature, or even in an extended sense when attached to character or to a life. I am not proposing in the aestheticization of culture a culture of aesthetics, of aesthetes, or of art. Yet the

---

[12] *Ibid.*, § 5.

concept of beauty does nonetheless crystallize the core of positive value that is fulfilled in the aesthetic. Understood in this way, beauty may be taken to represent or, better yet, to symbolize the fulfillment of a social aesthetic.

Perhaps, then, I can conclude this inquiry into the power of the aesthetic to transform the human world by turning to it as a standard of fulfillment and not only of criticism. For the aesthetic possesses the capabilities of both. The ambiguity of beauty can only be resolved by recognizing its inseparability from the moral. The experience of beauty, Schiller argued, brings people together; it reconciles conflicts within a person and among people. Beauty is thus not mere delectation but a conciliatory force. Its social significance lies in its capabilities for reconciliation, and it is this that gives beauty a moral standing.

Indeed, the multivalence of beauty appears in recognizing its bond with the moral. Ultimately the morality of beauty and the beauty of morality cannot be kept separate. Each enhances and contributes to the other. We can no longer look at any event as exclusively aesthetic in the conventional, narrow sense of beauty, for doing so only contributes to its isolation. So we must free ourselves from the myth of aesthetic disinterestedness, a view that rests on a contrived, even false ordering of the world.[13] It is one thing to identify and distinguish aesthetic value; it is quite another to separate it from its inherence in the objects, events, and conditions of the human world.

What is most forceful in a fulfilled experience with the arts is our complete absorption in perceptual experience that has temporal depth conjoined with the resonance of memory and meaning, what I have called "aesthetic engagement". Yet this account of aesthetic experience in the arts is at the same time a description of human relations, both personal and social, at their most fulfilling — of a social aesthetic. For in the aesthetic we discover the human world,

---

[13]   See Chapter Five, above. I have developed an extended critique of the notion of aesthetic disinterestedness in *Re-thinking Aesthetics, Rogue Essays on Aesthetics and the Arts* (Aldershot: Ashgate, 2004), Pt. I.

and in re-constituting the aesthetic we laid the groundwork for reconstructing a more humane world. This world is first aesthetic, and that is why the aesthetic verges on the political, where its transformative powers make possible its unique social contribution.

> I know the truth! All other truths—out of my sight!
> There is no cause for us to hold these fights and battles!
> Just take a look: there's evening, look: there's night.
> Why do we fight—O poets, lovers, and commanders?
>
> The grass is dewy and the wind has settled down,
> And soon, the vortex of the stars will stop,
> And we shall all sleep with our foes below the ground,
> Though on this earth, we kept each other up.[14]

---

[14]   "I Know the truth", Marina Tsvetaeva, 1915, trans. Andrey Kneller. Used by kind permission of the translator.

Index